THE LAST DURBAR

Shashi Joshi has a Phd in history from Jawaharlal Nehru University, New Delhi. She began her academic career as senior lecturer in history at Miranda House, University of Delhi, was Senior Fellow at the Nehru Memorial Museum and Library, New Delhi, and from 1983-97, was co-director of an Indian Council of Social Science research project. She is currently Senior Fellow at the Institute of Advanced Study, Shimla, India.

The author has several publications to her credit including *Struggle of Hegemony in India: The Colonial State, the Left and the Indian National Movement*, Volume I, and *Struggle for Hegemony in India: Culture, Community and Power*, Volume 3.

THE LAST DURBAR

A Dramatic Presentation of the Division of British India

Shashi Joshi

LOTUS COLLECTION
ROLI BOOKS

Dedicated to
Adya, Tia, and Tishya

Lotus Collection

First published in Pakistan, 2006
by Oxford University Press

First published in India, 2007
The Lotus Collection
An imprint of Roli Books Pvt. Ltd.
M-75, G.K. II Market, New Delhi 110 048
Phones: ++91 (011) 2921 2271, 2921 2782
2921 0886, Fax: ++91 (011) 2921 7185
E-mail: roli@vsnl.com; Website: rolibooks.com
Also at
Varanasi, Bangalore, Kolkata, Jaipur, Chennai & Mumbai

Cover design: Mukesh Singh

ISBN: 978-81-7436-583-5
Rs. 295

Printed at Anubha Printers, Noida.

Contents

Preface

Much history writing has emerged from the Partition of the Indian subcontinent. And yet the whys and wherefores of the decisions taken during the run-up from March 1947 by the leaders involved continue to remain unclear and intriguing. We still ask the most basic questions: how could such wise and clever political leaders not avoid the division of the country? How could they not anticipate the holocaust it would unleash? Continued dissatisfaction with the answers provided by scholars only tells us that the narrative mode of history writing cannot reflect the simultaneity and multiplicity of perpetually shifting positions and accents: the clashing wills and conflicting lines of argument as they are revealed in the minutiae of daily records.

The existing histories of the Partition have very little chance of capturing the moods and mindsets, the helplessness and frustrations, the anguish and final despair of those who steered the course. At times they appear to box at shadows, at other times they move slowly towards the apparently inevitable. The histories written in India thus far have either focused on political narratives or ideological analysis. More recently, the spotlight has turned upon the blood and gore, the madness and pathology of mass murders and hate. This work tells the story as it was—without the epic dimensions of conventional writing filled with the rhetoric of freedom and greatness, and also without the legalese and constitution-making vocabulary of the *Transfer of Power*. It captures the ticking of the clock in 'real time'—with a mix of cynicism, fair play, strategic advantage, pelf and profit juxtaposed with all too human and frail visions, desires, prejudices and isolations.

Bing Crosby sings as breakfast is eaten; the protocol and ceremony of the Order of the British Empire runs parallel to the columns of refugees; the gracious sophistication of the viceregal public relations machine and the bowing and curtseying at the balls intersect with the exercise of power with a capital P. Bach and Chopin play as the Indian world goes mad.

All this and more comes into play as the endgame reaches its final moment and denouement. The personal and the political meet and separate 'as the Last Durbar' with Louis Mountbatten on the throne, and the modern, constitutional *durbar* is to proclaim a republic and bid farewell to each other.

This work, based scrupulously and completely on the private papers of Mountbatten, including verbatim records and testimonies, discussions and suggestions of the leading Indian actors, is a blow by blow, nuanced and multilayered account of the months and days that led to the Indian partition. It exposes the palpable relationship of the leading actors in this drama, the moves and countermoves, the interactions and manoeuverings between a range of characters against the backdrop of momentous events and developments that transfigure their imagination for better or worse. Past policies and platforms mutate rapidly, often into diametrical opposites, and lifelong patterns jerk into new trajectories. Marginalized and shunned elements, traditionally kept out of the reckoning at Round Tables and parleys at the top, threw most of the figures that were centre stage into confusion and turmoil. The Journalist and the Administrator spin order out of chaos with words and prescriptions. And yet, the relentless speed of disorder defies any miracles. The prosaic and the poetic, the narrow and the expansive, the wise and the foolish, and the hopeful and the bleak are fused together.

It is only the dramatic genre of writing history which allows us to recover the complexity of such a process and frame the atmosphere of that concentrated moment. It also raises interesting issues about writing: the main concerning 'voice' and its textual representation. It also admits more documentary evidence than historical studies usually do. That evidence, here, takes the form of statements from the actors involved in the events who are all extensively quoted: it better inscribes the view of historical discourse. As Certeau remarks: 'History is never sure: made of "two series of data", namely of ideas we have about the past on the one hand, (and) of "documents" and "archives" on the other, the history book is a "book divided".'

Acknowledgements

Without the Fellowship and support given to me by the Hartley Institute Library, Southampton University, and its then Director, Dr Woolgar from May to July 1998, I would not have had the opportunity to research the 'Mountbatten Papers' housed there. I place on record my gratitude both to Dr Woolgar and the Hartley Institute Library.

Renuka Misra, Primila and Charles Lewis read the manuscript and encouraged me greatly. Charles, especially, was most generous in help and advice in the process of publication. My loving thanks to them.

I must also record my debt to some authors whose writing was invaluable in evolving a balanced perspective: Leonard Mosley, Trevor Royle, Penderel Moon, Richard Symonds and other accounts of the events that follow. The biographies and memoirs of many of the characters such as Lord Ismay, Edwina and Louis Mountbatten who figure in my work gave this writing a sense of their times, not least because of the language and vocabulary that prevailed then. My debt to all of them is great.

Alan Campbell-Johnson's *Mission With Mountbatten* provided 'structural support' in crafting the manuscript. After a thorough consultation of the 'Mountbatten Papers' it was clear to me that Alan's account was scrupulously faithful to the stenographical notes dictated by Mountbatten immediately after each interview with representative Indian leaders. I have taken no license with the words recorded in the archive.

Acknowledgements

History in Dialogue: An Introductory Note

The first thing that needs to be said is that this is not a play meant for the stage. It is a book of history in dialogue form, that is, a 'dialogical history' as opposed to narrative history.

This new form should not be misunderstood as an attempt to 'dramatize' historical events. All the drama in it is in the Mountbatten records itself. The 'officialese' some characters speak is also inherent in the records to which I scrupulously adhere to.

The sensitive subject of conversations, confabulations and negotiations between historical persons on the Partition of India ought not to be embellished or modified in any way to serve the interest of theatrical production. What obtains between the covers of this work is completely loyal to the actual words uttered by the characters.

So much so that friends who read the transcript wanted a more dramatic finale than I offered. 'But that was how it was,' I protested. While the murder and mayhem spread across the land it was mundane inventories and formal farewells that dominated Delhi, Nehru chasing rioters on the streets regardless.

Narrative history primarily offers political and institutional explanations and is invariably permeated by the emotion and agenda of the author. If Anita Inder Singh's book appears to justify Indian nationalists, Ayesha Jalal's writing air-brushes Jinnah by what she terms 'teasing out the "real" political aims of Jinnah'.

Such biases in historiography are logical as a narrative must move towards a conclusion in what may be called the 'who is to blame' school of history. The attempt underlying it always is to fix responsibility on to a person (Gandhi, Nehru or Jinnah?); an institution (British colonial state); or an ideology (Indian National Congress or Muslim League, Hindu nationalism or Muslim separatism?). In Jalal's words, the aim is 'to "rectify" the historiographical errors ...'

Most of the literature on Partition thus has been devoted to the rights and wrongs of the division and the responsibility for the bloodshed that followed. The question that moves scholars and lay readers is the same: why and how was India partitioned? Who were the villains and who the victims?

For Jalal the Congress and Gandhi were 'too clever' or too 'patronizing' for Jinnah. For Inder Singh, Congress was no match for 'Jinnah's obduracy and dialectical skill'. For Penderal Moon, the Congress was responsible for the 'fatal error' of offering the Muslim League not 'partnership but absorption'.

R.J. Moore saw the 'monolithic Congress' making the 'totalitarian claim to the Indian nation in microcosm', and Jinnah's two-nation theory as 'a psychological weapon and tyrannical idea against the Congress'.

The old language of 'divide and rule' survives in Mushirul Hasan's book holding the colonial government culpable for 'encouraging the Muslims to develop separately'.

The discourse of 'Hindu communalism' and 'Muslim separatism' a la Francis Robinson and David Page is of course widely prevalent.

The canonization of one's leader and demonization of the opponent also is *de rigueur* in both Indian and Pakistani nationalist history writing (see A.G. Noorani's review of Hector Bolitho).

The theory of a flawed Indian nationalism that compromised with communalism leading to Partition is propounded by Bipan Chandra and Mushirul Hasan. Sumit Sarkar's emphasis is more on Congress not rooting out social and economic reactionary elements as a causative factor.

More recent efforts (including my own earlier publications) at providing a bigger picture and to explore popular perceptions, the role of crowds and the power of symbols are helpful in mapping the terrain but stop short of the in-camera proceedings that divided the land. (See Shashi Joshi and Bhagwan Josh, Farzana Shaikh and Ian Talbot.)

Historians dismiss each other's arguments, even their motives: Tapan Raychaudhuri accuses Moon for reflecting 'colonial stereotypes'; Asim Roy charges Inder Singh for subscribing to 'orthodox historiography' and Jalal for advocating the 'revisionist position' on Partition and on Jinnah. And so on... Thus, interpretations are exactly that, while conversations re-told leave the space for every reader to develop insights.

The eternal question of what had irredeemably destroyed all chances for a united Indian state spawns other questions always impossible to answer definitively, convincing to all. Was it the failure of Gandhi and his non-violence, or Nehru's willfulness and haste, or Jinnah's paranoia and obduracy? Was it Gandhi versus his Congress colleagues, Jinnah versus the Muslim League, Nehru versus Patel, Jinnah pitted against Mountbatten or the masses against the leaders?

The questions themselves reveal the polemical impasse historians end up with. The emphasis on motives and assertions of their answers ridiculously turns historians into clairvoyants.

Almost all the aspects questioned above had roles to play in the final outcome. However, meta-narratives set out an interpretative argument while, the all too human contradictory trends can only emerge when multiple voices are allowed to speak. The operative word here is 'speak' not as an authorial claim but literally, as they are recorded in the minutes. As the film-maker Shyam Benegal, on reading this work so generously put it, 'What I learnt from *The Last Durbar* was how an aggregate of subjectivities lead to objective outcomes.'

The build-up towards any denouement cannot be grasped without mapping interactive, dialogical relations between various personae. Their psychological dispositions, reactions to others and to events flow gradually into the eventual outcomes. The usual rhetoric of British machinations, the out-manoeuvering, the motives and betrayals of various parties and people that litters partition literature can be shown in its shoddiness if the encounters and exchanges between the political actors are laid out in their movement from day-to-day. The story is as much about tensions, rivalries and intolerance as about co-operation or conflict.

Though the Partition occupies the larger share of this book, it is textured by the desire to communicate the mind-sets and mental baggage individuals carry. Barbs aimed at nationalism or imperialism, the 'memsahib's' world, the liberals or die-hards of different sides, the castes of men and women, so to speak, among the British as much as the Indians, all come in a few loaded verbal exchanges.

We historians forget that in all our analysis of historical 'processes' and 'forces', state structures and ideologies we have individuals at work in history. All the dialogues that occurred in Mountbatten's study in the Viceregal house could well have had a sign-board proclaiming: 'Historical Work in Progress'! The book traces the dialogical exchanges through which the final decision to partition was arrived at.

In sum the book is in lieu of answers to the most popular question: how did the principal actors – Mahatma Gandhi, Sardar Vallabhbhai Patel, Maulana Azad, Jawaharlal Nehru, Mohammad Ali Jinnah, Lord Wavell, Lord Mountbatten et.al. fare during the negotiations?

And where did they go wrong? I eschew all judgement. And plead for non-judgemental history.

A.G.Noorani, Review of Hector Bolitho, *Jinnah: Creator of Pakistan*, Karachi: Oxford University Press, Karachi, in *Frontline* 18 May 2007.

Ayesha Jalal, *The Sole Spokesman*, Cambridge University Press, Cambridge, 1985,1994.

Anita Inder Singh, *The Origins of the Partition of India*, Oxford University Press, New Delhi, 1987.

Bipan Chandra, *Communalism in Modern India*, Vikas Publishing House, New Delhi, 1984.

Farzana Shaikh, *Community and Consensus in Islam*, Cambridge University Press, Cambridge, 1989.

Francis Robinson, *Separatism among the Indian Muslims*, Cambridge University Press, Cambridge, 1974.

Ian Talbot, *Freedom's Cry: The Popular Dimension in the Pakistan Movement and Partition Experience in North West India*, Oxford University Press, Karachi, 1996.

R.J. Moore, *The Crisis of Indian Unity*, Oxford University Press, Oxford, 1974.

Mushirul Hasan, *Legacy of a Divided Nation*, Oxford University Press, New Delhi, 1997.

Sumit Sarkar, *Modern India*, Macmillan, New Delhi, 1990.

Shashi Joshi and Bhagwan Josh, *Struggle for Hegemony in India*, Volume 3, Sage, New Delhi, 1994.

Shyam Benegal, Personal Communication.

List of Characters

Abdur Rab Nishtar	Member, Interim Government (Posts and Air).
Abul Kalam Azad	Member, Interim Government (Education and Arts).
Acharya Kripalani	President, INC.
Alan Campbell-Johnson	Press-Attaché to the Viceroy.
Altaf Hussain	Editor of *Dawn*.
Amrita Kaur	Sometime Chairperson of All-India Women's Conference; worked as a secretary to Gandhi.
Arthur Henderson	Parliamentary Under-Secretary of State for India and Burma.
B.G. Kher	Chief Minister, Bombay.
Captain Ronald Brockman (Ronnie)	RN, Personal Secretary to the Viceroy.
Chaudhuri Mohammed Ali	ICS, Secretary-General of Civil Services, Pakistan, 1947–51.
Col. Douglas H. Currie	Military Secretary to the Viceroy.
Colville	Governor of Bombay, 1943–8.
Commander George Nicholls	RN, Deputy Personal Secretary to the Viceroy.
Cooverji Hormusji Bhabha	Member, Interim Government (Works, Mines, and Power).
Dr Bailey	Clergyman.
Field Marshal Sir Claude Auchinleck	Commander-in-Chief, Army, India up to January 1948, then Chief of Joint Defence Committee of the Indian and Pakistani armies.
General Lockhart	Acting Governor, NWFP, 26 June–13 August 1947.
General Roy Bucher	Chief of Staff, Army, India, August–

	December 1947; Commander-in-Chief, 1948–49.
George Abell, ICS	Private Secretary to the Viceroy.
Ghazanfar Ali Khan	Member, Interim Government (Health).
Ghulam Mohammad	Finance Minister of Pakistan, 1947–51.
Gordon Mosley	BBC representative.
H.M. Patel, ICS	Secretary, Viceroy's Executive Council.
H.S. Suhrawardy	Chief Minister, Bengal.
Ian Dixon Scott, ICS	Deputy Private Secretary to the Viceroy.
Ian Melville Stephens	Editor of *The Statesman* (Calcutta).
Indira	Daughter of Jawaharlal Nehru.
Jagjivan Ram	Member, Interim Government (Labour).
Jawaharlal Nehru	Member, Interim Government (External Affairs and Commonwealth Relations).
John Christie, ICS	Joint Private Secretary to the Viceroy.
John Lascelles	Personal Assistant to Lord Ismay.
Journalists: A, B, C	
Kiran Shankar Roy	Leader of Opposition, Bengal Legislative Assembly.
Krishna Menon	Representative of the Government of India at UNO General Assembly 1946–7; High Commissioner for India in UK from August 1947.
Lady Edwina Mountbatten	Vicerene of India.
Lady Ismay	
Lady Wavell	
Liaquat Ali Khan	Member, Interim Government (Finance).
Lord Ismay	Chief of the Viceroy's Staff.
Lord Louis Mountbatten	Viceroy of India, March 1947–June 1948.
Lord Wavell	Viceroy and Governor-General of India, 1943–47.

Lt. Col. de la Fargue	Chief Secretary to the Government of the North-West Frontier Province.
Lt. Col. Vernon Erskine-Crum	Conference Secretary to the Viceroy.
M.A. Jinnah	President, All-India Muslim League (AIML).
M.K. Gandhi	Leader of the Indian National Congress (INC). Also referred to as 'Gandhiji'.
Major Short	Personal Assistant to Sir S. Cripps during the Cabinet Mission to India.
Malcolm MacDonald	Governor-General of Malaya and British Borneo 1946–8.
Martin Gilliat	Deputy Military Secretary.
Mr Symon	Deputy High Commissioner for the United Kingdom in India.
Mrs Fay Campbell-Johnson	Wife of Campbell-Johnson.
Neville	Delhi Correspondent, *Time* and '*Life*'.
P.C. Gordon-Walker	Parliamentary Under-Secretary for Commonwealth Relations, 1947–50.
Pamela Mountbatten	Second daughter of Lord and Lady Mountbatten.
Penderel Moon, ICS	Revenue Minister, Bahawalpur State.
Peter Scott, ICS	Assistant Private Secretary to the Viceroy.
Rajagopalachari (Rajaji)	Member, Interim Government (Industries and Supplies).
Rajendra Prasad	Member, Interim Government (Agriculture and Food).
Russell	Businessman, Killick-Nixon and Company.
Sardar Baldev Singh	Member, Interim Government (Defence).
Sardar Vallabhbhai Patel	Member, Interim Government (Home and Information and Broadcasting).
Sheikh Abdullah	All Jammu and Kashmir National Conference.
Shyama Prasad Mukherji	President, All India Hindu Mahasabha.

Sir Conrad Lawrence Corfield, ICS	Political Advisor to the Crown representative.
Sir Eric Mieville	Principal Secretary to the Viceroy.
Sir N. Gopalaswami Ayyangar	Prime Minister of Kashmir 1937–43.
Sir Percival Griffiths	The British Ambassador.
Sir Terence Shone	High Commissioner for the United Kingdom in India.
V.P. Menon	Reforms Commissioner to Government of India.
Winston Churchill	Leader of the Opposition in Britain from 1945–1950.

Chamber of Princes

Diwan of Gwalior	
Jam Sahib of Nawanagar	
Maharaja of Dungarpur	
Maharaja of Patiala	Pro-Chancellor of the Chamber of Princes.
Mir Maqbool Mahmood	Secretary, States Negotiating Committee.
Nawab of Bhopal	Chancellor of the Chamber of Princes.
Rai Bahadur Kak	Prime Minister of Jammu & Kashmir.
Raja of Bilaspur	
Sardar D.K. Sen	Foreign Minister, Patiala.
Sardar K.M. Panikkar	Prime Minister of Bikaner.
Sir A. Ramaswamy Mudaliar	Diwan of Mysore.
Sir Brojendra Lal Mitter	Diwan of Baroda.
Sir C.P. Ramaswami	Diwan of Travancore.
Sir Mirza Ismail	Prime Minister of Hyderabad.
Sir Syed Sultan Ahmed	Legal Advisor to the Chamber of Princes.
Sir V.T. Krishnamachari	Prime Minister of Jaipur.

Hyderabad Delegation

Laik Ali	Prime Minister of Hyderabad.
Rauf	Minister.
Reddy	Deputy Prime Minister.
Sir Walter Monckton	Advisor on Constitutional matters to the Government of Hyderabad.
Zahir Ahmed	Secretary of External Affairs, Hyderabad.

Acronyms

BOAC – British Overseas Airways Corporation.
DSO – Distinguished Service Order.
GG – Governor-General.
GCMG – Grand Cross (of the order) of St. Michael and St. George.
HMG – His Majesty's Government.
INA – Indian National Army.
KCB – Knight Commander of the Bath.
PM – Prime Minister.
RN – Royal Navy.
RSS – Rashtriya Swayamsevak Sangh.
TOP – Transfer of Power.

Glossary

Chaach – Buttermilk.
Durbar – Royal Court.
Goonda – Hooligan.
Jat – Agricultural tribe found in Punjab, Western United Provinces and Rajasthan.
Jirga – A Council of Elders.
Khakhra – A crisp savoury typical of Gujarat.
Pathan – Generic name given to Pushto-speaking peoples of North-West Frontier Province of the subcontinent and Afghanistan.

THE LAST DURBAR

SCENE 1

A radio broadcast is on air.

This is London. Good morning listeners. We now bring you a special programme on Indian affairs presented by Nick Holt.

The reaction of the Press in Britain to the 20th February declaration by the British Government and the new appointment of Lord Louis Mountbatten as Viceroy of India has been generally favourable.

The American press has also made interesting comments in so far as the British Raj has been a traditional target for American criticism. The 20th February declaration and the time limit of June 1948 for transferring power to Indians has been described by the *New York Times* as an 'Ultimatum to India'. I quote: '*This declaration matches the American grant of independence to the Philippines; it marks the decisive step in Britain's self-imposed task to complete self-government for India. It is also an ultimatum, though of a kind never before issued by a power so often accused of being imperialistic. It is an ultimatum to the Indian leaders to end their quarrel.*' End quote.

The *Washington Star* goes further and asks whether Britain, in the event of the time limit producing no agreement between the Hindus and Muslims, would, as a humane nation, feel compelled to stick to its promise if the only clear prospect for India is a vacuum of fratricidal war?

In London, the parliamentary debate on the Indian question has ended today. The big fireworks were provided by Mr Churchill when he denounced the government's policy as an 'Operation Scuttle'. The appointment of Lord Louis Mountbatten was, Mr Churchill said, the government's attempt to make use of brilliant war heroes in order to cover up a disastrous transaction.

The socialist backbencher, Mr Zilliacus, made the most original suggestion: citing the example of the USSR, he suggested that India should enjoy multi-national membership of the United Nations which would enable the Muslim community, which was more than a national minority, to have the same status as the Ukraine and become a separate member. Mr Churchill surprised everyone by proposing that Mr Zilliacus' suggestion should be taken up and the problem of the Muslim minority submitted to the United Nations.

The Prime Minister, Mr Attlee rounded off the debate by raising the most pertinent question: '*The essence of the Indian problem*,' he said, '*is to get Indian statesmen to understand what real problems they have to face*.' As regards our responsibilities to the minorities, including the Scheduled Castes, he said: '*With one or two exceptions, our policy in the past has been to accept the social and economic system we had found. Why are we told now at the very end of our rule that we must clear up all these things before we go, otherwise we shall betray our trust. If that trust is there, it ought to have been fulfilled long ago*.' Essentially, Mr Attlee maintained, the dangers of delay, the dangers of hanging on, were as great as the dangers of going forward. And he would thus ask the whole House to wish the new Viceroy 'Godspeed' in his great mission—a mission of fulfilment.

SCENE 2

Viceroy Wavell hosts lunch party. Venue: the terrace of Mughal Gardens, Viceroy's House, New Delhi. Present are Lord and Lady Ismay, Sir Eric Mieville, Commander George Nicholls [Royal Navy], Lt. Col. V. Erskine-Crum, Martin Gilliat, John Lascelles [Ismay's PA], Mr and Mrs Campbell-Johnson, and Wavell's staff, Abell, Christie, Ian and Peter Scott, Col. Currie, Lt. Col. Taylor, bearers serving drinks].

Abell: Welcome to India Lord Ismay. How was the flight, comfortable I hope?

Ismay: Very fine George. I saw to it that I wasn't with Lord Mountbatten. He has no concept of stops and rest on the way. His plane left a whole day after us and he'll be here in two hours from now! A ruthless journey!

Well, let me introduce the rest of our party. Sir Eric Mieville, Commander Nicholls, John Lascelles....

[He introduces all members of Mountbatten's staff as Abell introduces Wavell's staff. Auchinleck walks in briskly]

Auchinleck: All done—your luggage has been sent off to your accommodation and their Excellencies will join you for lunch shortly. I have to run now to the airport to receive Lord and Lady Mountbatten. The Commander-in-Chief can't be late!

[Thanks and handshakes as Auchinleck leaves]

Mieville: It was really kind of the Field Marshal to receive us at the airport, especially as he had to go back for the Mountbattens in the boiling heat of an Indian noon!

Ismay: You know when I saw him in his beret I blurted out: have you gone mad, Claude? Where is your toupee? He replied that we had all been mad for over a hundred years to wear such uncomfortable headgear. We were brought up in the belief that anyone who failed to wear a pith helmet when the Indian sun was still in the sky was a lunatic. Remember Mieville, Delhi in 1931?

Col. Currie: You were both here in Lord Willingdon's time, were you not?

Mieville: Yes, till 1933. Ismay was the military secretary and I the private secretary to the Viceroy. But Ismay had been here earlier as a young Subaltern—in the Gloucestershire Regiment at Ambala, wasn't it?

Ismay: There I was merely a bird of passage, my own regiment was at Risalpur on the North-West Frontier. You know [in reminiscent mood] I had to travel half across India to get there, and arrived at the officer's mess, unkempt and travel-stained, just as dinner was finishing. The scene is indelibly stamped on my memory. The officers in magnificent kit of dark blue, scarlet and gold, were seated at the table. Behind them stood the waiters in spotless white muslin, with belts of the regimental colours and the regimental crest on their turbans. It seemed unbelievable—the table decorated with bowls of red roses and gleaming silver, laden with fresh meat, fish, fruit, vegetables, whisky, beer, and above all plenty of ice, all on the frontier. [A group forms around him as he talks. Crum and Campbell-Johnson stand apart, talking.] The 21st Cavalry, it was called. Belonged to the Punjab Frontier Force: the Piffers, as they were nicknamed. Ah, those were the days.

Lt. Col. Taylor: [Excitedly] I had an uncle who served the 21st around the turn of the century. He gave me Rudyard Kipling's *The Lost Legion*—it had a masterly pen picture of the cavalry. I grew up on it, and it led me to India.

Ismay: Then you would know that it played a heroic part in suppressing the Indian mutiny, and of course, fought gallantly in Afghanistan.

Lt. Col. Taylor: As a matter of fact, he never spoke of anything except the mountains and the horses—he was a great rider.

Ismay: Undoubtedly, to anyone who was fond of horses and riding, life with a cavalry regiment on the frontier was blissful. By lunch-time the day's soldiering was over. In the afternoons, most of us played polo or schooled ponies. There were races and rough shooting. It felt very odd to be paid a salary for doing what I loved above all else. But, [shaking a finger emphatically] when we were pursuing raiders from Mohmand country, life could be extremely uncomfortable. A fierce summer sun, an exclusive diet of bully beef and army biscuits, water so chlorinated it seemed undrinkable, the burning rocks boring holes into the soles of our boots. The churches and graveyards of Mardan, Kohat, Bannu and the rest bore witness to the price paid so proudly.

[A bearer—Abdur R. Khan—approaches diffidently and *salaams* Ismay]

Khan: *Salaam* Sahib. I am pensioner Abdur Rahman Khan. Sahib, I have come to serve you.

Ismay: Good God Khan! My bank manager in London told me you haven't drawn your money for the last two months, I feared something had happened to you. Where have you been?

Khan: Sahib, I heard on the radio many weeks before you were coming to India. They gave no date Sahib and I thought I must be here when you came and I took train for Dilli immediately. Sahib, I have been waiting for you, Sahib.

Ismay: Well, I'm very pleased to see you're alright.

Khan: Sahib, all the house servants are also waiting for you.

Ismay: Go back to the house, Khan—Lady Ismay and I will come after lunch.

Khan: Yes, Sahib. *Salaam* sahib. [Goes]

Ismay: Amazing! Khan joined the 21st Cavalry as a recruit about the same time as I did—he was my orderly on and off for about a quarter of a century.

Mieville: He still receives an allowance from you, Ismay?

Ismay: Oh it's nothing much—just to supplement his meager pension.

[The ADCs rush in and announce: Their Excellencies, Lord and Lady Wavell]

SCENE 3

Much preparation and bustle in the main courtyard and up the steps leading to the great Durbar Hall of Viceroy's House, New Delhi. The Mountbattens arrive in an open Landau with escort and outriders, and are conducted up a long flight of red-carpeted steps by Col. Currie and an ADC. At the top they're received by the Wavells, Edwina curtsies and Mountbatten bows head. They stand talking while cameramen take shots. The rest of the lunch party is lined up on one side. All go in.

Wavell and Mountbatten seated in the study, conversing.

Wavell: You've met Nehru earlier in Singapore, I believe. What do you think of him?

Mountbatten: Attractive man. And friendly.

Wavell: You know I always found him rather quixotic, emotional and socialistic. You, I'm sure, will be able to draw out more good from him than I could. The most difficult person is Gandhi—all lawyer's talk. You know when I expressed my horror over the killings in Calcutta and my fears that India was on the brink of civil war, he kept repeating that we had promised the Congress would be allowed to form an interim government on its own.

[Shaking head] Disgusting! Wouldn't listen to reason at all. I explained that if I allowed Congress to form a government without the Muslim League, they would decide that direct action was the only way and we would have the Bengal massacres all over again. At which Gandhi, fully supported by Nehru, mind you, accused me of surrendering to the League's blackmail. He actually commiserated with me for being 'unnerved by the Bengal tragedy'. The death and devastation in Calcutta was abominable and he asked me to leave the matter of peace-keeping to the Congress. Can you believe that? What kind of peace can a butcher maintain in a slaughter house? Do you think the emboldened Hindus wouldn't give short shrift to the Muslims? It was utter nonsense—and Nehru and Patel knew that even if Gandhi did not. Patel came to me several times to request military help in restoring order in Bihar. The Hindus there had begun to rape, kill and mutilate in reprisal for Calcutta.

Mountbatten: My impression is that Nehru considers Patel a non-idealist and non-intellectual type. Nehru's friend Krishna Menon had a long chat with me before I came down.

Wavell: So much the better for Patel. One can talk sense with him.

Mountbatten: Well, I am hoping to bring Gandhi and Jinnah together. Perhaps I can help them come to some agreement.

Wavell: Harrumph. [Looks quizzical] Then you need all the luck I can wish you to deal with those two gentlemen.

Mountbatten: Do you think we must seriously consider the issue of partitioning the country?

Wavell: We cannot rule out partition as a final solution but only if all efforts to transfer power to a united India fail. Of course, there must be detailed arrangements so as to avoid confusion when we leave. And that would take time. The Commander-in-Chief thinks about ten years! I have only one solution, which I call Breakdown Plan, withdrawal of the British province by province, beginning with women and children, and then the army.

Mountbatten: Thank you, Lord Wavell, for giving me your mind, I have been well warned.

Wavell: Well, I must wish you the best of luck, my wife and I leave tomorrow morning at 8.15 a.m.—we are looking forward to England again.

[Edwina and Lady Wavell enter the study]

Edwina: Lady Wavell has briefed me so helpfully on the daunting task of running Viceroy's House. I think we should leave now, Dickie—they have to leave so early in the morning.

[Thanks are said, Mountbattens bow and curtsy and are escorted out by the Wavells. Sound of car and outriders' bikes as the Wavells return]

Wavell: You know, after talking to Mountbatten's staff at lunch and with him now, I don't think they really know very much about India, nor do they have any new or definite policy.

Lady Wavell: Just stop worrying about India now, You heard what Churchill said: 'This is Operation Scuttle'.

SCENE 4

24 March: Swearing-in ceremony inside the Durbar Hall. Red and gold thrones set in bold relief by the lighting concealed in rich red velvet hangings. Arc lights play down. Film cameras whirr and flash-bulbs go off. Audience is already in place, Nehru and Liaquat Ali Khan flank the thrones.

Harsh movie lights are switched on as the trumpets sound the prelude to the arrival of the Mountbattens in the Hall. ADCs lead them in stiff procession.

Mountbatten in pale blue robe of Grand Master of the Star of India over full dress of Admiral's uniform, dark blue ribbon of the Garter above array of 3 Grand Crosses, various orders and decorations, for example, the KCB and DSO.

Edwina, in ivory brocade, tiara, a blaze of diamonds in her coronet, and at her neckline and wrists, a delicate pink ribbon of the Crown of India across her dress, and a few medals, for example, St. John's Ambulance Cross.

The Master of Ceremonies: Ladies and Gentlemen please rise to welcome the Viscount Mountbatten of Burma, Knight of the Most Noble Order of the Garter, Member of His Majesty's Privy Council, Grand Master of the Most Exalted Order of the Star of India, Grand Master of the Most Eminent Order of the Indian Empire, Knight Grand Cross of the Royal Victorian Order, Knight Commander of the Most Honourable Order of the Bath, Companion of the Distinguished Service Order, Rear-Admiral in His Majesty's Fleet, Honorary Lieutenant-General in His Majesty's Army and Honorary Air Marshal in the Royal Air Force, the Governor-General of India.

The Oath is administered by Chief Justice Sir Patrick Spens, and Mountbatten repeats it, with his formidable string of Christian names: I, Louis Francis Albert Victor Nicholas, Viscount Mountbatten of Burma, do solemnly swear…

Mountbatten at microphone begins to speak. His diction, short, straightforward, typical manner of addressing troops.

Mountbatten: Although I believe it is not usual for a speech to be made at the swearing in ceremony, I should like to say a few words to you, and to India.

This is not a normal viceroyalty on which I am embarking. His Majesty's Government are resolved to transfer power by June 1948. I believe every political leader of India feels, as I do, the urgency of the task before us. I hope soon to be in close consultation with them and will give them all the help I can.

In the meanwhile, every one of us must do what he can to avoid any reaction which might lead to further bitterness or add to the toll of innocent victims.

I have many Indian friends. Some I made when I was out here twenty-five years ago—it was here in Delhi that my wife and I became engaged. In the three years that I was with the South-East Asia Command I made many more among the Indian fighting forces, with whom I am proud to have been associated.

It will not be an easy matter to succeed Lord Wavell, who has done so much to take India along the path of self-government. I am under no illusion about the difficulty of my task. I shall need the greatest goodwill of the greatest possible number, and I am asking India for that goodwill.

[Mountbatten sits down beside Edwina on his throne; audience applauds; Nehru and Liaquat Ali Khan sit on either side of the thrones; the trumpets blow, and artillery is heard firing the 31 gun salute. As the firing dies down the Mountbattens stand and are escorted out by the ADCs. The senior ADC, Peter Howes, and three Indian ADCs—one from each service]

SCENE 5

Viceroy's study: Only Mountbatten's special group present.

Ismay: Phew! It was terribly warm inside that Durbar Hall. [Wipes his forehead vigorously].

Mieville: He's setting us a killing pace. I hope I can last out. When is the meeting to begin exactly, Ronnie?

Ronnie Brockman: Dickie said half-an-hour after the swearing in. He's gone to change 'to shed his finery' he called it.

Campbell-Johnson: A correspondent just handed me this at the ceremony [waves a broadsheet], the usual bombast from the leftist press [reads out]: '*P.C. Joshi, General Secretary of the Communist Party of India, assured the faithful that the British had no real intention of leaving.*' He said: '*A Tory Field Marshal goes, but a Tory Admiral, accompanied by one of the cleverest imperialist generals, Ismay, both Mr Churchill's favourites, comes.*'

Vernon: I don't suppose the communists matter too much—the bad news is I've been told the British sentiment here is definitely anti-Mountbatten. They say he knows nothing about India and that he is a playboy.

Campbell-Johnson: Hmm. We shall have to tread carefully and avoid tender, British corns. We could very well say that Dickie has been called in after the situation has become hopeless. Only he himself is incurably optimistic!

Ismay: I think you should present a frank picture to all the foreign correspondents, Alan.

We have inherited inter-alia communal rioting which is spreading by chain reaction; in the Punjab, the Hindu–Muslim and Sikh communal tangle is contained only by an emergency decree; the Wavell plan is nothing but a phased military evacuation; the Congress has a formula for an independent sovereign republic resisted by the Muslim League formula of Direct Action; and the principle of paramountcy, which returns power to the Indian princes, contains no machinery to provide a new relationship with our successors in British India.

What could be more impossible!

[Mountbatten walks in briskly]

Mountbatten: Gentlemen, have a look at this morning's masterpiece. [waving newspaper] On the front page of *Dawn*—a photograph of Ronnie and Elizabeth described as 'Lord and Lady Louis arriving'.

[The paper is passed around as Mountbatten settles at his desk]

Mountbatten: Well, I won't keep you long, just wanted to tell you that beginning today, I will be holding one-hour meetings with all the Indian leaders. Nehru and Liaquat Ali Khan are coming to see me this afternoon. From tomorrow morning, all of us in this room—we shall include George Abell of course—will meet for informal round table moots on a day to day basis. This will enable us to think aloud without any reservations. I instituted this technique at Combined Operations and in the South-East Asia Command during the war and found it extremely useful. Till tomorrow morning, then.

[All start to leave]

Ismay: Dickie, I noticed at the swearing in that the Nawab of Bhopal and the Maharaja of Bikaner were absent. Aren't they two of your oldest personal friends in India?

Vernon: I was waiting to tell you Dickie, there was an urgent message, that they want to see you today.

Mountbatten: Well, I better see them and find out what their problem is—please give them time after Liaquat Ali.

[Ismay leaves. Ronnie places a file on Mountbatten's table]

Ronnie: It's almost time for the first interview with Nehru, you know him from earlier on don't you?

Mountbatten: Ah yes. Wavell called him quixotic, emotional and socialistic, rather deprecatingly. But I took greatly to him at our first meeting in Singapore. He has charm and intelligence and his socialism is tempered with worldly-wise sophistication. He responded very warmly to me at that time.

Ronnie: Lord Ismay was saying that you won his affection by ignoring the heavy-handed officials in Singapore and inviting him to lunch.

Mountbatten: I also gave him a car to drive around and meet his Indian admirers. He returned my goodwill by agreeing not to visit the memorial to Indians who fought on the Japanese side against us. He is able to see reason. And he found Edwina very sympathetic, of course. They had a long chat together.

[Knock on the door—Vernon peeps in]

Vernon: Pandit Nehru is here Your Excellency. [Lets Nehru in and goes out with Ronnie, closing door. Mountbatten and Nehru sit down]

Nehru: That was a very effective and crisp speech this morning. Everyone was impressed.

Mountbatten: I'm glad you think so. I hope I conveyed the urgency of our task. Let me take the bull by its horns—tell me, what is the main problem that you face with the Muslim?

Nehru: The Muslim League. Really, Lord Mountbatten, Lord Wavell's biggest mistake was to invite the League into the Assembly instead of waiting for them to ask to be brought in. I know for certain that a private League meeting had already decided to capitulate when the Viceroy invited them.

Mountbatten: You feel Wavell created the problem?

Nehru: Actually, it was his predecessor, Lord Linlithgow who raised Jinnah's stock as leader of the Muslim League. Since then Jinnah has exercised a virtual veto on every constitutional issue. The Simla conference in 1945 was held to ransom by Jinnah—he insisted all Muslim members of the executive council should belong to the League.

Last year they accepted the Cabinet mission plan in May and then withdrew agreement in July.

Mountbatten: That, I'm told, was because of the Congress party's attitude towards the grouping scheme. The clause was introduced to avoid division of the country. And then followed the Great Calcutta Killings last August, and the Muslim attacks on Hindus in Noakhali which were then followed by revenge killings in Bihar. In private, can you give me your own estimate of Jinnah?

Nehru: There's nothing secret about that—I have publicly done so in my recent book. You know the essential thing to realize about Jinnah is that success has come to him very late in life—at over sixty. Before that he was a successful lawyer, but not an especially good one. His success lies in his capacity to take up a permanently negative attitude.

Mountbatten: But he was in the Congress party—what offended him?

Nehru: He left our party only because it ceased to be a party for gentlemen, and he was a snob. He cannot forgive Gandhi for that. He accepted leadership of the Muslim League only to lash back at Gandhi—and especially Muslim Congressmen who had snubbed him. He doesn't really believe in Islam and Pakistan—his separatist policy is prompted purely by the desire to win easy attention and secular power. I don't believe he is sincere.

Mountbatten: Mr Nehru, what do you think is the biggest single problem facing India today?

Nehru: The economic one. But the Muslim League is determined to sabotage all economic planning as it entails planning for a unified India.

Mountbatten: Therefore, is not the problem of communalism more serious? And what about the Princely States? You cannot plan for a united India till you have sorted out these issues.

Nehru: All issues would be resolved if our economic policy were allowed to be implemented.

Mountbatten: But the situation in the Punjab cannot wait—the deadlock between the three communities is increasingly grave.

Nehru: The Sikhs and Hindus will now in no circumstances willingly accept the rule of an unrepresentative League ministry. As they will not in Bengal either.

Mountbatten: I have seen the resolution of the Congress advocating partition of the Punjab and of Bengal. But I believe Mr Gandhi is opposed to this resolution?

Nehru: I have not yet discussed this with Gandhiji. But he would be willing to pay an immediate cost for a long term benefit.

Mountbatten: And is Mr Gandhi's sojourn of Bihar after the riots of any help?

Nehru: Certainly it is helpful. But it is like going around with ointment trying to heal sore spots instead of diagnosing the cause of the sores and treating the body as a whole.

Mountbatten: I will discuss everything with Mr Gandhi, and of course with Mr Jinnah, as soon as they will come and see me and will do everything I can to help. [Warmly] Mr Nehru, I want you to regard me not as the last Viceroy winding up the British Raj, but as the first to lead the way to the new India. [Shakes Nehru's hand]

Nehru: [visibly moved] Now I know what they mean when they speak of your charm being so dangerous. [Smiles and leaves]

SCENE 6

Two journalists A and B are at lunch. Venue: The Imperial Hotel, New Delhi.

A: So. Mountbatten's coronation is over.

B: Lord! That was a pain! Did you see the little king's regalia? Every medal and order was on show.

A: It is the sick who are obsessed with their bodies, the impotent with their virility and the faithless with their faith. Without the majestic titles, silver thrones and ceremonial durbars the fraudulence of British pretensions would be all too apparent. [Pause] I do believe Mountbatten wanted to be Viceroy because of the grandeur and pomp, the ceremonial and uniforms. An immature schoolboy who loves to dress up and look handsome.

B: [Slowly] I think he has some sense of history, you know. The great-grandson of Queen Victoria, proclaimed first Empress of India giving away the 'brightest jewel', etc. Mountbatten, and his wife, I daresay, love posing as radicals of some sort. So he is a socialist Viscount behaving treacherously to his class. [Pause] The lady, actually, was less decorated. I hear, though, that makes her unhappy—she'd like to match medal for medal with Dickie boy.

A: Well, she seems to be a great hit with Nehru. I attended last evening's At Home that Nehru hosted for the delegates to the Asian Relations Conference and [leans back] saw the two cozying up all evening. Seems they've a lot to talk about for persons who've just met.

B: As a matter of fact, they met in Singapore when Mountbatten was Chief of South-East Asia Command. They had Nehru over for dinner and softened him up to the extent that he didn't go to the INA memorial—which was the main agenda of his visit! [Laughs] By the way, I presume Nehru invited you due to your socialist credentials?

A: Probably, though I'm not his kind of socialist! What seems to hold Nehru and Lady Edwina in mutual admiration is that both have earnestly absorbed editorials in so-called progressive publications, such as the *New Statesman* and the *Manchester Guardian*. They remind me strongly of the Webbs.

B: Shh! Here comes Mountbatten's PR man, and Nehru's PR man too!

[Campbell-Johnson and Krishna Menon walk in and settle at table near the journalists and while they order, the journalists pay and leave].

Campbell-Johnson: Krishna, who was with Mr Patel at breakfast in Pandit Nehru's home today? He was pleading with Nehru to open a new factory of his in Bombay.

Krishna Menon: Must be another of Sardar Patel's men—they are all a bunch of crooked businessmen.

Campbell-Johnson: You sound like that conservative editor I lunched with in Fleet Street in London. He was very bitter about some of India's business magnates: he said they were men with no principles save the acquisition of money, [laughingly] men without taste or culture, who eat bad food in ugly houses. Their outlook, he said, was in striking contrast to the idealism of the political leaders they were backing.

Krishna Menon: Sardar Patel is no idealist, let me tell you. Nehru has great difficulties with him. But the comment on the food is rather obnoxious—it's a question of habit and taste. [Smiles] You can't complain about that in the Nehru household though—you got an English breakfast, eggs and tomatoes, tea and coffee, toast and marmalade. Nehru should invite that editor of yours to dinner, perhaps. His cook is a great hand at European food.

[Journalist C passing by, stops at table]

C: Mr Campbell-Johnson! How are you sir? That was a great show you put up at the swearing in! It was a brilliant idea to put up the tri-forum platform for the cameramen, the first time such a film has been made in the Durbar Hall.

Campbell-Johnson: Thank you Sidney—but that was Lord Mountbatten's idea totally, not mine. Tell me, have you planted that story in *The People* today?

C: Not at all, I'm a *Daily Express* man; I don't work for the Odhams.

Campbell-Johnson: Don't they own *The People* and the *Daily Express*?

C: No, no. They own the *Daily Herald*! But, is it true sir? I suppose you wouldn't tell me....

Campbell-Johnson: Let me introduce you to Mr Nehru's friend and advisor, Mr Krishna Menon of the India League fame. He can tell you more than me.

Menon: I haven't seen the story, I'm afraid. Well, goodbye.

C: [Leaving reluctantly] Good day Mr Menon. [To Campbell-Johnson] Good day Sir, we shall meet at the press conference.

Menon: This place seems to be crawling with pressmen! The two who left the next table, I've seen them in London. What's *The People's* story, Alan?

Campbell-Johnson: On Nehru's alleged deal with the British government and his acceptance of Dominion Status for Hindustan, etc. I showed it to Mr Nehru, he shrugged it off as a two days' wonder.

Menon: I think you should put the record straight at your press conference. We've discussed it, Nehru and I. The suspicions about Churchill are so great, and as he is prepared to accept dominion status, no Indian can believe it means real freedom. I stressed to Nehru that we should press for common citizenship on the principle of reciprocity.

Campbell-Johnson: Well, I'm sure that will come up at Mountbatten's next meeting with Mr Nehru. Meanwhile, what do you think he's going to do about the Muslim League members in the cabinet, they simply and completely reject him?

Krishna Menon: He's been very tolerant so far, but there is a limit to his patience. I'm sure he won't put up with their obstructionism for too long now—their behaviour is intolerable!

Campbell-Johnson: What do you think the Mahatma's attitude is going to be? I think Mountbatten is a little anxious about him. They are due to meet this afternoon.

Krishna Menon: Oh, Mountbatten is starting with a decided advantage—Gandhi regards him, I'm told, as an honest man, an upright admiral. But, I must warn you, a conversation with the Mahatma is always unpredictable—there's a constant danger of Gandhi side-tracking it in to some project of his own!

Campbell-Johnson: [laughs] By the way, Nehru's charming and brilliant sister, Mrs Pandit, appears to have made a great impression at the United Nations in New York. Do you think she would influence Nehru in matters of international relations?

Menon: Absolutely to the contrary! She takes her brief completely from him, actually idolizes him.

Campbell-Johnson: Oh, I see.

Menon: Alan, there's something I have to speak with you about, I think it hasn't been very wise to retain George Abell on Mountbatten's staff. The ICS staff of most Viceroys is never trusted, and there is tremendous criticism of Abell in particular.

Campbell-Johnson: That's unfortunate, very discouraging. George Abell is a man of high calibre and patent objectivity. Ismay was saying just the other day that Abell is one of those rare birds, a first at Oxford and a triple Blue, destined for the highest offices in the land if the British Raj was not willingly being ended.

Menon: Well, the attacks against him may be unjustified, but they must be recognized by Mountbatten as a political reality. I suppose I can discuss it with Mountbatten himself when he can see me—when he has run through all the big guns he's meeting these days.

Campbell-Johnson: You knew him fairly well in London did you not? So you can mention it to him if you like, though I'm absolutely convinced he has implicit faith in Abell's impartiality.

[They begin to eat]

SCENE 7

Viceroy's House, Delhi. Mountbatten, Edwina, and their 18-year-old daughter Pamela, at breakfast.

Edwina: So here we are in India, in this labyrinthine monument. Any regrets Dickie?

Mountbatten: Well, I resisted it as you know, but I was relentlessly cornered. Amazing! I made all sorts of conditions and each one was met. I will choose and take my own staff from London and keep Wavell's as well—agreed; I must have Pug Ismay, all my staff must be allowed to bring their wives, they must be given cars and air conditioners—granted; I said my old York aircraft had to be fitted out just as I liked it and complete control over the Honours list at the end of my term—every condition was met! Now, all the balls are in my court and I have to deliver. And I quite like the challenge of steering warring leaders into a sensible course.

I told Wavell I was trying to get Gandhi and Jinnah together, and he gave me a pokerfaced look. He probably thought: here comes the new, smart boy who thinks everything is a cakewalk. He would've been amazed at the way I handled Bhopal and Bikaner yesterday.

Edwina: [To Pamela] Daddy's like a dynamo isn't he? He slathers on the charm, becomes ruthless next, and then flashes his Germanic arrogance.

Pamela: I heard the younger staff, Ian and Peter, say that he was called 'democratic Dickie' because he sits familiarly on the ground with Indian hosts.

Mountbatten: Don't make fun of me ladies! Well, both of you are my secret weapons, your job is to get the women on our side.

Edwina: Oh! Is that official? O-n-l-y the women?

Mountbatten: Jokes apart—it's a strange coincidence, perhaps, but have you noticed the four important leaders of India, Nehru–Patel–Jinnah–Gandhi—are all widowers.

And three have women with strong personalities behind them—Nehru's sister, Vijayalakshmi, Jinnah's sister, Fatima, and Patel's daughter. You have to get to know them so that a general fund of goodwill can be generated.

Edwina: Of course, Dickie. I'm genuinely interested in knowing them. And I'm most eager to meet Mr Gandhi. So is Pammy.

Mountbatten: Capital! Everything, absolutely everything, is going to depend on personal relationships. Nehru, for example, I like him and he's very friendly towards us. Though I must say that it helps that he is a great snob and pro-English, even if the English put him in jail so often. He's always been one for rank and titles. [Moment's silence] You know, I still can't get used to being treated like an Emperor. [Laughingly] I find you have to hold ladies' hands very firmly while they make a deep curtsey as they seem to steady themselves on your hand and are apt to pull themselves up by it.

Edwina: It's all so stuffy. Oh, I must tell you, some of the old hands here refer to me as the Vice Queen. Isn't it delicious? It makes me feel like Mrs Meyrick.

Mountbatten: And it seems they are infecting Pug with nostalgia. He was very gloomy last night and said we would be going out 'to the last *chukka* twelve goals down'.

[Campbell-Johnson comes in with a record in his hand]

Campbell-Johnson: Good-morning. Viceroy's House is like the Versailles of South Asia—I tend to get lost in it.

Edwina: And Dickie loves it despite his protests. But I am doing my best to straighten out the bad protocol of this place. I looked at the lists of invitees to the regular Viceregal luncheons and evening receptions and could barely find any Indian names in it. Well, I've made the rule that not less than fifty per cent of those present must be Indians. Last night, the large crowd of Indian leaders we had saw the inside of Viceroy's house literally for the first time. And I could see their barely-suppressed curiosity. Pammy overheard an English lady say that it made her sick to see this house full of dirty Indians.

Mountbatten: That's horrifying! I shall quote this at the Governor's meeting today, such people should be sent back home straightaway.

Edwina: And I'm going to introduce some measures of austerity in the kitchen. It's obscene to have such lavish meals when there is a near famine in parts of India.

[A visitor is announced. Mountbatten and Edwina start to walk towards the door]

Campbell-Johnson: I've brought Pammy the record I promised, Bing Crosby's 'Moonlight becomes you'. It's still very popular in India. [To Pammy] Shall we listen to it? [They leave by another door. The song is heard, then fades.]

SCENE 8

Mountbatten's staff meeting in a dark, air-conditioned study at the Viceroy's house is about to begin. Abell, Christie, and Peter Scott are putting papers in files on table. Mountbatten's group has yet to arrive.

Christie: Here you are—all files in order.

Abell: Yesterday the Dickie birds had a meeting in camera. Today, I was told I would also attend the morning sessions. Want to pick my brains no doubt.

Christie: I just heard a gem of Jinnah's on the great Dickie. Having heard of his Lordship's ambition to be Admiral of the fleet, Jinnah said that he would devote Pakistan's first budget to building him a battleship and even supply him with a crew: Azad as laundryman, Nehru as steersman, to keep him miles away, and Gandhi for hot air to breathe into the boilers.

Abell: Jinnah's interview with him will be exciting. Now, both of you better leave—I hear the Dickie birds arriving. [Sounds of talk, laughter approaching]

[Mountbatten and team arrive, all settle around table]

Mountbatten: So far, I've seen Nehru, Liaquat, Bikaner, Bhopal, John Matthai, and not least, Patel. These bods are heavy, not one stays less than three hours. At the end of these sessions I feel like a boiled egg despite the air-conditioning. [Pause] You have read the resume of each conversation, haven't you? Nehru really surprised me by his statement that the economic problem was most serious despite the utter confusion India faces in communalism and the problem of the Princes. Nehru's letter to Wavell almost two weeks ago recommends the division of the Punjab into a predominantly Muslim area and a predominantly non-Muslim area. He assures us that the Sikhs also desire this. We must get all the information from the Governors of the two provinces.

Mieville: There is a telegram from Sir Evan Jenkins, the Punjab Governor, that the Sikh leader, Giani Kartar Singh insists on the partition of the Punjab and threatens to resist with all his Sikh resources any attempt to set up a Muslim League ministry there. He says it was the Sikhs who persuaded the Congress to put up the resolution in favour of partitioning the Punjab.

Campbell-Johnson: I have here a report from the *Manchester Guardian*. It says '*the partition of Punjab and Bengal seems to be a political folly at first sight and gives an additional argument for Pakistan. But it has been taken up by Hindu politicians with the stated object of reducing the Muslim majority provinces to such a small dimension that the idea of Pakistan no longer appears workable or attractive to the most ardent Muslim.*'

Mountbatten: We must coordinate information from the governors of both provinces. The second meeting I had was with Liaquat Ali Khan. As we know, he put Nehru in a difficult position by producing a poor man's budget and hitting capitalists. Nehru now is in the invidious position of seeking relief and protection for the industrialists backing the Congress at the expense of his own progressive views. I'm certain some compromise will be found on this—there is a limit beyond which the Muslim League cannot go in taxing wealthy subscribers. Liaquat Ali told me that the League was convinced I had made my swearing-in speech at the request of the Congress—a good example of the prevailing communal suspicion.

Campbell-Johnson: The Congressmen believe we put Liaquat up to making the budget proposals which soak the Hindu rich and are calculated to widen the breach between their millionaire and four-*anna* subscribers. What else did Zinkin say?

Campbell-Johnson: He put forward the thesis that Pakistan was economically viable—we mustn't readily assume it has no survival value. I asked him to prepare a memorandum on this. And last, he spoke of Nehru as Gandhi's western face.

Mountbatten: Ismay tells me that Patel seems to share this view of Nehru. He compares himself as a simple village follower of Gandhi to the westernized Nehru. But his reputation as the strong man of the Congress was apparent in his very blunt statement that India must get rid of the Muslim League once and for all.

Campbell-Johnson: That was exactly the view of K.M. Panikkar who is the *Diwan* of the Prince of Bikaner. Maurice had invited him to meet me and he was very forthright on Pakistan. '*Hindustan is the elephant*,' he said, '*and Pakistan the two ears. The elephant can live without the ears*'. As for the Princes, he thinks they must seek security within the structure which will take over from the Raj. The Princes who have already joined the Constituent Assembly, probably under his influence, are trying to reinforce the right wing of Congress and act as a counterweight to the socialists.

Mountbatten: Right. Time now for my letter to London. [Stenographer called in, Mountbatten dictates] Dear Secretary of State, etc. I am already persuaded, after one week here, that the decision regarding the future of India must be taken at a considerably earlier date than was envisaged in London before I left, if further trouble is to be avoided here. The cabinet, as the viceroy's executive council is now colloquially called, is divided on communal lines and each party insists on its own solution.

The country is in a most unsettled state. There are communal riots even here in Delhi, besides the Punjab, UP, North-West Frontier Province, Bihar, Calcutta, and Bombay. I have received a report that so far in the North-West Frontier Province the Muslim Pathan felt the British Raj to be his natural enemy and was happy to find an ally in the Congress party. Now that the Congress looks like it is taking over from the British, cries such as 'No Hindu Raj' and 'Muslims Unite' appeal to the Pathan in spite of the influence, reportedly high character and intelligence of the Pathan Prime Minister and his friendship with Gandhi. The Punjab is busy preparing for a civil war. The Sikhs plan to seize the main irrigation centres in order to exercise physical control over the whole province. There are demonstrations by Muslim immigrants on the Assam border and further disorder is threatened. The Bihar police is a washout and in constant trouble.

The only conclusion I have been able to come to is that unless I act quickly I may well find the real beginnings of a civil war on my hands. As for the Princes of India, the King had entrusted me with ensuring their welfare in any plan of transferring power. It was very distressing to me to find how completely the Maharaja of Bikaner had thrown in his lot with the Congress party, along with the Maharajas of Jaipur, Jodhpur, Patiala, Baroda and Gwalior, and split the Princes whose unity the Nawab of Bhopal has struggled for so long to ensure. [Breaks off dictation] Can anyone tell me what politics the Princes have been playing?

Abell: The most important are the communal politics they are being pulled into. Patiala, Mysore, Jodhpur and Kashmir are being successfully wooed by the Hindus. All of them are major benefactors of Malaviya's Hindu University. The Nizam and the Begum of Bhopal, on the other hand, gave several *lakhs* to the new Muslim University at Aligarh. Patiala and Nabha gave a big sum to the Sikh Khalsa College at Lahore, and Bikaner has been a large benefactor of the Servants of

Hindu Society and Gandhi's Hindi campaign on behalf of untouchables.

Mieville: But surely those are worthy causes! They would demolish their ill-deserved reputation as bejewelled loafers.

Abell: It is not an innocent pattern. During the war, Patiala spent heavily on armaments, and is known to have an ambitious scheme to rebuild the kingdom of Lahore. Bhopal augmented his army with Pathan mercenaries from the North-West Frontier Province and it was widely rumoured that he intended to use them in his kingdom.

Ismay: It is understandable that Muslim Princes should worry when the Chamber of Princes is being run by a man who is described as a 'most bitter Brahmin' obsessed with a desire to avenge the disappearance of the Brahmin power of the Peshwas. He plans to create blocks of Hindu ruled states. I am told the Nizam himself feels threatened by Haksar.

Vernon: Friends of mine in the service at Bhopal tell me that the Nawab calls himself an Indian nationalist. He is relatively young, and a modern prince. Quite contrary to the stereotype of the oriental despot.

Abell: His modernism is well suited to resisting government power. There was a story of how he did not arrange a formal Durbar for Colonel Heale as required by protocol. When asked about it, he explained that he had been trying to do things in the European way.

Mountbatten: This bit about oriental despots is the legacy of the evangelicals who wanted to civilize the heathen, I'm afraid. I have some good friends amongst the Princes. Though mind you, some of them are as profligate as they come.

Ismay: Oh, yes. I have spent time with some of them and a half-century of public school education at 'Chiefs' Colleges plus educative trips abroad have turned them into proper cricketers.

Campbell-Johnson: V.P. Menon tells me that Bhopal has shifted his stance of Hindu-Muslim unity. He doesn't like the Congress republicanism.

Abell: I think his anger was born of the nationalists failure to concede the Muslim claim for fair representation in the Central Legislature. He was also influenced by the Nizam's closeness to the Muslim League. After all, he got a lot of financial help from the Nizam. Moreover, the Hindu rulers of North and Central India make no secret of their financial backing for the Mahasabha.

Ismay: It's true Bhopal is quite unfairly attacked by Haksar. He calls him an out and out Pakistani. And Panikkar recently charged him with being a Muslim partisan and an enemy of the Hindus.

Mountbatten: Tell me about Panikkar, Abell. He is to see me in regard to Bikaner's affairs and all I know is that he is the Prime Minister of the state.

Abell: A very suave gentleman. He was the editor of a nationalist newspaper at Madras and helped Gandhi to defuse the Akali temple agitation in the Punjab. He also took part in the temple *satyagraha* in his home state of Travancore. He is very ambitious, likes rubbing shoulders with powerful people and is busy canvassing closer relations between the Princes and the nationalists. He was responsible for bringing together the present Mr Nehru's father and Mr Patel's brother with the rulers of Bikaner and Kashmir. And now he has effectively sealed a deal between the Hindu Princes and the Congress.

Mountbatten: So that explains Bikaner's cozying up to the Congress. Right. Time for lunch.

[All move out except Mountbatten and Campbell-Johnson]

Campbell-Johnson: I must tell you Dickie, Panikkar is highly urbane and respected among Indians. They are very proud of him—he is a graduate of Oxford, Sorbonne and the Middle Temple. He wrote a scholarly book on the relations of the states with the Government of India. He was the first Indian ever to get a scholarship to Christ Church and received an Oxford first. I think Abell doesn't like what he considers his overambitious style.

SCENE 9

Mughal Gardens, outside the Viceroy's study. Crowd of pressmen, cameramen quizzing Campbell-Johnson about photograph opportunities clamouring to go inside.

Gandhi arrives, Mountbatten's ADC takes him in. Mountbatten and Edwina come out with Gandhi. Frenzied scramble for posed shots. As they turn and go back inside, Gandhi places his hand on Edwina's shoulder, and a cameraman leaps forward and takes a shot.

Campbell-Johnson herds out all present urging them to get 'some refreshment'.

The scene shifts inside to the Viceroy's study. Gandhi and Mountbatten are sitting in armchairs away from the table where

Mountbatten conducts his daily 'interviews' with Indian leaders. Gandhi with feet folded beneath him in chair.

Gandhi: It was very naughty of you to release pictures of me eating curds at tea yesterday.

Mountbatten: Edwina and Pamela were really very thrilled to meet you. Both of them feel honoured that you invited them to your prayer meetings. It seems you already knew Pamela as a regular speaker at Indian youth groups.

Gandhi: I am very impressed by their genuine interest in our problems and Lady Mountbatten's compassionate nature. I'm afraid you encouraged me to bore all of you with reminiscences of my early life in England and South Africa.

Mountbatten: They were fascinating. And your accounts of meetings with the Viceroys in the past really helped me to understand so many developments. Campbell-Johnson, you know, my press attaché whom I introduced at our first meeting, tells me that the Press refused to believe that momentous decisions had not taken place.

Gandhi: I have a proposal of great importance to place before you in all seriousness. I would like to avert partition at all costs.

Mountbatten: Yes, so would I. It really makes me unhappy to think of Indian unity being broken up.

Gandhi: Therefore, I will ask Nehru to resign and you can call Jinnah to form the interim government. He can appoint an all-Muslim cabinet.

Mountbatten: What would Jinnah say?

Gandhi: [Grins] He would say, '*Aha, it's that wily Gandhi again*'.

Mountbatten: Won't he be right?

Gandhi: No. I am absolutely sincere. Lord Mountbatten, the old Roman policy that the British executed in India, of divide and rule, has come to roost. It has brought about a situation in which there are only two alternatives: either a continuation of British rule, to keep law and order, or an Indian blood-bath.

Mountbatten: What must I do then?

Gandhi: You must face the blood-bath. Accept it. [A moment's silence] So, what do you think of my proposal to ask Mr Jinnah to take over?

Mountbatten: I shall ask Lord Ismay to make a draft of the details of your proposal—how you think it can be implemented.

Gandhi: I will give him a detailed plan. By the way, I have been scolding Aruna Asaf Ali, the young Socialist lady, for being so aggressively anti-British. I am very anxious that she should meet Lady Mountbatten and discover the immense goodwill both of you have for India.

Mountbatten: Certainly. I shall ask Edwina to invite her again, though she refused an earlier invitation. [Stands up] Come, let us go and talk to Lord Ismay.

Gandhi: [While walking out with Mountbatten] You must consider my proposal seriously, I can assure you of Congress cooperation, and I will tour the whole country and convince everyone about my plan.

SCENE 10

Viceroy's staff meeting. All seated around table.

Mountbatten: As you know I have had five meetings with Gandhi during the past week. The first two days I purposely spent in getting to know him and hearing the story of his life. The presence of Lady Mountbatten and my daughter helped to produce an air of friendliness.

It was only on the third day that we got down to business and he produced the plan which Lord Ismay will read out. In sum, he has come out definitely for inviting Jinnah to form an administration and pledged himself to get Congress support for it. I am rather impressed by him. He reminds me of the phenomenal Mr Pyke—the scientist at Combined Operations who put forth the plan of the floating, self-propelled airfield made of ice—far-fetched but potentially feasible.

Ismay: It is an utterly mad plan. He calls it 'a scheme for an interim government pending transfer of power'. 1. Mr Jinnah to be given the option of forming a cabinet. 2. The selection of the cabinet is left entirely to Mr Jinnah. The members may all be Muslims or all non-Muslims, or they may be representatives of all classes and creeds of the Indian people. 3. In the assembly the Congress have a decisive majority. But the Congress would guarantee to cooperate freely and sincerely so long as all the measures Mr Jinnah's cabinet brings forward are in the interests of the Indian people as a whole. 4. The sole referee of what is or is not in the interests of India as a whole will be Lord Mountbatten, in his personal capacity as a man and not in his representative capacity. 5. Mr Jinnah must stipulate, on behalf of the League or of any other parties represented in his cabinet, that they will do their utmost to preserve peace throughout India. 6. There shall be no National Guards or any other form of private army. 7. Within the framework hereof Mr Jinnah will be perfectly free to present for acceptance a scheme of Pakistan, even before the transfer of power.

Abell: It was always very risky to negotiate with Gandhi.

Mountbatten: There is no question of negotiation. I told him that unless he could get Nehru to back the plan as practicable and was certain to get Congress backing, I would not have anything to do with it.

Ismay: We could write and make clear to him that the Viceroy was only asking for advice and nothing more. It is important to get out of Gandhi's mind any idea that we consider his scheme as a draft agreement of any sort. Possibly he has mentioned it to Nehru who may have disagreed and he thinks he can push our hand this way.

Mountbatten: He must be reminded that I always insisted it would be necessary to talk about his scheme with Nehru—I must be convinced that Nehru agrees with him. What's next?

Vernon: Lord Ismay to present his report on discussions with the Governor of Punjab, Sir Jenkins and Governor of the North-West Frontier Province, Sir Olaf.

Ismay: [Reads] Punjab first. Jenkins says a general election here would solve nothing. The League would probably get a bare majority and would then proceed to form a Muslim ministry without Sikh or Hindu representation. This would properly touch off the mine. Then, the Sikhs are brewing up trouble. Their objective is the mastery of their old kingdom and they wish to establish a Sikh state. They have been extremely uneasy since it became clear that the British intended to transfer power to Indian hands. They threatened militant agitation during 1946 claiming they had been unfairly treated by the cabinet mission and demanded a communal veto. They were placated by the selection of Sardar Baldev Singh as Defence member and by his visit to London with the other party leaders. All Sikhs were deeply disturbed by the Muslim League agitation of January–February 1947, and Master Tara Singh aroused Sikh feeling. The resignation of the coalition ministry increased the anger and apprehension of the Sikhs and inflammatory speeches by Tara Singh led to communal outbreak. The Muslims, for their part, especially in Rawalpindi division, have made a dead set at the Sikhs and there is no doubt that the Sikh leaders are preparing for retaliation. Intelligence reports suggest that the Sikhs will wait until the British leave India before making any big move. But further attacks by Muslims on them might force their hand. There is a strong Jat versus non-Jat feeling among the Sikhs complicated by the fact that those in office are seldom active party managers. Sardar Baldev Singh and Sardar Swaran Singh have influence within the community but have never been in the front rank of the Shiromani Akali Dal, the Sikh party. Therefore, the governor recommends the viceroy should call Baldev Singh, whose wealth and position in the cabinet gives him standing, and ask him to get hold of Master Tara Singh and Giani Kartar Singh who are clever party managers. The viceroy should also tell Nehru and Jinnah, who will not like it though, that he proposes to call the Sikhs into consultation. Finally, Jenkins said that partition in the Punjab would be a dirty job requiring a lot of troops.

In the North-West Frontier Province, Olaf Caroe says the clash is between Hindu-financed Muslims and the Muslim League. It is immensely complicated by the tribes who are in sympathy with the League. The Congress inspired government has thrown Muslim League members in jail and their methods are completely totalitarian. Feelings are running high, and the government there says it will not hold a general election until the new constitution is decided. Meanwhile, the tribes may flare up at any moment and the frontier will disintegrate. According to the governor, three courses are open to us. The Viceroy can take over tribal affairs himself. This would be resisted by the Indian cabinet but the tribal response would be immediately welcoming, we should take the line that it is necessary to ascertain beyond any shadow of doubt that in a province where power is so evenly balanced, to whom should power be transferred: in short to have a general election. Since the Congress is opposed to it, we can induce them somehow to agree to the election, though it would almost certainly be rigged. The only way of assuring a clean election would be for us to take the initiative and force it on them. This would mean dismissing the ministry, dissolving the house, and taking powers under section 93. This is what both the League and the tribes demand. Caroe told me that he recommends forcing a general election, though he appreciates that it is a difficult move which might infuriate the Congress.

Mountbatten: Before I take any decision I would like to visit the Frontier myself. Please let Caroe know that I will fly to Peshawar as soon as possible and would like to hold discussions with the Prime

Minister Dr Khan personally. Meanwhile, all of you can briefly note down your views.

Anything else before Mr Jinnah arrives to see me?

Campbell-Johnson: I have a file of press cuttings from the British press on your first meeting with Gandhi. That photograph, in which Gandhi is seen with his hand on Lady Mountbatten's shoulder, has created an unholy row in England. The conservative reaction is to call it outrageous—that a British Vicereine should permit such a familiar gesture by a native.

Mountbatten: [Takes file] Edwina will be greatly amused to see this—she loves a controversy. Alan, when you come to dinner with us tonight we can discuss whether we should send any response to any newspaper. It's time now for my notoriously difficult customer to arrive.

[All leave. A moment later, Ronnie brings Jinnah in, then goes out. Mountbatten and Jinnah formally shake hands, sit]

Mountbatten: I hope you have given thought to accepting the Cabinet Mission Plan, as I urged upon you yesterday?

Jinnah: That is quite impossible, as I said yesterday.

Mountbatten: I must warn you the Congress is adamant that the Muslim League should either enter the Constituent Assembly or be expelled from the interim government. Lord Wavell had only offered you seats in the interim government on the understanding that you would enter the Constituent Assembly.

Jinnah: [Heatedly] I deny that implication. If you search the files you will find that I have carefully preserved my position in this matter—all my letters are crystal clear. And I have nothing to add to what I stated in the letters.

[*There is palpable tension and a long silence. Mountbatten is reading something*]

Jinnah: You see, Lord Mountbatten, it is quite valueless for us to enter the assembly or try to go back to the Cabinet Mission Plan, since the whole spirit of cooperation and mutual trust with which we were supposed to work is completely absent. In fact, the atmosphere is taking a turn for the worse, and it is absolutely clear that the Congress has no intention of working the Plan either in spirit or letter. India has now passed beyond the stage at which any compromise can work. I would call upon you to hand over power as soon as possible—preferably province by province.

Mountbatten: And who will defend the country—who will take charge of the defence forces?

Jinnah: On the question of defence I have come to the conclusion that the Defence forces must be separated, and Pakistan and Hindustan must be responsible separately for their own defence. It will not be possible to have any form of central organization on terms of parity.

Mountbatten: I must point out to you that in discussing your proposals I am very far from agreeing with you. But I naturally have to consider every proposal put to me. Even if your proposals prove to be the correct solution, they can only be satisfactorily implemented if I have the necessary time at my disposal for each step to be properly carried out. Brigadier Cariappa and five other senior officers have told me that it would take a minimum of five years before the present Indian army can expect to be efficient and stand on its own, without the help of British officers. You are asking me to perform the miracle of cutting the army into half. Do you seriously consider that it can be implemented by the time I have to leave in June 1948?

Jinnah: [Cryptic smile] How then do you propose to leave in June 1948—is it then your intention to turn this country over to chaos, bloodshed and civil war?

Mountbatten: There is one thing of which I'm quite certain—that I am going in June 1948, and withdrawing all British personnel. [Stands up] Unless, by some miraculous event all Indian parties unite together to beg us not to go in the interests of the Indian people, as a whole.

[Mountbatten calls 'Alan' who enters and is introduced]

Mountbatten: Mr Jinnah, this is Alan Campbell-Johnson—my press attaché. Perhaps you could see him to help with press problems?

Jinnah: Ah yes, I will be pleased to see you. You may call on me at 11 a.m. at my home tomorrow. [Stands up] I will take your leave then.

[Jinnah moves slowly as Campbell-Johnson walks him to door and returns]

Mountbatten: You know I quite like the old boy really. His hat and monocle, raised finger slicing the air with emphasis, solemn looks and cold voice, like watching a pantomime.

SCENE 11

Staff meeting, all are seated waiting for Mountbatten to arrive.

Ronnie Brockman: I believe Alan went over to 'Gimlet's' house yesterday [to Alan] how did it go?

Campbell-Johnson: His house looks rather like a mosque—full of red and black inlay. On his mantelpiece he had a silver map of India, and Pakistan is marked in green. He dismissed the All-India Editor's Conference as a bunch of Hindus. It was quite funny, he said that he never exercised direct influence over the policy of his paper, *Dawn*, and then added without a smile, 'The editor has always been in agreement with my views'. [All laugh]

Ismay: Is Dickie meeting 'His Nibs' today, Ronnie? I have a letter from him for Dickie.

Abell: 'His Nibs'?

Ronnie: [to Abell] Gandhi. No, he's not due today.

Ismay: He doesn't give up! He's still conjuring up a 'Gandhi–Mountbatten pact' out of nothing more than Dickie's sympathetic interest in helping along Hindu–Muslim rapprochement. King George did urge the Prime Minister to give a clear directive to Dickie: Is he to lead the retreat out of India or is he to work for the reconciliation of Hindus and Muslims?

Mieville: The problem is, nobody knows. Dickie is putting on a marvellous show though.

Ian Scott: Do you know what he told Peter? He said, '*We shall be incredibly unpopular, and the odds are we shall end up with bullets in our back.*'

Ismay: I think he is very lucky. Look what a great success he is with the Indian leaders. And I like working for lucky men.

Campbell-Johnson: He is a wonderful conversationalist and puts across his own sincerity. I was at lunch at Viceroy House when the Indonesian Premier, and Nehru and his daughter were guests. Dickie and Nehru seemed like the best of friends.

Ismay: By the way, have you heard Lady Edwina has imposed rationing in Viceroy's House? The helpings are so small that the hungrier members of the staff [smiling at the two Scotts] are seeking invitations to houses where they can be sure of a square meal.

Ian Scott: How was the food at the big state dinner for the British Residents of the Princely States?

Ismay: The silver plate was brought out, but it somehow did not improve the flavour of the food.

Campbell-Johnson: Did you notice the string band played a strange blend of Gilbert and Sullivan and Indian rhythms?

Mieville: What I found very moving were the portraits of former Viceroys—Minto, Mayo, Halifax and Reading looking down upon the scene under the Persian ceiling.

Campbell-Johnson: Before I forget, I must tell you the story of Jinnah's first visit. When he was being photographed with Dickie and Lady Edwina, he spoke of a rose between two thorns. Unfortunately, it turned out that he was in the middle himself.

[Laughter as Mountbatten enters]

Mountbatten: What is the joke?

Ismay: Jinnah.

Mountbatten: My God, he is cold. That's no laughing matter. When I saw him first he was in a most frigid, haughty and disdainful frame of mind. He started off the conversation abruptly and said, '*I will enter into discussion on one condition only.*' I interrupted him before he could finish his sentence and told him I was not prepared to discuss conditions or even the present situation at that stage and the object of the meeting was to make each other's acquaintance. He was taken aback but he remained reserved and aloof. I had thought of asking him to dinner that very night but put it off to the next day, I simply could not sustain two sessions with him in one day. He came with his sister to dine alone with Edwina and myself and stayed until well after midnight, and it was only by then that the ice was really broken. Though even through dinner he kept harping on Muslim massacres and described the horrors at length. He says the Congress will even accept dominion status to deprive him of Pakistan, and wants me to perform a surgical operation. I did tell him that an anaesthetic is required before the operation but he kept demanding a quick decision. He is coming today, and I will have a difficult talk with him. [Opens a folder] My conclusions thus far are this: 1. The only way to get his cooperation is to tell him that the British accept Pakistan, a truncated version if necessary. 2. We must strengthen the centre by getting him into the government by providing such safeguards as he agrees upon, and 3. We make use of Gandhi to put through a solution with the aim of eventually creating a truncated Pakistan.

I believe Jinnah is not opposed to an interim government under a British Viceroy. Can the Muslims not be given some sort of parity in the interim government?

Abell: It is not likely that the Congress will agree to that. There is really no justification on census figures for such parity. Congress has never agreed to it and I think they never will.

Ismay: A committee can be established from members of the interim government to work out the ultimate solution, and there can be parity in this committee under the chairmanship of the viceroy. [Turns to Mountbatten] Perhaps you could tell Jinnah you want him in the government so that he can present his views directly in the committee conferences.

Abell: I am extremely doubtful that Jinnah will agree to join the government on such terms.

Mieville: Whether or not Jinnah joins the government, a small committee of two Congress representatives, two from the Muslim League, one Sikh and perhaps the Nawab of Bhopal should be set up under the Viceroy to hammer out the final plan.

Mountbatten: I am opposed to this, it would mean throwing away my present strong position whereby I alone make the decision. There will be no agreement nor will I ask for acceptance. But the Indian leaders must be made to believe in the impartiality, competence and firmness of whatever decision I make as a testator on behalf of His Majesty's Government. My ideas at present are: 1. The earliest possible transfer of power, 2. India should be offered Commonwealth status as soon as possible, 3. I will remain as constitutional head until June 1948, and 4. The British will remain at the beck and call of India for any assistance required during the period India chooses to remain a member of the Commonwealth.

Ismay: Do you intend to obtain the sanction of His Majesty's Government before telling the Indians of your decision? I am very concerned over the early introduction of Commonwealth status. If power is transferred before 1948 what will happen to the British army in India, and indeed to the Indian army with British officers owing allegiance to the king? It would be wise to avoid any premature grant of dominion status.

Mieville: If dominion status is granted in say, June 1947, the Viceroy would remain in an advisory capacity only. He would attend meetings of the cabinet. He would have no powers.

Mountbatten: I understand these objections but some formula will have to be devised to reserve powers for me. However, a decision in principle should be taken right away and the Indians themselves left to work it out in detail. Only short notice and a time limit can make the Indian leaders face up to reality.

Mieville: The strife between communities in the Punjab is heating up very rapidly—I doubt they can work out any details without your help.

Ismay: I have another letter for you from Gandhi, asking for your advice. [Gives letter to Mountbatten, who looks at it and hands it back]

Mountbatten: I can't make out the handwriting—please read it.

Ismay: [Reads] '*Dear friend, I have pressing letters from the Punjab asking me to go there. Pandit Nehru agrees. Nevertheless, I would like your guidance as well. Then Noakhali calls. If the wires received by me during the last two days are to be relied upon, there is increasing lawlessness in Noakhali. Attempts at roasting people alive have been traced, and looting etc. is going on. This outbreak of violence is not a mere detail. If it cannot be dealt with now, it won't be fourteen months from now. Signed: Yours sincerely, M.K. Gandhi.*'

Mountbatten: Ronnie, please take down the reply. [Dictates] Dear Mr Gandhi, Many thanks for your letter of today. I find it difficult to advise you. I doubt whether you ought to exhaust yourself by undertaking any tour in the Punjab at this time of the year. I quite agree that these outbreaks of violence are not a mere detail. What we have to secure is a settlement between the parties at the centre, and if possible, a combined front against violence. It is the effort to find a solution which will occupy all my efforts in the near future, and I know I can rely on help from you wherever you may be. I enjoyed meeting you so much and found all you had to say of the greatest interest. Yours sincerely, Mountbatten of Burma. Do it now, I'll sign it right away. Alan, was it any help going over to Jinnah?

Campbell-Johnson: It was helpful in so far as it will enable me to make contact with the Muslim press, but there are no chances of any working arrangement between the Hindu and them. I had tea in the afternoon with the Nehru household. It was most interesting—Nehru's daughter, Indira, and Krishna Menon alleged that the League had grown under British encouragement.

Mountbatten: I'm going to do some tough talking today with Mr Jinnah. Do you know I was somewhat apprehensive about my first meeting with Patel? But he had quite a twinkle in his eye. While Jinnah! The nickname 'Gimlet' really becomes him.

SCENE 12

Sardar Patel reclines in chaise longue in his house; his daughter, Manibehn, serves him some snack. V.P. Menon enters, bows in greeting and the latter welcomes him benignly; asks Manibehn to also serve their guest.

Patel: So? While the Viceroy holds his Durbar what have you been doing? How are you trying to help us?

V.P. Menon: I've drawn up a scheme to solve the problems in the transfer of power, but I'm sorry to say that the only way we can move forward is to accept that Jinnah will never back down from his Pakistan. Sardar, with all due respect, I feel you should accept the fact that Jinnah has the support of influential British opinion in his claim to Pakistan. Even more important, he is supported by most of the high officers of the army.

Patel: [With a wave of his hand] They are all pro-Muslim. Jinnah is the worst headache we have. [Pause] What do you suggest then?

V.P. Menon: My personal view is that it is better to divide India rather than let it gravitate towards civil war. If we agree to partition, Jinnah can obviously not ask for those portions of the Punjab, Bengal and Assam which are predominantly non-Muslim.

Patel: What happens to the transfer of power to independent India then? What will be the basis?

V.P. Menon: In a divided India the transfer can be to two central governments, but it should be on the basis of dominion status.

Patel: The Congress has opposed it all these years, how can we accept it now?

V.P. Menon: Sardar, you must use your power over the Party members. [Becomes excited] You see, by consenting to dominion status Congress will gain great advantages. Firstly, it will ensure a peaceful transfer of power. Secondly, it will be warmly welcomed in Britain. Jinnah has been insisting that Pakistan must remain in the Commonwealth and if we also accept, we will have British friendship and goodwill to counter him. Thirdly, the British officials in the Civil Service and Indian army, air force and navy—will all be willing to help if we stay in the Commonwealth. Last, but not least, the Princes who are so fond of their connection to the Crown will be reassured and more willing to federate. [Stops and looks at Patel who is frowning] Sardar, what have we got to lose? Whatever Constitution India eventually makes for herself will be unaffected by dominion status. We can get power immediately by accepting it, and we can walk-out of the Commonwealth at any time we like.

Patel: [Slow, measured tone] If your scheme can get power transferred at once, then I will see that the Congress accepts dominion status. Though, Jawaharlal will be the main opponent I think.

V.P. Menon: No, No! I have heard different things. Krishna Menon, who is so close to Jawaharlalji has been convincing him that dominion status means a sovereign state within the British Commonwealth. And he has won him over at least halfway. Mountbatten has asked me to discuss it with Jawaharlalji and I will convince him completely now. He objects mainly to the phraseology, and we will change that, there will be no references to Empire and King Emperor.

Patel: Have some more *chaach*—and you haven't tasted the *khakhra*? It's absolutely fresh, and no fat in it. [Presses the plate upon V.P. Menon, suddenly in a lighter mood] You know, when it was announced that Mountbatten would be the new Viceroy, I sent for a report from my contacts in London. They told me Mountbatten was a liberal aristocrat with revolutionary leanings. [Laughs] Well, I thought, well! He will be a toy for Jawaharlal to play with, while we arrange the revolution. Incidentally, have you been attending their staff meetings? As Reforms Commissioner to the Viceroy you are part of Mountbatten's new team aren't you?

V.P. Menon: I have no doubt that Abell is responsible for advising Mountbatten in keeping me out of their meetings—though his name is not mentioned. I was told it was better not to have me there as Muslims would be convinced the viceroy was becoming partial to Hindus because of me. [Fuming] Anyone who knows how Abell's mind works will know that a pro-Muslim League man is already present, so they should have me there to balance him. I conveyed this to Mountbatten. He said I would soon be asked to attend.

Patel: We have to call the Muslim League's bluff, and if Jinnah persists in his policy, then good riddance to him!

SCENE 13

Viceroy's study. Mountbatten looks up frowning at Jinnah as he is shown in.

Mountbatten: Mr Jinnah, the communal situation is getting completely out of hand. Will you be willing to join with the other high commands of Hindus and Sikhs in issuing an appeal for no further provocative acts which can lead to bloodshed?

Jinnah: Have you seen in the newspapers an account of my speech in Bombay yesterday? I have made so many speeches in various cities deploring massacres and assaults. I can send you a complete file of my statements to the press also.

Mountbatten: Unilateral appeal is almost valueless. Your followers can claim provocation to bloodshed by the actions of the other side. I want a joint appeal: settle your differences by negotiations instead of direct action. Of course, if you find it embarrassing to renounce the use of force, please consider the matter closed.

Jinnah: If you wish me to join in an appeal against provocative action I am prepared to do so.

Mountbatten: As both Pandit Nehru and Sardar Baldev Singh have told me that their own high commands are prepared to do the same, I'm hopeful we can quieten things down.

Jinnah: Lord Mountbatten, perhaps you have a misconception about our 'direct action'. We have never instigated bloodshed anywhere. Until I resorted to 'direct action' the League position was becoming more and more insecure. The most you can say is that by our organization we created a situation which angered the Congress and it started the bloodshed.

Mountbatten: Mr Jinnah, I am going to make my decision without necessarily obtaining the agreement of the major parties. I am merely hearing your views. My approach is different from that of the cabinet mission which tried to get all of you to come to some agreement. It will be for the major parties now to try and get round me to make a decision which will suit them.

Jinnah: I quite see your point. But you must carry out a surgical operation. Cut India and its army firmly in half and give me the half that belongs to the Muslim League. Time does not permit any negotiations and details. I would urge you to give an overall decision quickly. And the first act of the Pakistan government will be to apply for admission to the British Commonwealth.

Mountbatten: Unless we know what mechanics are required to implement it, it is impossible for us to consider such a decision. Come what may I will leave India in June 1948. You must base your plans on British officials being out of India by that date. And I certainly cannot be party to any suggestion that Pakistan should enter the Commonwealth.

Jinnah: This deadline has been a shock.

Mountbatten: Please give me your views on the way I should give my decision, together with your reasons.

Jinnah: No other solution except full Pakistan can possibly bring peace to India. Anything less will be sure to produce further strife and bloodshed. I can even promise peace on the Frontier—the tribes there will beyond any question accept Pakistan with great relief. You may take the example of the Islamia College, it is 15 miles from Peshawar, in the jungle, and full of valuables, a natural target for tribal raiders, people think. It has never been attacked in 30 years, simply because it is a Muslim College.

Mountbatten: You are adamant that you will not discuss the cabinet mission plan, even if I can hammer out the maximum concessions short of partition? I find that the present interim government is working better everyday and in a more cooperative spirit. It is a daydream of mine to be able to put the central government under your prime ministership.

Jinnah: [Grimaces] I have explained to you that it is useless to resurrect a plan which could only have been tried if the utmost goodwill had prevailed between all parties. Now, it is foredoomed to failure.

Mountbatten: I have seen your arguments for partition in writing—they are the classic ones you put forth before the Cabinet Mission. I must point out that all your arguments apply also to the partition of the Punjab and Bengal. By sheer logic, if I accept them in the case of India as a whole, I have also to apply them in the case of these two provinces.

Jinnah: You are trying to give me a moth-eaten Pakistan, and it is most upsetting. This demand for partitioning the Punjab and Bengal is a Congress bluff to try and frighten me off Pakistan. I am not to be frightened so easily. I will be sorry if you are taken in by the Congress bluff.

Mountbatten: I will not be taken in by anybody. If I agree to partition India, it will be on your able advocacy. But I cannot allow your theories to stop short at the provinces. You claim the right of a large minority to partition on a big scale. If I grant you this, how can I refuse Congress, who will press for exactly the same right for the large Hindu minorities in the Punjab and Bengal to be partitioned?

Your arguments for not agreeing to partition the Punjab and Bengal are very convincing—but they apply with even greater force to India as a whole. Mr Jinnah, if you insist on the partition of India, you will be breaking up a great subcontinent of numerous nations, which could live together in peace and harmony. United, you can play a great role in the world; divided, you would not even rank as a second-class power. What is worse, you evidently intend to destroy even the mere vestiges that remain of the Indian army.

Jinnah: You can take it from me Lord Mountbatten, the 'Be all and end all' of Pakistan is to have our own army. Nothing short of this can possibly satisfy us.

Mountbatten: I have insufficient expert knowledge to say how long it would take to partition the armed forces. The complete nationalization of the three services by June 1948 will so greatly weaken them that I do not see how they can possibly stand partition on top of nationalization.

Jinnah: Of course, I am also no expert. We will require the views of experts as to when partition can be implemented in the services.

Mountbatten: I remain statutorily responsible for law and order in India until June 1948 and I have no intention of weakening the efficiency or even the morale of the army. The difficulty can be overcome, if indeed I finally decide on some form of partition, by setting up a committee of experts to work out a time-table. Meanwhile, the armed services should remain under the control of a central body presided over by me while I am here.

Jinnah: That seems very reasonable. But I must appeal to you once again: please do not give me a moth-eaten Pakistan. You must make it viable. The partition of Poland has not been made on the basis of counting heads or taking into account the will of the people.

Mountbatten: Although I have not made up my mind in any way whether to agree to partition or not, I simply cannot visualize being so inconsistent. I cannot agree to partition India without agreeing to partition the provinces in which the same problem arises. I must follow a course that would be generally acceptable, and so far as possible, ascertain the will of the people.

Jinnah: The Congress is deliberately drawing a red herring across your path. If you fall for their ploy, I will demand the partition of the province of Assam. I would like to see the Congress proposals for carving up Punjab and Bengal so that I can submit my counter proposals.

Mountbatten: I shall ask Pandit Nehru for the proposed boundaries and also discuss with him the solution you are proposing. Mr Jinnah, I entirely agree that your moth-eaten Pakistan is almost unworkable, but that is all I can possibly offer you. It will be a tragedy for Pakistan to cut up the provinces.

Mountbatten: Mr Jinnah, I regard as a great tragedy that you are trying to force me to give up the idea of a united India. Imagine, the greatness India could achieve—four hundred million people of different races and creeds, all bound together by a central Union government, with all the economic strength that would result from increased industrialization. India would play a great part in world affairs as the most progressive single entity in the Far East.

Jinnah: Nothing would have given me greater pleasure than to have seen such unity. It is indeed tragic that the behaviour of the Hindus has made it impossible for the Muslims to share in this. As you said, you could have seen me as the Prime Minister!

[Ismay comes in with cabinet papers]

Ismay: Your Excellency, these are the un-circulated cabinet papers—it is almost 6 o'clock, and the cabinet meeting is due to begin.

Mountbatten: Mr Jinnah, I will leave you with Lord Ismay. He will take your proposals in writing for further consideration. Please give him all the details.

[Mountbatten leaves. Ismay takes his place]

Ismay: Mr Jinnah, what would you recommend instead of the cabinet mission plan if you were in the Viceroy's shoes?

Jinnah: Lord Mountbatten has already asked me that question. There is no earthly chance of working that plan.

Ismay: Your original objection to the plan had been that certain provinces could not opt out of, but could only transfer to another group. Congress has now agreed to opt out, but want to hold on to the concept of a Union government of India.

Jinnah: Lord Ismay, India has now passed beyond the stage at which any such compromise solution can possibly work.

Ismay: Even if His Excellency gets the Congress to accept the plan in full?

Jinnah: The Congress will never do so. And we could never trust them anyway. The plan lays down that a difference of opinion on a major communal question should be decided by the federal court. I asked the Chief Justice what he would do if his ruling were disregarded and he replied that the court would refuse to give any more rulings. That would leave it open to Congress to impose their will by majority vote.

Ismay: We should consider then, the hypothetical case of partition. What are your ideas about arrangements between Pakistan and Hindustan in all essential matters of common interest?

Jinnah: I am afraid I do not understand what arrangements need to be made.

Ismay: The case of assets and liabilities for example. Who is going to decide what proportion of India's existing assets should go to the two dominions? And who is going to decide what proportion of India's present obligations for pensions etc. are to be taken over by Hindustan and what proportion by Pakistan?

Jinnah: This is a case of a company going into liquidation and it is the job of the liquidator to say how the company's assets and liabilities are to be proportioned to the new firms taking over the business.

Ismay: I disagree absolutely! We would be very ready to help with advice, if desired, so long as we remain in India. But we cannot possibly take any responsibility for a division of resources and obligations. The companies taking over the concern in this case will have to agree among themselves.

Jinnah: If His Majesty's Government remits power to the provinces, the provinces will immediately get into groups and elect their own parliaments. In each group, a government will be formed and their cabinets will meet together to consider all matters of common interest such as defence and communications, etc.

Ismay: And no central authority?

Jinnah: I will deprecate anything in the nature of a supreme council sitting over the federal governments even it were purely consultative. Sovereign nations, Lord Ismay, do business with each other on all matters by an exchange of delegates, and not by setting up any formal machinery. I assure you with the greatest earnestness that once partition has been decided upon, everyone will know exactly where they are, all troubles will cease, and we will live happily ever after. I once had the case of two brothers who hated each other like poison as a result of the portions allotted to them under their father's will. They brought the case to court and I defended one of them. The case was fought with the utmost venom. Two years later I met my client and asked how he and his brother were getting on and he said: 'Oh! Once the case was decided, we became the greatest friends'.

Ismay: It is not so simple, is it Mr Jinnah? I have prepared various schemes as a result of the discussions the Viceroy has had with so many Indian leaders the last fortnight. They have yet to be considered before we can recommend any new plan to London.

Jinnah: The arrangements to be made after the transfer of power will take a lot of time. It is therefore most important that the Viceroy should announce his decision as soon as possible. Time is the essence of the contract.

Ismay: The partition of Bengal and the Punjab, especially Punjab, will be most difficult and requires time.

Jinnah: You must not do that—it is a Congress ramp! I beg of you, do not take a decision on Punjab and Bengal solely on a counting of heads. Look at the case of Poland after the First World War, and the recent case of Trieste.

Ismay: I do not quite see the analogy. In these days of democracy, the counting of heads is practically decisive.

Jinnah: Let me tell you, Lord Ismay, the present population of Bengal is entirely fictitious owing to the large number of labourers who are not Bengalis at all. They have been imported from other parts of India. I pray that there will be no question of a moth-eaten Pakistan, shorn of half Bengal and half the Punjab. May I see the various schemes you have prepared, Lord Ismay?

Ismay: [Hedging] I'm sorry, they are still to be circulated officially and in any case the final plan the Viceroy decides to send to London will be only partially based upon earlier ideas, you know.

Jinnah: Lord Ismay, Pakistan will not be able to stand alone. We will require a big power as a friend. Russia has no appeal for us, France is weak and divided. There remain only England and America, and of the two, England is our natural friend. Apart from anything else, the devil you know is better than the devil you don't. [After a moment's silence, smiles] I do not wish to make any improper suggestion to you, but you must realize that the new Pakistan is almost certain to ask for dominion status within the empire.

Ismay: A truncated Pakistan will be a severe liability to the empire and the Viceroy cannot recommend that. [Affably] It has been a great pleasure talking with you. I will send the typed version of the points we have covered to you soon.

Jinnah: I am also very happy to have discussed things with you frankly—I do look forward to another talk with the Viceroy and yourself.

SCENE 14

Viceroy's study: Staff meeting.

Mountbatten: So that is the full account of my dialogue with Mr Jinnah. I'm afraid I drove the old gentleman quite mad; because whichever way his argument went I always pursued it to a stage beyond which he did not wish it to go. And the funny bit was that though he ignored my personal remark about wishing to see him the Prime Minister of India, thirty-five minutes later he suddenly made a reference to it out of the blue. There is no doubt that it had greatly tickled his vanity, and he had been turning over the proposition in his mind. Mr Gandhi's famous scheme may yet go through on the pure vanity of Mr Jinnah!

Campbell-Johnson: The press is raving about your success in getting Jinnah to sign the peace appeal along with Gandhi as a great personal triumph and as an impetus to producing an acceptable plan.

Mountbatten: The stern and forceful tone and the timing are designed to create a detente without which no political solution will be worth a pin's fee. It is a victory for open diplomacy.

Mieville: It certainly enhances your prestige and exploits to the maximum the goodwill that surrounds you. It should be disseminated widely.

Campbell-Johnson: I have gone into that. The engine of All-India radio will be at full throttle and a plan to show it at cinemas and to distribute it by leaflet from the air over the disturbed areas.

Vernon: It's time for the first interview—you have six bods coming to see you today, Dickie.

Mountbatten: You better leave then. The air-conditioning doesn't seem to be working.

Ian Scott: It's a 100 degrees outside. And the Indians find your room freezing! Mr Gandhi was wearing a shawl on his last visit!

[All leave. Baldev Singh is ushered in]

Mountbatten: Good morning Sardar Baldev Singh! How did the first meeting of the Defence committee of India work out?

Baldev Singh: Excellent, Excellency, excellent! But I hope you appreciate how very weak Indian defence will be with a budget of Rs.107.5 crores per annum?

Mountbatten: That is a matter you should point out to your colleagues. Since the weakness will occur after June 1948 it will purely be an Indian responsibility.

Baldev Singh: I am also worried about how many British officers will agree to employment to help the Indian forces until nationalization is efficiently completed. I am under no illusion, the Indian army definitely requires British help for five years, the navy for more than ten years and the air force about ten years.

Mountbatten: You should not count on getting more than a few British officers if India leaves the Commonwealth.

Baldev Singh: I agree entirely. I have already told Pandit Nehru that for the sake of the Defence forces alone, India should remain within the Commonwealth.

Mountbatten: The difficulty is that the Constituent Assembly has already passed a resolution that they will be a sovereign independent republic. A formula has to be found to save the face of Congress.

Baldev Singh: I have thought of one: the resolution should be accepted in principle, but the date should be postponed until nationalization of the forces is complete, in say, ten years time. Then it can be reconsidered. The trouble is to get anybody to listen to me.

Mountbatten: The position of a defence minister is regarded in England as being so powerful that it rivals the position of the prime minister. You hold the key portfolio at the moment, if you assert yourself in a much stronger way. I am sure you could get the support of minority members to this scheme of yours.

Baldev Singh: That is a very good suggestion. I can speak to Dr Matthai, Mr Bhabha and Mr Jagjivan Ram individually.

Mountbatten: You could even obtain their joint signature to a proposal which can be put to the Congress at the appropriate time.

Baldev Singh: Excellent! I'm sure this will be the real solution.

Mountbatten: You are of course at liberty to mention the fact that you have had this discussion with me, but I think it will greatly diminish the prospects of success if you say that you had consulted me first.

Baldev Singh: I agree! I will not mention your name.

Mountbatten: His Majesty's Government is not particularly interested in having India within the commonwealth since it is clearly the Indians who would lose most by severing their connections with England. The resolution to leave the Commonwealth has already brought disadvantages. His Majesty's Government has decided not to call any more Indian officers to the Imperial Defence College or the Joint Staff College in England, or to attend the Commonwealth Defence conference, until the position in India has been clarified. Of course, I regret the decision, but it is not surprising.

Baldev Singh: That is very bad news. But I'm certain Pandit Nehru will persuade everyone. Look at the admirable way the INA issue has been handled. Pandit Nehru's speech was courageous and statesmanlike, and very generous to Commander-in-Chief Auchinleck.

Mountbatten: I trust you will counter any Sikh who speaks against the motion? I will request Mr Liaquat Ali Khan to do the same in the case of Muslim Leaguers.

Baldev Singh: Certainly. I am responsible for supporting the motion. But I must tell you that Siddique Ali, who is a commander of the Muslim National Guards, has made a most disgraceful speech in Urdu, glorifying the INA and bitterly attacking Pandit Nehru for not supporting the resolution to release them. Mr Liaquat Ali should have spoken up against this. I regret that he has not done so.

Mountbatten: I will refer to this when I see Mr Jinnah. [Stands and ushers Baldev Singh out while talking] I must suggest to you that it would be better not to use the term 'dominion status' or talk about deferring independence for ten years—it will needlessly ruffle the feathers of your Congress colleagues. [Smiling] An expression like 'the free nations of the British commonwealth' is preferable.

[Mountbatten returns from door, sits down as Ronnie peeps in]

Ronnie: Dr Rajendra Prasad is here. [Opens door for R. Prasad]

Prasad: Good morning, Excellency.

Mountbatten: Welcome, Dr Prasad. I believe you have been away to the hills?

Prasad: Yes, Lord Mountbatten. Actually, not to the hills—I went to visit the Kosi Dam project. It is really a magnificent project and will bring great benefits to people in the area.

Mountbatten: That is what the Sutlej Project was designed to do, but the Punjab is heading towards civil war and it will come to nothing. Tell me, what would you do in my place about the transfer of power?

Prasad: I find it very difficult to say. I cannot set aside my association with being a Hindu and a member of the Congress and put myself in your place.

Mountbatten: It has become clear to me that Mr Jinnah is thinking only along the line of partition.

Prasad: There will be disastrous consequences of the breakup of Indian unity, after all, we are all really one people. We have spent all our lives working for the future of our motherland. It will be a big blow to have partition.

Mountbatten: Do you think I could override the danger of civil war, which is likely, if I enforce unity against the wishes of the Muslim League?

Prasad: The position we have now reached makes civil war likely because the Muslim League is dead set against us.

Mountbatten: Let me put it this way: will the Congress voluntarily decide to partition if that was the only way I could transfer power without risking civil war?

Prasad: If that becomes the position then we would have to accept it. There is no alternative. You cannot allow civil war.

Mountbatten: Perhaps, introducing a time element into the stages by which partition is implemented will help reason to prevail over communal emotional sentiments.

Prasad: Yes, perhaps that will help.

[Mountbatten stands and thanks him for the visit. Prasad leaves slowly]

Ronnie: [Brings in Kripalani] Mr Acharya Kripalani to see you, Your Excellency.

Mountbatten: Ah! Good day Mr Kripalani. I'm sorry I have very little time before my next appointment but I was keen to see you today. It is becoming very impractical to deal with fifteen men. I really must ask for the minimum number who can be responsible to answer for Congress. Would you say, you as the party president, Pandit Nehru as leader of Congress in government, and Mr Gandhi as the spiritual factor behind Congress, are sufficient for me to negotiate with as representing the Congress view?

A. Kripalani: Oh yes, that will be alright.

Mountbatten: I cannot move towards a final decision without keeping in constant touch with the Congress and the Muslim League. And I must say it is much easier to deal with the League, since Mr Jinnah can speak firmly on their behalf without his working committee repudiating any agreement he makes.

A. Kripalani: If you will not take it amiss, may I say that is the way that all organizations built up on a Hitlerite principle work. May I ask, Lord Mountbatten, whether you propose to give a decision yourself or are you considering calling in an outside authority to arbitrate?

Mountbatten: What and who do you have in mind?

A. Kripalani: No, no, I have no special ideas—I was wondering about United Nations arbitrators.

Mountbatten: Do you think a committee of arbitrators would come to any different conclusions than mine?

A. Kripalani: No, that is unlikely.

Mountbatten: Also, are you prepared to accept the additional delay, to set up such a body and give them time to complete their work? Will not the country deteriorate irreparably in that time?

A. Kripalani: Yes, there would be problems of unnecessary delay. Lord Mounbatten, the Congress is ready to place its services at your disposal to help you in your difficult task. You do realize that it is a democratic institution of which I am the elected president only for a term of office. I have no authority to speak except to a brief supplied by the working committee, nor can I give any undertakings unless ratified by the same.

Mountbatten: You do agree that Mr Gandhi and Pandit Nehru, apart from yourself, can be taken as the chief spokesmen?

A. Kripalani: They too are subject to the working committee's sanction, [smiles] but I think you can take it that they will carry the others along.

Mountbatten: Thank you very much for coming in. [A. Kripalani stands up] I do hope you and your wife are coming to luncheon with Lady Edwina and myself tomorrow?

A. Kripalani: Certainly. We are looking forward to meeting Lady Edwina over lunch.

[Abell walks in with Liaquat Ali, he and A. Kripalani greet each other before A. Kripalani leaves with Abell]

Mountbatten: Please take a chair. I hope Mr Abell has given you a full resume of my conversation with Mr Jinnah?

Liaquat Ali: Yes, I have also read the typed notes Lord Ismay kindly gave me.

Mountbatten: Therefore we should begin our talk with my last remark to Mr Jinnah: I will in no circumstances prevent provinces from being partitioned if I accept the principle of Pakistan.

Liaquat Ali: Your Excellency, what are you going to do to ensure continuity after you leave in June 1948?

Mountbatten: I intend to make a public statement setting down the programme that ought to be followed and the principles for conducting negotiations.

Liaquat Ali: Ah, but supposing they do not adhere to what you have laid down?

Mountbatten: That would be just too bad. That is one of the penalties you have to pay for being free.

Liaquat Ali: But do you not recognize that your responsibilities extend beyond June 1948? If your government fixes a date which cannot be adhered to, are you going to imperil the implementation of your decision?

Mountbatten: Most certainly. It has nothing to do with us after June 1948.

Liaquat Ali: What have you decided about the partition of the army?

Mountbatten: As long as I am responsible for law and order I will not take a single step to imperil the efficiency of the army. I will put up proposals to set up the machinery to produce plans and finally implement a split. It will take its own time. The final details, in any case, have to be worked out by the Indian parties themselves.

Liaquat Ali: After June 1948, who will see that the centre uses the army correctly and not unfairly?

Mountbatten: Presumably you will have two Defence ministers meeting on equal terms and giving joint agreed instructions to a single commander-in-chief.

Liaquat Ali: [Long pause] Is there any chance of the commander-in-chief being British?

Mountbatten: That is entirely dependent on the Congress and Muslim League getting together and asking to retain connection with the Commonwealth to enable them to have a British commander-in-chief.

Liaquat Ali: But there is no doubt that Pakistan wants to remain a dominion. We want to have your officers.

Mountbatten: I am not prepared even to discuss the suggestion of any part of India remaining within the empire unless the suggestion comes from all parties together. Even then I cannot say what the answer of His Majesty's Government would be. If you discuss this matter during your visit to London please remember I have given you no encouragement.

Liaquat Ali: I understand, I will respect your attitude. I have to raise the question of the appointments committee with you. Sardar Patel has been trying to ensure that even in those five portfolios which Muslim League members hold, the Congress can put in whomever they like.

Mountbatten: How is that possible?

Liaquat Ali: He wants it to be settled by a majority vote in the cabinet. The League would rather have only five out of 17 departments than be defeated in even these five by cabinet vote.

Mountbatten: I can't share your views on this since I am a trustee for the government of India as a whole and not for any one particular party. I think you should accept the External Appointments Committee consisting of Pandit Nehru, Sardar Baldev Singh and yourself, and the Internal Appointments Committee consisting of Sardar Patel, Dr Matthai and yourself.

Liaquat Ali: Lord Mountbatten, the procedure should be changed. At present, the Committee puts their recommendations to the Viceroy and if the matter has to come before the whole Cabinet, it will be intolerable. Personalities will be discussed, and finally a vote will be taken which you will find almost impossible to overrule.

Mountbatten: I will go into this matter and let you know what I decide. Meanwhile, do try and work with Pandit Nehru—I'm certain you can cooperate with him.

Ronnie: [Peeps in] Mr Patel is here.

[Liaquat Ali leaves as Patel is shown in]

Mountbatten: Sardar Patel! We meet at last. I trust Lord Ismay has given you a full account of my negotiations with Mr Jinnah?

[Patel nods assent]

Mountbatten: I must explain why I have not consulted you—or any member of the Congress before this. I wanted to tell Mr Jinnah of my own views without being suspected of having got my ideas from any member of the Congress. Mr Patel, do you think the Congress can accept the Cabinet Mission plan without reservations?

Patel: Which interpretation of the plan? HMG's statement of 6th or 7th December?

Mountbatten: What I mean is that if Mr Jinnah can be made to accept it then the Congress should agree upon one interpretation with him.

Patel: It was I, Lord Mountbatten, who finally got the Congress to accept the plan earlier, and I remain its strongest advocate in my party. The mistake the British have made with Jinnah is always to give way to him, as a means of his face saving. I can tell you he will only accept that plan when the force of circumstances give him no alternative. You should announce the partition of Bengal and the Punjab soon and you will see the Muslims of Bengal secede from the League. This may even happen in Punjab, it is likely there will be a revolt against Jinnah.

Mountbatten: You seem hopeful but we shall see. How is the interim government working?

Patel: Why has His Majesty's Government not given us control over the services yet? How do you imagine we can govern if we have no power to get rid of disloyal members of the services who are harming the interim government?

Mountbatten: You only have to report to me any cases of disloyalty, of course, supported by good evidence, and I will take the necessary steps. Mr Patel, it now seems highly doubtful that you can have a unified India—in fact Pakistan is looming before us—to whom then can the services be turned over? It is not even clear who will be in Pakistan and who in Hindustan.

Patel: You know, Lord Wavell created a lot of problems for us. Before the formation of the interim government he governed with a strong centre, and kept law and order in the provinces. Since we formed the government he allowed such power to go the provinces that they could defy the central government. By introducing Muslim League members in the government against the advice of Congress he so weakened the centre that India is rapidly disintegrating into a lawless state.

Mountbatten: I'm afraid the League could not have been kept out of power, and I hope you are not suggesting that. Thank you for coming in Mr Patel. We will meet again very soon.

[Patel leaves. Ronnie announces Mr Rajagopalachari.]

Mountbatten: I have been unable to get Mr Jinnah's cooperation for a unified India, Mr Rajagopalachari. Civil war is certain if we try to impose Union on the Muslims.

Rajaji: I deeply regret that the ideal of united India should fail but have to admit that if imposing it by force should lead to civil war, it would be a tragic paradox.

Mountbatten: I have to be guided by what is practicable and will produce a peaceful solution.

Rajaji: Of course, that is the only way. I must point out to you that most of the leaders take a long time to acquire sufficient influence to become leaders, and by that time they are usually embittered old men who have become obstinate and not open to reason.

Mountbatten: If such leaders, for example Mr Jinnah, are brought into the government, the added responsibility might modify their views and make them more balanced, don't you think?

Rajaji: That might be true—it is admittedly true in the case of Pandit Nehru, but I would be very surprised if it were to come true in the case of Mr Jinnah. His great reputation has been made in the legal profession but his knowledge of administration is nil.

Mountbatten: What do you think of the armed services being completely Indianized by June 1948—will that help in good administration?

Rajaji: I have never shared the general view of our politicians that Indianization can be completed in so short a time without the gravest effect on efficiency. Five to ten years must elapse before it would be sound to withdraw British officers.

Mountbatten: Your most senior Indian officer, Brigadier Cariappa, stated in London that it would definitely take five years before they can do without British officers. All other senior Indian officers I have seen share this view. In the case of the navy, the most senior officer, Commander Choudhury, considers ten years to be necessary.

Rajaji: I am glad that Brigadier Cariappa has had the courage to say this since it is due to the senior Indian officers themselves that the politicians have been misled. As far as I know, all Indian officers had combined together to give the impression that the sooner the British were pushed out the better. I presume they are looking forward to rapid promotions for themselves.

Mountbatten: The British might not wear their hearts on their sleeves, Mr Rajagopalachari, but they are all the more emotional for repressing their emotions. I cannot imagine any officer of calibre being prepared to resign his King's commission in order to take on a contract with a foreign power—as you will be. The only way you could keep them would be for India to remain in the Commonwealth.

Rajaji: I think we are pretty well committed to do this—the Congress party, that is. The difficulty about it would come if it was generally known in the country.

Mountbatten: You could counter that by promising to review it after five years.

Rajaji: That may be a solution, I will have to give it consideration. There is, of course, the analogy of Ireland.

Mountbatten: In any case it is absolutely no concern of mine what happens to your services after June 1948. The only people who would gain by not severing the link with the crown would be the Indians. It has been a great pleasure talking with you. I'm sure you will come up with good suggestions to your party. Of course, if you quote me to anybody else it will not help you to pursue the matter.

[Rajaji leaves. Abul Kalam Azad ushered in]

Azad: I'm amazed, Lord Mountbatten at what Lord Ismay has been telling me. Even after you explained to Jinnah that the Cabinet Mission plan would give him a full Pakistan he insists on accepting a truncated country. It will spell disaster for the *Mussulmans*. Jinnah will be committing suicide!

Mountbatten: You have seen the lines on which I negotiated with him, but he is intransigent.

Azad: After all, the Cabinet Mission gave him the right to secede at the end of ten years if he wished. He is being purely destructive. [Shakes head]. You should try to meet his objections, Lord Mountbatten. His main worry was Bengal and Assam, but that was solved by His Majesty's Government. Then he had insisted that he should have the power to fill any vacancy among the minority seats in the Cabinet. The Congress can well agree to this request even now if it is put up for action. I will go to any length to support you if you can get the plan accepted by Jinnah. I am certain the Congress will fully cooperate.

Mountbatten: He has stonewalled all such suggestions Mr Azad. He is in no mood to listen.

Azad: Then you should quickly announce the partition of the Punjab and Bengal. The Muslims of Bengal will separate from the League immediately. Even in the Punjab once it is known that Jinnah has agreed to partition it there will be a violent reaction against him, it will lead to revolt. Things are bad in the frontier as well. The Prime Minister, Khan Sahib, formed the ministry in the province on my assurance that Lord Wavell would make the British Governor cooperate. But no sooner had Sir Olaf become the Governor he was violently anti-Congress and pro-League. He did not bother to conceal his deliberate hostility.

Mountbatten: I have had similar reports from Pandit Nehru, Mr Gandhi and Mr Abdul Gaffar Khan. This appears to be the general Congress point of view. I have only been here three weeks and one hour and have been fully occupied on my first priority: an overall solution for India. Anyway, there will have to be a new election in the Frontier Province.

Azad: I am sorry to hear that we will have another election. Very fair elections were held only a year ago. Nothing has changed except League propaganda. The Congress will be re-elected.Why is it necessary there and not in other provinces?

Mountbatten: Pandit Nehru thinks Congress might not be re-elected since the frontier people are always against the government, whichever it might be. In all other provinces, Mr Azad, the separate electorates enable one to forecast accurately the results of elections, since all Muslims voted for the League. In the Frontier Province, however, the election was largely an issue between the Congress Muslims and the League Muslims and there is no separate electorate here. The results will clearly show whether they want a League or a Congress Government.

Azad: If you are determined to hold an election, I presume it will be after giving a decision in favour of Pakistan. If the Cabinet Mission plan gets accepted I assume that a coalition government will be formed in most provinces, including the Frontier Province.

Mountbatten: Let us hope we can avert partition, Mr Azad. I shall ask you to come and see me again when things are clearer.

[Azad leaves. Jagjivan Ram shown in]

Mountbatten: Well, Mr Ram, what is your view on the strike of the ordnance depot with which your defence department is faced?

J. Ram: We have to face this strike like all others, Your Excellency. The government has to resist unreasonable demands.

Mountbatten: And what do you think of Mr Jinnah's demand for Pakistan?

J. Ram: No impartial and balanced man can doubt that any form of partition will be disastrous for India as a whole, and even for a weaker unit like Pakistan.

Mountbatten: Is there any hope of creating a unified India by the consent of all parties?

J. Ram: At one time it had looked possible but now the situation has gone too far even to consider it. Nowadays, the creed of Pakistan is even being preached in mosques. I doubt whether Mr Jinnah himself can reverse the feeling which he himself has instilled in the Muslims. But I think they should be allowed to do what they want. They will find their Pakistan unworkable and will voluntarily rejoin the Indian union. Specially, if they are restricted by a partition of Punjab and Bengal.

Mountbatten: Mr Ram, I met Dr Ambedkar yesterday. He says the Cabinet Mission and His Majesty's Government had betrayed the Scheduled Castes. He says, as in the past, they will continue to be exploited and oppressed in the future. He quoted a most monstrous case from the UP where, he said, four Scheduled Caste men had recently been burnt alive by caste Hindus. I am making enquiries about it. What is your position?

J. Ram: The majority of Scheduled Castes disagree with Dr Ambedkar. He is trying to make them a separate minority community who would be too poor, too uneducated, and too ill-equipped to enter the fight in a big way. I am among those who think that our only hope is to be absorbed by caste Hindus. Only by a voluntary arrangement can the concept of untouchables be finally eradicated.

Mountbatten: Do you agree with Dr Ambedkar that certain safeguards should be provided in any new constitution and the British government should ask the Constituent Assembly to introduce them?

J. Ram: I entirely agree with that. This should be the aim. Seats should be guaranteed to the Scheduled Castes in the same proportion to the total number as is our ratio to the total population. I have submitted a memorandum to the Constituent Assembly on this point. I will send you a copy, and I hope Your Excellency will be able to help me. I feel the real opposition will come when the Scheduled Castes demand a share of seats in all the cabinets and governments, and a share of the appointments in the civil and the fighting services.

Mountbatten: I will certainly do whatever is possible to get the Constituent Assembly to incorporate your ideas. Anything else that you would like to suggest?

J. Ram: There is one matter on which I would like advice. The International Labour Conference is being held in Geneva in June, and my departmental officers are very keen that I should head the delegation to it.

Mountbatten: That is an excellent idea, I will certainly back you. But you should not go for more than ten days or a fortnight. I would urge you to go to London and see the Ministry of Labour and the India Office on your way. I will write to them on your behalf.

J. Ram: Thank you Excellency, I'm most grateful.

[J. Ram leaves. After a few moments Krishna Menon peeks in with Vernon hovering behind him]

Krishna Menon: Are you going to interview the entire Congress today or do you have time for an old friend, Dickie?

Mountbatten: [Looks up from papers] Oh Krishna! Come in. It's alright Vernon, you can ask them to send in tea for two. When are you going to London, Krishna?

Krishna Menon: I'm staying out here especially for you. I hope to be of use to you. [With a wave of hand] You know, give you the background of what is going on in Congress circles and help you put over any points that you find too delicate to handle directly yourself. Can't ditch a friend of…how many years is it? Four, I think.

Mountbatten: Thank you very much. Stay on for a week more at least. So what is the Congress saying?

Krishna Menon: I have got very encouraging reactions from the party, both to Edwina's and to your activities. But I must warn you: don't let the pressure of events and the many people you meet every day lead you into missing the wood for the trees. That is a fault which has obscured the minds of so many English people in recent times out here.

Mountbatten: I am full with complaints about the governors from Congressmen, while I am trying to focus on the big picture.

Krishna Menon: The Congress is convinced that the governors of the North-West Frontier Province, Punjab, Bihar, and Sind are acting in the most suspicious manner. They are all notorious imperialists who have always worked on the divide and rule principle. Mudie joined forces with the Muslim League to get them into power; Dow's reputation is of open hostility towards Congress; Jenkins is partly to blame for the critical situation in the Punjab; Caroe and all his officers have been preaching anti-Congress doctrines to the tribes for so long they cannot sing a different tune even if they want to. [Shrugs] How did you get along with Jinnah?

Mountbatten: I may have to give him a truncated Pakistan.

Krishna Menon: The Congress will be unhappy but they will not resist it any more. I can help you put the idea over with Nehru. Do you remember, at our talks in London last March I put forward partition as necessary to a solution? But the outer line of India must remain intact, all secession must be subject to it. I warn you not to try anything clever. I can easily forecast that if the Frontier Province and Kashmir go to Pakistan we will see many years of conflict.

Mountbatten: Jinnah even demands a split in the army. As a serving officer I hate to see the magnificent Indian army grossly weakened. As for the navy and air force, they will be strangled at birth.

Krishna Menon: Would you be prepared to keep British officers with our three services for as long as we wished, and would you turn them over officially to us?

Mountbatten: No British officer worth his salt would willingly resign his King's commission to become an adventurer in the Indian services. The only way out is for India is to stay in the empire and not sever the link with the Crown.

Krishna Menon: You know that India's wish to shake the dust of the British Empire off her feet originated with your official attitudes, we have always been pushed to a corner. I myself suggested the term 'Independent Sovereign Republic' for the resolution in the Constituent Assembly. Perhaps such drastic terminology was hasty so early on in the negotiations.

Mountbatten: You could postpone the resolution for five years and openly give the reason that it was to enable British officers to remain and assist a handover throughout the army. You could also avoid the term 'dominion status'. Use a term like 'free nation of the Commonwealth'. Even Ireland has a link with the Crown.

Krishna Menon: That is the crux of the problem, the link with the crown. In the political war waged by the Congress it has always attacked the Crown as a symbol of oppression. It would be very difficult to explain to the people such a fundamental change in political outlook.

Mountbatten: That is your headache. You can't have your cake and eat it too. If you can't find some way of accepting the Crown, I'm not prepared to play. I have strict instructions not to try and keep India in the Commonwealth—I might well be shot down by the powers that be for talking about it. The Princely states and Jinnah have, of course, already said they wish to be within the Commonwealth.

Krishna Menon: Unless you take the first step and approach us, nothing will be done.

Mountbatten: Then nothing will be done. It is entirely your loss and I am not going to allow any sentimental reasons make me pull your chestnuts out of the fire. If you do not take the first step, you will have a rotten army; you will lose all the benefits of the Commonwealth; and you will save us the expense, anxiety and responsibility of your defence. His Majesty's Government, I fear, will not think it worthwhile to have India. After all, British commercial interests are adequately safeguarded by the sterling balances which tie India to Britain for years to come.

Krishna Menon: I did not mean that there cannot be private off-the-record discussions. But the first step can't be taken publicly by the leaders without reversing everything they have preached to the people.

Mountbatten: What are you proposing then?

Krishna Menon: If the British were voluntarily to give us dominion status now, much before June '48, we will be so grateful that not a voice would be heard in June '48 suggesting any change, except possibly the word 'dominion'.

Mountbatten: If the Muslims were to stay in a Union of India, I would recommend dominion status next month. But since I know they are not, how can the present government be given dominion powers? The Muslim League will violently object to a position of a permanent minority in the cabinet.

Krishna Menon: Can you propose equal dominion status to Hindustan and Pakistan and the Princes who join these two confederations?

Mountbatten: Certainly, provided I can retain full powers over defence since I would have to coordinate the use of the single army for both dominions.

Krishna Menon: Dominion status without control over the army would be laughable. It will never be accepted by the Indians.

Mountbatten: You should go home and think of a solution by which dominion status can be granted and which will satisfy the Muslim League that the army will be fairly administered and operated.

Krishna Menon: I will have to think about this problem.

Mountbatten: [Shaking a finger] You have no authority to quote me, but you can discuss the tenor of our discussion with Nehru. But make it clear, I will never take the first step.

SCENE 15

Get-together at Nehru's house. Present: Nehru, Krishna Menon, Campbell-Johnson, Mountbatten and Edwina, Indira, and three other Indian women and two Englishmen. While all of them are grouped in a semi-circle in the middle, Mountbatten and one Englishman sit at the back talking in low voices.

Nehru: Of course, the caste system is an abomination! But I have to say that the structure of British society in India has been more rigid than the caste system. The British have formed a separate caste, with several sub-castes, strictly preserving the usual characteristics of endogamy, commensality, and mutual control by members.

Krishna Menon: You only need to look at 'The Warrant of Precedence', the rule book of the British caste-system which sets people in their place, and not only at the dinner table. At the top of the pile are the heaven-born members of the ICS, the Brahmins of British India. Next, are the lower Brahmins, members of other administrative services; then comes the army. Very much below them are ranked those in trade and commerce, contemptuously referred to as the *boxwallahs.* The sub-caste further divides itself into two, an upper of those engaged in commerce and who spend their time in offices, and a lower of those who actually trade and work in shops and stores. Below that again is a range of untouchables, country breeds and poor whites, of pure British blood, but born in India.

Indira: You've left out the truly wretched of the earth, at the bottom of the pile, the half-caste Eurasians who are beyond the pale.

Nehru: Kipling learnt his lesson well when he wrote: a man should, whatever happens, keep to his own caste, race and breed.

Englishman: The whole elaborate system is an amalgam of British class and Indian caste. The warrant of precedence is a joke. A very superior general from the brigade of guards observed angrily to me, '*I cannot help thinking that these people who go into dinner ahead of me are the wretched people who put up little bungalows round my place in Hampshire.*'

Edwina: I've had my encounter with the infuriating order of precedence. When Dickie was last here with the Prince of Wales, he went back to England and told everyone that he had not understood the meaning of royalty until he stayed at the residence of the Governor of Bombay. There was quite a fracas over inviting a businessman to dinner and an instance of wrongly placing a civil servant in an inferior position to a director of dairy farms. Nothing's changed much, has it? Our dinners at vice-regal lodge follow the same semi-regal protocol: full evening dress, curtsy and bow, and the [mockingly] order of precedence!

[One of the men with Mountbatten has, meanwhile, joined the main group and Edwina gestures at him]

Edwina: Malcolm and I were saying just yesterday how appalling is the attitude of the civil servants towards the Indians.

Krishna Menon: I'm not surprised. A young fellow, say, the son of an Ulster farmer, is pitch forked by a successful examination into high authority in Bengal. He quite naturally looks upon the educated Indians as 'the damned nigger party'.

Malcolm: I've always thought that the services, particularly the police, have forever been filled by the kind of men portrayed by Trollope. You know, the amiable detrimental, the younger son, or the sporting public schoolboy, too lazy or too stupid for the army, but prepared to go anywhere or do anything which does not involve prolonged drudgery. In my travels as a journalist I've found the empire is awash with ignoramuses, narrow-minded lower-middle-class attitudes, and Tommies in the British army with no more than ten words of Hindustani, ruling the roost.

Englishman: As children we used to sing a music-hall ditty which ran, 'The men who live in Poona would infinitely sooner play single-handed polo, a sort of solo polo, than play a single chukka with a chap who isn't pukka'.

[Loud laughter]

[Indira has been with the bearers laying ice-cream at a side table while Malcolm speaks, and now calls them]

Indira: The ice-cream is melting rapidly in this weather. Come and eat it fast.

[All move towards it]

SCENE 16

Viceroy's study, staff meeting. Abell and Mieville are chatting, waiting for Mountbatten and others.

Mieville: Dickie's Durbar yesterday was amazing! He handled each chap so effortlessly. Too exhausting a pace for me. And today promises to be equally gruelling.

Abell: A pity he's here to wind up. He has made a very great impression on the Indians. [Voices approaching closer] Here they come.

[Mountbatten and the rest settle down]

Mountbatten: The first item on our agenda is Mr Jinnah. I have had six meetings with him.

Mieville: I do not believe that Pakistan is an economic possibility.

Abell: In my opinion the political objections to Pakistan are greater. Economically it could be made to work—Zinkin has sent in a paper on its viability.

Mountbatten: The time factor is of over-riding importance and Jinnah has no idea of the mechanics and time-table of establishing Pakistan. Everyone must bear in mind that the sheer logic of events and mechanical difficulties are likely to wield the greatest influence.

Ismay: If only Jinnah could be invited to be prime minister of the central government—there is a tendency for responsibility to improve people beyond recognition.

Abell: I do not think he will accept such an invitation.

Mountbatten: I am meeting Nehru this afternoon and I intend to take him fully into my confidence, which I have not done so far.

[Tea-tray arrives and as it is served the staff break up and talk softly to each other. Mountbatten continues to look through papers while drinking]

Mountbatten: Let us move to the next item. The two main plans under consideration now are, first: Plan Union, which is the Cabinet Mission plan, with some possible modifications, and second is Plan Balkan which will leave to each province the choice of its own future. This will certainly result in a truncated Pakistan and the abolition of a centre. A centre will be retained to deal with defence until the armed forces are divided. Comments everybody?

Abell: There is no chance of the Congress accepting the first without conditions.

Ismay: It is not impossible, though indeed, it would mean a complete change of heart.

Mountbatten: My impression is, the Congress leaders desire a united India above all and might accept 'Plan Union' to achieve this end.

[Stenographer enters with letter and gives it to Vernon]

Vernon: From Mr Gandhi, a handwritten note.

Mountbatten: Read it.

Vernon: [Reads] '*Dear friend, I had several short talks with Pandit Nehru and an hour's talk with him alone and then with several members of the Congress working committee last night, about the formula I had suggested to you. I am sorry to say that I failed to carry any of them with me except Badshah Khan. Having failed to carry both the head and heart of Pandit Nehru and the working committee I have to ask you to omit me from your discussions. The Congressmen who are in the interim government will be your complete advisors so far as the Congress point of view is concerned. I would still love to take the place that the late C.F. Andrews took. He represented no one but himself. And, if you ever need my service on its merits, it will be always at your disposal. I hope the constant interviews are not proving an unbearable strain. Yours sincerely, M.K. Gandhi.*'

Mountbatten: So his kite falls down.

Mieville: Patel and Nehru appear to have decided to accept partition—I gathered that from my talk with K.M. Panikkar, the Diwan of Bikaner state. He is particularly close to Patel—thinks no one else understands strategic defence issues like him. He positively welcomed Pakistan since it would enable a really strong centre to be formed at Delhi, which the inclusion of Muslim majority provinces would have rendered impossible.

Mountbatten: Perhaps we have no choice now except to act on Jinnah's advice.

Ian Scott: Before accepting Mr Jinnah's opinion as final perhaps Dickie can appeal to a representative Muslim body such as the All-India Muslim League council, the All-India Muslim League committee and the Muslim members of the Constituent Assembly who have been elected although they have not taken their seats.

Mountbatten: Indeed, that is a worthwhile suggestion. Obviously, I can't address them in person; perhaps Eric or Ismay can read an appeal from me. It would be useless to leave Jinnah to put my point of view forward.

Ian Scott: Maximum publicity would be necessary for an appeal to a Muslim body—the issue must be put before the whole world. In a private meeting without the glare of world publicity, Mr Jinnah will undoubtedly have his own way.

Mountbatten: Hmm. I could call a press conference. I have Nehru's permission to convene a press conference whenever I think it is necessary.

Ian Scott: The Muslim League's main fear is what is going to happen to them after June '48.

Mountbatten: Yes. Liaquat Ali Khan even suggested that an impartial British head of state should remain. It would be a most difficult position, as impartial decisions are always apt to annoy both sides.

Ismay: An impossible position, having responsibility with no authority.

Mountbatten: Back to plan number two. If 'Plan Balkan' is eventually chosen it must be pointed out what a long time I devoted to get the leaders to accept a united India but in the end found that it was impossible to impose it without a recrudescence of bloodshed and civil war. We have to carefully present to the world our sincere attempts to find a peaceful solution.

Ismay: We should not rule out the possibility of making use of the United Nations.

Mountbatten: That sums it up. Now I should finish my report to London.

[All leave except Ronnie who opens a file] Ronnie, read out the letter from the secretary of state.

Ronnie: [Reads] '*Gandhi's scheme appears to be remarkably detached from the realities of the situation. As I anticipated, the road you had to tread with Jinnah appears to have been up-hill all the way, but it was a great personal triumph for you that he agreed to put his name to a joint statement with Mr Gandhi. I note your remark that if any attempt is made to impose the Cabinet Mission plan on the Muslim League, they will resort to arms to resist it. It is only natural that as the Muslims refuse to accept what they represent would be a Hindu raj, the non-Muslim elements are beginning to agitate for a partition of provinces. I am afraid the Sikhs are giving you your worst headache. I suppose the basic fact of the situation is that the Sikhs have an exaggerated idea of their proper status in the future set-up. No doubt this is partly due to their historical position as the rulers of the Punjab, partly to the rather flattering treatment they have received from us as one of the great martial races of India, and partly to the fact that they consider that they have contributed out of proportion to their numbers to the economic wealth of the Punjab. On the other hand, their numerical community is a not even a major minority. In no single district do they constitute a majority. It is, therefore, out of the question to meet their claims by setting up a separate state. During the Cabinet Mission these considerations were put to the Sikhs in answer to their case but evidently it has all been like water off a duck's back*'.

Mountbatten: Hmm. Back to my report: More than numbers, the communal problem appears to be psychological. Bhimsain Sachar remarked that Muslims were arrogant, treated Hindus as inferiors and they would no longer submit to undiluted Muslim rule. Sardar Swaran Singh declared that Sikhs were not going to be treated as serfs under Muslim masters. The divide in the communities is getting sharper: a Resolution passed by the formerly pro-Congress Ahrar Party makes it clear. Its President, Mr Bukhari, lays the responsibility for riots on 'the fascist Congress leadership, which in its lust for power, set out a pre-planned programme of aggression to deprive Muslims of their rightful place.' The Resolution adds: 'Our foremost duty is to strive for the maintenance of honour and integrity of the Muslim nation'.

Another body of Muslims known as the Nationalist Momin Conference has issued the following statement: '*The only guarantee for the safety of Muslims today lies in establishing Pakistan. All Momins, Ahrars and Khaksars alike should gird up their loins and throw full weight on the side of the Muslim League*'.

Meanwhile, communal riots are on the same scale as last week. A 24 hour curfew in Amritsar, looting and arson in the Frontier Province, the tribes are restless and tension is very high. Half the city of Dera Ismail Khan is in flames and the situation is explosive. There have been more incidents in Calcutta, night curfew in Bombay, and also in Benares. I wish I could paint a more optimistic picture of the state of the country. After three weeks of incessant talks with all the leaders I am convinced that our decision must be announced before the end of May at latest, if we are to avert civil war. On this there is complete unanimity of opinion, both European and Indian. All the governors urge the greatest possible speed, for even the quieter provinces feel we are sitting on the edge of a volcano and an eruption may occur in any of the major craters: Bengal, Punjab and the Frontier, with sporadic eruptions in Assam, Bombay and Bihar. I am afraid that partition is proving to be the only possible alternative.

About the joint peace appeal, Gandhi signed there and then in three scripts. When Mieville took the appeal to Jinnah, informing him that Kripalani, as the president of the Congress, would sign after him, Jinnah refused to sign saying he could not have an unknown nobody like Kripalani signing on the same sheet of paper. Nehru was furious and wrote two pages of protest but finally left it to me. And so I issued the statement only under Gandhi and Jinnah's names. I relate these details to give an idea of the fantastic difficulties with which the simplest negotiations are hedged. Jinnah and I are meeting regularly but we keep going round the mulberry bush. When I told Jinnah I would like to see him in the present government, he visibly recoiled. If I had invited the pope to take part in the Black Mass he could not have been more horrified. He said: '*I do not care how little you give me as long as you give it to me completely*.' In fact, until I met him I would not have thought it possible that a man with such a complete lack of administrative knowledge and sense of responsibility could achieve or hold so powerful a position.

[Ismay and Mieville enter with Auchinleck. Latter's manner is measured and incisive throughout the meeting]

Ismay: The C-in-C Field Marshal Auchinleck is here, Excellency.

Mountbatten: Ah, commander-in-chief, I believe Lord Ismay has given you the outline of 'Plan Balkan'. Don't you think both parties will accept it?

Auchinleck: The Congress will do their best to wreck it as soon as it is put into operation.

Mountbatten: Jinnah is very obdurate—he will get what he wants. His great fear is of being swallowed by the Congress unless he has his own army.

Auchinleck: The fear is genuine, but largely self-induced. There is no other solution unless both sides should agree to a change of heart and be generous. They must acknowledge that they have both been wrong in the past.

Mountbatten: What is likely to happen next?

Auchinleck: If matters go on as they are, with no settlement, no agreement, the situation is bound to deteriorate. The army is bound to be affected—the Muslim League will ensure this if they do not get their way.

Mountbatten: Field Marshal, we have a problem with the Muslim League. Mr Liaquat Ali Khan complains that Muslims are not adequately represented in the armed forces. And he wants us to reorganize the forces on community lines so that they can be split if partition is declared.

Auchinleck: To say there is inadequate representation of Muslims is unfounded. The proportion of Muslims in the army is 29 per cent, that is a larger percentage than the total Muslim population of India. The complaint is due to their earlier figure of 37 per cent having dropped because we had to increase the Madrasis from 3 per cent to 20 per cent after the war. Anyway, if Pakistan is created they would not be able to afford a bigger army than the 29 per cent they form in the total Indian army. Of course, the Hindus dominate from behind the scenes, most of the senior officers are Hindus. For one reason or another, the Muslim senior officers have faded out. As for reorganizing the forces on a communal basis, it would be a very complicated and difficult process. It would take months, if not years. I am not prepared, Your Excellency, to take responsibility for that.

Mountbatten: My idea is to make a committee of Indians responsible for that. Perhaps, you and other senior British officers could appear before the committee as expert witnesses.

Auchinleck: That would be a good procedure. We had prepared a plan for re-organization on communal lines some years ago but it was seen to be very impracticable. The units would be out of action for at least one year. By no means do all the Muslims in the army have homes in what might become Pakistan—they cannot be expected to join the Pakistan army.

Mountbatten: Liaquat Ali sounded me on the possibility of retaining British officers by remaining in the Commonwealth. Of course, I told him we would not be ready to sacrifice the unity of India by considering side-offers of this nature.

Mieville: Field Marshal, what effects on the army will the declaration of Pakistan have?

Auchinleck: Very serious effects. If the Punjab is split there will definitely be civil war. The Muslims will not take orders from Hindu officers and vice versa. It would be appalling. It could be controlled so long as British officers are there but a stage is fast being reached when they no longer want to stay on. Anyway, the retention of British officers will be opposed politically, backed by the Indian officers themselves. The British officers hold is already loosening, and will continue to do so as the Indian soldiers fully realize we are leaving. [Pause] My strategy paper on the prospects of partition, written in June 1946, clearly shows how Hindustan and Pakistan would be a menace to each other.

Mountbatten: Perhaps Mr Jinnah could profit by reading it. Thank you very much, commander-in-chief. I will convey your opinion to the leaders, it should bring a little sanity to them.

[Auchinleck leaves]

Ismay: Very pessimistic. Dickie, perhaps we can use the British officers from Gurkha regiments which are being handed over to the Indian army?

Ronnie: [Enters] The chief secretary of the Frontier province is here, Lt. Col. De la Fargue.

[Ronnie goes out and la Fargue enters]

Mountbatten: I called you in, Lt. Col., for your views on holding an election in the Frontier province.

Fargue: Your Excellency, a free, clean election in the Frontier is likely to return the Congress to power.

Mieville: My impression is that Abdul Ghaffar Khan is the most unpopular man on the Frontier.

Fargue: That is true, but his brother the premier, Dr Khan Sahib is absolutely first class. All the stories about his being neurotic have arisen due to his ungovernable temper.

Mountbatten: Lt. Col., in normal times I would consider it highly reprehensible to discuss your governor with you, but in this time of crisis I need a British opinion on the shocking reports on him I receive from Pandit Nehru. In fact, he has asked me to remove the governor.

Fargue: Your Excellency, I must honestly tell you that although Sir Olaf is a man with great knowledge of the Frontier, he is, in fact, biased against the Congress government and has lost the confidence of all fair-minded people in the province. I am sorry to have to say the governor's continuation in office is a menace to British prestige.

Mountbatten: Thank you for being frank and speaking with courage. We shall find a solution for this soon. [Fargue leaves. Mountbatten turns to Ismay and Mieville] I'm expecting Patel, I'll speak to him alone. [Both leave]

Ronnie: [Peeping through door] Sardar Patel is here, Your Excellency. [Opens door wide as Patel walks in]

Mountbatten: Please sit down Mr Patel. I'm sorry to call you twice in one day, but I have just seen the file of the Appointments Committee. I propose to talk to you pretty straight. I am extremely offended by the tone of your minute.

Patel: In what way is my tone offensive?

Mountbatten: [Picks up paper and reads] '*I regard a reference to the selection board as both pointless and inappropriate.*' This is the most direct criticism of myself. It is discourteous and disloyal to the president of the cabinet that he should receive from a colleague a minute of this kind. It cannot be tolerated by anyone, least of all by me since I do not take behaviour of this sort kindly.

Patel: I meant no offence. I myself was put in an embarrassing position by your order that my recommendation should be reviewed by a committee of secretaries including my own.

Mountbattenis: If, you had consulted the establishments committee in the first place, you would not have put yourself in this position.

Patel: There is a written ruling saying that the establishment committee are not to have appointments of secretaries referred to them.

Mountbatten [Rings and Ronnie peeps in] Please ask Sir Eric to come in. [Mieville enters a moment later] Eric, is there a ruling that secretaries' appointments are not referred to the establishments committee?

Mieville: That is a ruling of Lord Linlithgow's which Lord Wavell, by convention, had reversed. In fact, he insisted that they should be referred.

Mountbatten: Thank you Eric. [Mieville goes out]

Patel: I had no knowledge of this convention, had I known I would, of course, have abided by it. I have only been carrying out the written orders. And I was greatly embarrassed at your referring my nominee to the committee.

Mountbatten: Clearly there has been a misunderstanding about the written rule and unwritten convention. But nothing can possibly excuse the tone of your minute to me. What do you propose to do about that?

Patel: [Moment's silence] what would you like me to do about it?

Mountbatten: Withdraw your remarks.

Patel: I cannot do that—I am convinced the selection board's remarks are out of place and uncalled for.

Mountbatten: But you have criticized my remarks as well! They tell me you are a tough guy. Well, so am I. Now will you take back your minute or do you want me to bring it up in cabinet?

[Patel is silent]

Mountbatten: Take back the minute, tear it up and send me a perfectly straightforward minute re-submitting the proposal. I will then agree to it.

Patel: Alright. I will re-submit it.

Mountbatten: And I will accept it. But I repeat, I will not stand for any further treatment from you of this sort. I have two more items to discuss with you that you will not like much. First, do you want to get rid of Mr Williams? In fact, are you trying to get rid of all Englishmen from your department?

Patel: Of course not! I have a high opinion of Williams. Just because I have chosen an officer who was senior to him does not show any lack of confidence. I am one of those who have publicly stated that I would like to retain British officers after the transfer of power.

Mountbatten: I am glad to have a good report of Williams from you because I would like to offer him the job of secretary to the Governor-General.

Patel: But that post was becoming redundant, there is not enough work.

Mountbatten: I will find more than enough work for him in view of the pressure at which we are working. [Satirically] If you can spare him, please sound him out on my job offer.

[Patel nods grimly]

Mountbatten: The second case is that of the Chief Commissioner of Delhi. Please explain the criticisms you have made of him, because I do not agree with your conclusions.

Patel: It had been agreed that prosecutions would not be made unless the Press Advisory committee said there was a case. Since they said there was no case, the chief commissioner had no right to imply that it was for me to decide. He was trying to imply to the Muslims that the matter was in my hands, instigating communal trouble.

Mountbatten: I see your argument, perhaps Mr Christie has acted incorrectly.

Patel: Next, Mr Christie did not inform me that Mr Ghazanfar Ali Khan was going to tour the riot areas in Delhi to see what the police were doing. Since he is in the health department and not in the police department it is clear he was only going for communal propaganda. I should have been informed of his visit.

Mountbatten: I cannot see that Christie has committed any great crime in this matter and it certainly does not merit your drastic remarks.

Do you want to get rid of the British chief commissioner? Because you have only to say so and then we shall know where we stand.

Patel: I do not specially want to remove a British chief commissioner, only I do not think Mr Christie is able to shake off his pro-Muslim League feelings and therefore he is not a suitable chief commissioner.

Mountbatten: I will discuss your view candidly with Christie and then meet you again. I would also like to know with whom you propose to replace Christie.

Patel: There are four vital posts in Delhi: the deputy commissioner is a Sikh; the judge is a Hindu; and the superintendent of police is an Indian Christian. Mr Christie had made a great point about inadequate representation of Muslims, therefore I will find a Muslim to replace the British chief commissioner. Incidentally, the Delhi police force has ten European officers, four Muslims, and only one Hindu. For seven months I have been trying to make Christie change the proportions of the Hindu and Muslim police officers, but without success.

Mountbatten: I will speak to Mr Christie about this also. Please come at 3 o'clock on Friday for discussions with members of my staff about the plans for transfer of power.

Patel: Since you have come out here things have got much worse. There is a civil war on and you are doing nothing to stop it. You won't govern yourself and you won't let the central government govern. You cannot escape responsibility for this bloodshed.

Mountbatten: Kindly elucidate what you are trying to say.

Patel: I am not trying to link your arrival with the bloodshed—since it has been instigated by the desire of the Muslim League to seize power wherever they can in the hope you will transfer power to them. If you will not act yourself, then turn over full authority to the central government and let us stop the Muslim League war in the Punjab and North-West Frontier. Let us govern.

Mountbatten: You have no idea of the immense problems you will face. Your communal press adds to our difficulties by tendentious and one-sided reports. To start governing the first thing you should ensure is that the press reports events objectively.

Patel: I will immediately issue instructions to the press and send you a copy. [Looks at watch] May I take your leave now? The Congress Working Committee is meeting in half-an-hour.

[Mountbatten stares with narrowed eyes as Patel slowly rises and leaves, wishing him a 'Good Evening']

[Ronnie comes in with Altaf Hussain, editor of *Dawn*, introduces him and leaves.]

Mountbatten: This is an entirely informal talk Mr Hussain, everything I say is off the record.

Hussain: Of course Excellency. Do you have any complaints against me?

Mountbatten: Not more than all this partisan-community press out here. I appeal to you to tone down the bitter note in the reporting of news and above all in your leading articles. I have now enough evidence on which to make my recommendations for the transfer of power. The only result of further provocation by any side will be to throw me against that side. Therefore, the interests of the League lie in establishing peace and proving that they are not the instigators of bloodshed and rioting. I am going to tell this to the League leaders. I will never give in to any form of violence. I warn you, stop inciting the Punjab. Governor's rule there is in the interests of the Muslims themselves. You will have to trust me to be fair. Believe me, any further bloodshed from rioting is likely to rebound to the disadvantage of the Muslim League. [Pause] Thank you for coming to see me.

SCENE 17

Viceroy's study, staff meeting.

Ismay: The latest reports from the governors have arrived. [Begins reading] '*The police situation in Calcutta is deplorable. Till recently there are 1,200 policemen, mainly Gurkhas, as recruitment from the Bengal plains has never been resorted to. When the IG asked for an increase of 50 per cent Mr Suhrawardy the chief minister, insisted they must all be Muslims. As there were none suitable in the province, 600 Muslims were secured from the Punjab. They were given preferential treatment by the Muslim government which resulted in armed conflict with the Gurkhas. The Muslim government has just imposed a pre-censorship on news criticizing the police force in Bengal. In Bihar,*

Dow says the Congress government is incompetent and weak—its members would not qualify even for a seat on a Parish Council in England. They employed 300 ex-INA men against the advice of the governor who prophesied they would kill innocent people and the next day they accidentally killed an important local Congressman named Abdul Bari. In the Frontier, the Muslim League is continuing its violent agitation. A striking commentary on the state of the country is a proposal put before the Cabinet by banking and business communities to sponsor compulsory insurance against civil disturbances. This is a scheme which was operated throughout the war but is now demanded in peacetime.'

Mountbatten: For my part, I have been busy with the Punjabis. First, I saw the Raja of Faridkot. He handed me a letter from Tara Singh and Kartar Singh, inviting him to 'take over the entire policy, organization and safety of Sikh life and property in Ludhiana, Ferozepur and portions of Lahore, and consolidate the Sikh ideals of life'. The letter promised the support of the Akali Dal and the Panthic brotherhood to him. Faridkot also claimed he had the personal assurance of Muslim League leaders in the Punjab, the Nawab of Mamdot and Sir Firoz Khan Noon, that certain areas disputed between Muslims and Sikhs would be included in a new Sikh state. Of course, Ismay and I gave him no hope for supporting a separate Sikh state and advised him to join the Indian or Pakistani Constituent Assembly when the time came. He also expressed the great value all Sikhs have for the British connection and their wish to remain within the Commonwealth. We snubbed that again. Next, I met the Maharaja of Patiala who is completely wedded to the Congress. Patiala said he was trying to keep Tara Singh and Kartar Singh in order but they were apt to be inflammatory. He said he had warned them that they and Faridkot were being extremely foolish in the plans they were hatching. Any idea that the departure of the British could be an occasion of a grabbing match was out of the question. He fears the Sikhs are preparing for all out civil war, and have appealed for a 'war fund' of 50 lakhs, which sounds ominous. Finally, I had my interview with Tara Singh and Kartar Singh. They charged us with letting them down badly and presented me with a book called *The Betrayal of the Sikhs*. These two unkempt, *jungly*-looking old men were immensely learned. They have an encyclopaedic knowledge of every letter with the secretary of state, all statements in the House of Commons, and they brought copies of all the correspondence and the Hansard with them. Before they left I pulled their leg about the enormous swords they were carrying. I told them the Muslims also want the right to carry swords as they were at a disadvantage in street fights with the Sikhs. These scholarly, wild men actually said they wouldn't mind!

Liaquat Ali came in briefly to tell me that he was very grateful to God that Congress had refused the Cabinet Mission plan when the League had accepted it since it was now clear that they would merely use their permanent majority at the centre to manipulate the army and establish a stranglehold on the predominantly Muslim provinces. Two interesting meetings were with minority representatives. C.H. Bhabha, the Parsi was very keen to keep the link with the crown. And the Indian Christian Assembly member, John Matthai, was convinced that Jinnah is the main difficulty for a settlement. He believes Liaquat Ali and Nehru can work together as a team. I also saw Shyama Prasad Mukherji—the Hindu leader. He told me that Congress does not represent Hindus as it was a purely political party and all creeds could join it. Indeed, he accused Congress of not looking after the interests of Hindus sufficiently. Krishna Menon had also remarked last week that Nehru, especially, is becoming unpopular with the Hindus.

Ismay: There is the matter of Brigadier Cariappa's offer to me that he is prepared for a dictatorship of the army to replace British Raj. Some other senior officers have been talking similarly.

Mountbatten: A quick statement from us will stop such ideas.

Mieville: Corfield, who is in charge of the Princely states called me for dinner and complained bitterly of Nehru's speech threatening the princes. Did you have a word with Nehru about it, Dickie?

Mountbatten: I hauled him over the coals over it. I told him I was disappointed to find that a man who was so statesmanlike in Cabinet could be such a demagogue when let loose in public.

He took my ticking off in good part and took pains to explain that he was speaking only in his personal capacity as President of the States People's movement and not on behalf of the Cabinet or even the Congress.

Ismay: That's putting a fine point on it. I had two of the princes running to me after that speech.

Mountbatten: He has agreed that the rulers must not be harried to join the Constituent Assembly till I make the public announcement on the plan for transfer of power. But do tell Corfield that the rulers would be well advised to consult the will of their people.

Mieville: Suhrawardy, the Muslim League Premier of Bengal, must have arrived outside. Shall I call him in?

Ismay: Eric and I have already talked with him, you should see him alone now Dickie.

Mountbatten: Right! Send him in.

[All leave and Suhrawardy walks in]

Suhrawardy: Sir Mieville and Lord Ismay have told me the way your minds are working, and I am unhappy at the idea of partitioning Bengal.

Mountbatten: I am against all forms of partition, but regretfully it appears unavoidable.

Suhrawardy: In Bengal that is not the case—we would like to remain independent. If you give me enough time I am confident I can get Bengal to remain united. Jinnah sahib will agree to it.

Mountbatten: It is certainly better to keep Bengal as one economic unit but will you ask for a separate army as well?

Suhrawardy: Of course.

Mountbatten: That is the difficulty. It would be appalling to divide the army into three parts! It would take five years.

Suhrawardy: Oh no, it can be partitioned easily if we get help from the British officers and Bengal will remain in the Commonwealth as an independent nation.

Mountbatten: You are quite wrong on both counts—forming a Bengal army will be daunting and we will never accept Bengal if India as a whole is not in the Commonwealth. We cannot get mixed up in supporting one side if there is a civil war.

Suhrawardy: I cannot see how you can kick us out. What have we done to be expelled if the rest of the country does not join?

Mountbatten: I will report your point of view to London. Let me know about developments on the united Bengal front.

[Suhrawardy leaves. Ronnie from door: 'Mr Kiran Shankar Roy, leader of the Congress opposition in the Bengal Assembly']

Mountbatten: I have already recommended joint electorates and even a coalition government to Mr Suhrawardy. You might consider working closely with him as both of you desire unity.

Roy: [Excited] Please advise me on what I should do—a coalition would really preserve Bengali unity!

Mountbatten: I suggest you go straight back to Calcutta and see Mr Suhrawardy. Then go to Darjeeling and see the governor. You have not a moment to lose.

Roy: [Stands up dramatically, warmly shakes Mountbatten's hand] Thank you—thank you Your Excellency.

[Roy leaves room. Ismay rushes in saying Jinnah is outside, then brings him in]

Mountbatten: Mr Jinnah, why are you encouraging the Nawab of Mamdot—he is creating problems.

Jinnah: What is the problem Lord Mountbatten? He has up to 93 supporters out of 175 in the Punjab Assembly—he can form a government immediately and really govern. You have often proclaimed that you do not like governor's rule there, why don't you remove it now?

Mountbatten: After my talk with Messieurs Tara Singh and Kartar Singh, I am convinced that any attempt to impose a one-community government on the Sikhs will produce immediate armed retaliation and might well end in civil war. The Sikhs are so bitter about Muslim atrocities that they are only waiting for their revenge. If I am to give you Pakistan and have to divide Punjab what is the point of installing a Muslim League government? It will only bring bloodshed. [Holds up hand as Jinnah tries to speak] Nothing will induce me to change my mind, I am informing the governor not to entertain the Nawab. Can I tell the governor that you agree with me?

Jinnah: Certainly not. I definitely do not agree.

Mountbatten: Do you see my point of view and understand my reasons?

Jinnah: I see your point of view though I do not agree with your decision.

Mountbatten: [Impatient] It is very difficult to deal with somebody who admits he sees the point yet will not express agreement merely to score a political point! [Cold manner] You want to get into a mess in the Punjab. I am making this decision in the interests of the Muslim League, one day you will be thankful to me.

Jinnah: [Slowly] I respect your sincerity Lord Mountbatten, but I have my pressures also. [Pause] Your talks with the Sikhs must have had a good effect because Kartar Singh sent an emissary suggesting we should discuss about the future of 'Sikhistan' and hinting they might join up with Pakistan. You know, the Sikhs like me personally. They have always trusted me. I have publicly stated that I will support them against the Muslims whenever unfair action is taken against the Sikhs. The Muslim League would offer them very generous terms.

Mountbatten: That is good news. Mr Suhrawardy was also positive about Bengal, he thinks he can keep it united on condition that it does not join either Pakistan or Hindustan. Would you be prepared to support a united Bengal at the price of its remaining out of Pakistan?

Jinnah: I should be delighted. What is the use of Bengal without Calcutta? They had much better remain united and independent. I am sure they would remain on friendly terms with us.

Mountbatten: He also said that independent Bengal would wish to remain within the Commonwealth.

Jinnah: Of course, just as I said Pakistan would wish to remain.

Mountbatten: No—you told me that you might ask to be admitted.

Jinnah: You misunderstood me completely. It is not a question of being admitted but of not being kicked out against our wishes. I saw Mr Churchill in London and he told me that we have only to stand firm and demand our rights not to be expelled from the British Commonwealth and we are bound to be accepted. Britain would never stand for the expulsion of loyal members of the Empire. We Muslims have supplied a high proportion of the army which fought in both wars. None of our leaders have ever had to go to prison for disloyalty. Not one member of the Muslim League was present in the Constituent Assembly when the Congress passed the resolution for an independent sovereign republic of India. There is no precedent for forcing parts of the Empire to leave against their will.

Mountbatten: Emotionally and sentimentally, I not only see your point of view but share it. Rationally, I cannot support it, for if you have Commonwealth support and British officers and civil war broke out with the other part of India, then the British would be in a quite impossible position.

Jinnah: What about the other dominions, Australia and New Zealand, will they accept our being expelled? We will appeal to them over Britain's head.

Mountbatten: I shall put forward your argument to London. Meanwhile, I urge you to stop all the violence in the Frontier Province. Obviously, you want to get the province into Pakistan and you will only gain by quietly calling off the agitation there. I will in no circumstances yield to violence.

Jinnah: Unless a fresh election is announced it is impossible to control the movement there. Did your visit to the Frontier satisfy you that the Congress government there should be dismissed or not?

Mountbatten: No, definitely not. The Congress government there is duly elected for a full term. The election was suggested solely on the issue of whether the province should go to Pakistan or Hindustan.

Jinnah: But in the Punjab you don't allow the League to form a ministry. You should be consistent and face up to Sikh violence there just as you are condemning League violence in the Frontier province.

Mountbatten: This is not a parallel case. The previous ministry was thrown out through Muslim League violence.

Jinnah: The League movement was started in the Frontier because the Khan Sahib ministry sought to crush us—the victimization, persecutions, suppression and oppression of the people, especially top ranking leaders of the Muslim League knew no limits. The resentment of the people led to mass civil disobedience. If the Congress government is allowed to continue in the Frontier and I call off the campaign, I will be reduced to dust in the eyes of my followers. I have no hesitation in saying that they will not remain peaceful. Neither you nor I will be able to control the people.

Mountbatten: Then I shall have to send in the army and air force! I will not hesitate to impose bombing. My first requirement is peace—if I cannot have it by cooperation then I will make it completely disastrous for the aggressors.

Jinnah: Lord Mountbatten, the Congress government there is provoking violence and imprisoning all my people. They know perfectly well that they are finished in the Frontier. They are playing the game of the gambler's last throw. Their whole idea is to keep up the bloodshed and force you not to have an election there.

Mountbatten: My conscience will not allow me to yield to force in any way. Listen carefully. I have seen Mr Gandhi and he has agreed that the right to hold meetings with free speech cannot be denied. If there is any shooting at the meeting site, the government is to be blamed. But you cannot take out processions or indulge in picketing. And not too big meetings, mind you. They should be in out of the way places. I do not want to see any incidents in the newspapers.

Jinnah: All right. I will suspend the campaign on the condition that I can assure my people that you are recommending a referendum in the NWFP to decide whether its people are in favour of Pakistan or Hindustan.

Mountbatten: But London might over-rule my recommendation.

Jinnah: I understand that—but I have to give them a reason for toning down the agitation.

Mountbatten: Are you sure you want the province? It costs the present government three and half *crores* a year to keep the tribes quiet.

Jinnah: After you make your announcement on partition, I propose to go to the Frontier myself and have a straight talk with the tribes. I am sure I will not have to pay them anything, at least not so much. I will come to some arrangement with them.

Mountbatten: May I offer you a word of advice, Mr Jinnah? Drop the unfortunate term 'direct action'—the world at large takes it to mean a violent, armed action. It contrasts badly with the Congress non-violence creed.

Jinnah: Their so-called non-violent campaigns have always resulted in terrible bloodshed. And although we passed the resolution of 'direct action' we never launched the campaign.

Mountbatten: Then call the European correspondents together and explain it to them. You have a very bad world press.

[Jinnah leaves] [Add some miscellany with staff before next visitor]

Ronnie: Mr Ghazanfar Ali Khan, Muslim League, Minister of Health to see you, Your Excellency.

Mountbatten: Lord Ismay has explained the idea of partition in Punjab to you, I believe, since that is your home. Do you think there should be a referendum or will a vote of the representatives of the Constituent Assembly suffice?

Ghazanfar: A referendum will take too long, Your Excellency. And it is liable to instigate rioting.

Mountbatten: The Sikhs, unfortunately, will be cut in half in the process—18 *lakh* on one side and 20 *lakh* on the other.

Ghazanfar: Yes, the partition will be a great tragedy for the Sikhs. And it will be difficult to impose it against their will. Though I remember they made tremendous threats twelve years ago, at the time of the Communal Award, that they would die to the last man, in fact, they did not even die to the first man.

Mountbatten: This time you should take them seriously, because they are in earnest. If you are genuinely against partition then the best service you could do for the Punjab is to discuss the matter with Mr Kartar Singh.

Ghazanfar: Kartar Singh is an old friend but ever since the riots he has been saying terrible things.

Mountbatten: I think it is up to you to make the first move. And let me know if anything comes of it.

[Ghazanfar leaves]

Ronnie: Mr B.G. Kher, the Chief Minister of Bombay is here, Your Excellency.

[Kher arrives, smiling broadly]

Mountbatten: So are you happy Mr Kher? Mr Patel told me you have succeeded in getting rid of your pro-Muslim IG.

Kher: No, no, I don't think he was pro-Muslim. Actually, he was too soft-hearted and he fell over backwards in trying to be fair to minorities. The new IG has restored complete law and order in Bombay within three days. There has been no trouble since he came.

Mountbatten: I congratulate you on having a quiet province now, it is rare these days.

Kher: Our communal trouble was relatively small compared to other provinces. My government passed a law that the aggressive community was to pay for the damage to property of the grieved community. This had a most salutary effect in reducing the damage and also encouraged members of both communities to join together in putting out the fires.

Mountbatten: It is a very good idea—it should be the general law in all provinces. I will put this proposal in my letters to the governors.

Kher: Lord Mountbatten, I have a very happy government and relations with the Europeans are extremely friendly. I must give credit for this to the leavening influence of the Parsi community. I would really like you to visit one of the clubs in Bombay and see the friendly and free spirit among the British and the Indians there.

Mountbatten: If I can find the time. Tell me, Mr Kher, what truth was there in the Muslim League charges that the Congress government between 1937 and 39 repressed the Muslims?

Kher: Completely baseless charges! They brought up two points. First, they complained that Muslim children in schools were obliged to sing the Hindu national song.

We ordered that if even one member of a class objected to the singing of the song it was not to be sung. Next, they did not want the Congress flag to be hoisted on public buildings. My ministry directed that if anyone objected, it was not to be hoisted. This was a matter for local authorities.

Mountbatten: All this doesn't sound very harmful.

Kher: I assure you, Lord Mountbatten they have been very well treated. They are being well looked after—they have no genuine cause for complaint.

Mountbatten: Well, thank you for coming to see me. It will not be long now before I announce my new plan.

[Kher leaves]

[Ronnie announces K.M. Panikkar]

K.M. Panikkar: Thank you, Your Excellency, for giving me some time today, I have to urgently return to Bikaner tonight.

Mountbatten: Any trouble? Your Maharaja has got in well with the Congress by leading the group of princes who joined the Constituent Assembly last month.

K.M. Panikkar: No, no, there is no trouble, it is a personal matter. The Maharaja acted on my advice, Lord Mountbatten. After all, we must make our people feel that they have a voice in the Constituent Assembly. In any case, the states cannot possibly stand by themselves—a strong centre is absolutely essential for us. In fact, I positively welcome the idea of a separate Pakistan as it will enable a really strong centre to be formed at Delhi. The inclusion of Muslim majority provinces would have rendered that impossible. I am sure Mr Jinnah intends to set up an equally strong centre for Pakistan. You know, I am one of the very few Indians who have made a study of Strategic Defence and none of the leaders except Sardar Patel understand the problem. He told me he is so worried that he is determined to get a really good settlement with the British because, after independence, there may be new people in government who do not understand defence.

Mountbatten: Any settlement that fails to include India within the British Commonwealth to enable British officers to continue serving here will be no good to India. Unless all the secrets of modern equipment are at the disposal of India, any arrangement with us will halve the value.

K.M. Panikkar: I will talk to Sardar Patel about this as soon as I return. There is an immediate problem regarding equipment for the police force in Bikaner for which I need your help, Lord Mountbatten. I have a miniature Punjab problem in the Ferozepur area which borders on the northern corner of Bikaner and I must have modern rifles, field guns and Bren gun carriers to deal with the troublemakers. There is a large colony of Sikhs, Hindus and Muslims there who were involved in the rioting. On the other side, Bikaner borders on Bahawalpur which will join Pakistan, and we are faced with 150 Hindu refugees migrating from there into our territory everyday.

Mountbatten: The whole question of equipment for states is being considered—an overall policy has to be settled. Of course, your situation is tricky, I will follow up your request as a matter of urgency. One word about discussing my point on the Commonwealth with Mr Patel, please do not quote me. I am not prepared to raise this matter with any Congressman unless they raise it first.

K.M. Panikkar: Of course, Excellency. I understand the position. I will put it forward on my own logic. I do hope you are going to visit us in Bikaner in December, the Maharaja asked me to repeat the invitation.

Mountbatten: It will be a pleasure. Let's hope all goes well till then.

SCENE 18

Mountbatten in study: Dictating report to Ronnie.

Mountbatten: Up till this moment, I felt it my duty to push the Cabinet Mission Plan as the only reasonable solution for India. Jinnah refused absolutely to discuss it. He says he knows that the Congress do not mean to play fair, and intend to use their permanent majority at the centre to crush his project. I discussed with Patel a possible compromise, a system of voting on communal questions similar to that in the Constituent Assembly. Patel warned me, '*If you raise this question of parity you will incur the everlasting enmity of Congress; what you suggest is the one thing we have been fighting against and will never agree to it*'. My staff has now prepared a final draft of the new plan and I am sending Ismay to London with it. He will be able to explain it to the Cabinet in London. The essence of the plan is to make it apparent to the people of India and to the world in general that we are allowing Indians themselves to choose how they wish us to transfer power. In fact, the *Hindustan Times* launched an attack on me on the ground that I had recommended fresh elections under section 93 in the NWFP in the plan being sent home with Ismay. Fortunately, the leaders of Congress were not long in rallying to my defence. Gandhi himself castigated the *Hindustan Times* and his secretary Rajkumari Amrit Kaur issued a written statement denouncing the story.

As the editor of this paper is Devdas Gandhi, the Mahatma's own son, the situation was not without humour. I received commiseration and apologies from Nehru and Mr Birla, who finances the paper and in fact this attack, I think, has strengthened my position. In the process I was able to negotiate with Congress the idea of substituting a referendum for a re-election in the NWFP, on the simple issue of 'Pakistan or Hindustan'.

It is impossible to exaggerate the need for speed as the shocking deterioration in so many provinces continues. Every day now counts here if we are to prevent the communal conflict from spreading to unmanageable proportions. I have first hand information of the situation in the NWFP which, at the moment, is the greatest danger spot in India and the bone of contention between the Congress and the Muslim League. I spent 26 hours at Peshawar and up the Khyber and except between 2 a.m. and 7 a.m. when I was overcome by sleep and had to retire to bed, I saw an absolute stream of officials and delegations. I had separate talks with sixteen British and Indian officials from every part of the Frontier besides the Governor and Chief Minister. The Muslim League was a great problem during the visit. Jinnah had arranged for a demonstration of one hundred thousand in Peshawar and wished them to march in procession to Government House to hand in their resolutions. I absolutely forbade this. The greatest crowd ever seen on the Frontier had collected to see me and the Governor told me they would not disperse till I showed myself. The chief minister of the Congress Government there sensibly assented to my showing myself to this League demonstration. I simply stood on a railway embankment and neither spoke nor waved to them—yet there were tremendous bursts of clapping. Among the cries for Pakistan one could hear cries of 'Mountbatten *ki jai*', It was most awkward that the League should look upon me as some sort of saviour. However, the GOC, the IG of police and the DC thanked me as they said the crowd was determined to break through to Government House and they would have had the biggest killing ever known on the Frontier if I had not shown myself. I realized the risk I took in appearing to be partisan and I sent a full explanation of the incident to Nehru. I also told the Muslim League deputation that, as they were trying to overthrow the Congress Government by violence, I must support the government. I held a *Jirga* with representatives of all the tribes and there was remarkable unanimity among them. They say, in no circumstances will they come under Hindu domination—they would sooner make terms with

Afghanistan. They pressed hard for Pakistan and the dismissal of the Congress Government. Subsequently, I received a delegation of Hindus with a horrible tale of woe against the Muslim League, of murder, rape and violence. My wife and I drove to the small town of Kahuta which was set ablaze by Muslims from the rural district around it. The Hindu Sikh part is an absolute wreck, as though it had been subjected to an air raid. The massacres were distinguished by sadistic violence—tying whole families together and lighting them as a single torch. Many Hindu and Sikh women have taken their own lives rather than be raped or forcibly converted. Until I went to Kahuta, I had not appreciated the magnitude of the horrors which are still going on. The Muslim League campaign is assuming dangerous proportions, already they have destroyed millions of rupees worth of property and laid up bitter hatred. Jinnah tells me he now cannot stop it and further violence is inevitable.

The partition of the Punjab is going to be very difficult—almost impossible to produce a demarcation which will be accepted by both parties. The Sikhs, in their endeavours to obtain a real 'Sikhistan' want to take a large part of the area where they own most of the land but the Muslim population predominates. They also want their holy places, including Lahore itself, the capital-designate of Pakistan. The Maharaja of Patiala came rushing to tell me, that Sikh leaders were very perturbed because I was ruining the idea of Sikhistan. He appealed to me to make the partition line on the basis of Sikh landed property, Sikh sacred buildings and Sikh interests. I told him that world opinion would undoubtedly be against any attempt to put Muslim majority populations of the west Punjab under Sikh domination merely on ownership of land and religious grounds. Patiala was rather worried and said '*In that case I greatly fear the Sikhs will fight*'. I replied '*If they do, Maharaja Sahib, they will have to fight the Central Government. I will send in tanks and armoured cars and artillery—they will be bombed and machine-gunned from the air. You can tell your Sikhs that they will not be fighting the Muslim League but the whole might of the armed forces*'. He was visibly shaken and promised to report this to the Sikh leaders.

If it were possible to have a worse headache than the NWFP and the Punjab, then Bengal provides it. I asked the governor if, as he said two weeks ago, he was still sitting on a barrel of gunpowder, he replied '*Good Lord, no, we got off that a long time ago. We are now sitting on a complete magazine which is going to blow up at any time*'. Suhrawardy claims that he and the Congress leaders and Sarat Chandra

Bose had successful discussions on the unity of Bengal. I told him that if Hindus and Muslims reached an agreement to run a coalition government I would urge the Congress and League high commands to accept an independent Bengal. I know that Gandhi would help. Of course, I warned him that Nehru was not in favour of an independent Bengal unless it was closely linked to Hindustan, as he feels that a partition now would anyhow bring it back to Hindustan in a few years. Jinnah's view is to the contrary. He argues that a referendum is needed since the communal award was modified by the Poona pact, leaving the Scheduled Castes completely at the mercy of the caste Hindus in the electorates. Therefore, he says, only a referendum can secure any effective voice of the Scheduled Castes who, he believes would prefer to be with Pakistan. Calcutta has been very unsettled with the Muslims planning an anti-partition day and the Hindu Mahasabha organizing an Indian mutiny day on the same date. Even Nehru is infected by alarmist rumours and told me that the Muslims would sack Calcutta rather than let it be handed over to the Hindus. Almost everyone in this country is affected by a state of jumpiness. [Interrupted by Campbell-Johnson's entry]

Campbell-Johnson: Sorry Dickie, but I thought you might want to include Jinnah's statement published in the *Dawn* today.

Mountbatten: What does he say ?

Campbell-Johnson: [Reads] '*The question of partitioning Bengal and the Punjab is a sinister move actuated by spite and bitterness as the Congress want to unnerve the Muslims by openly and repeatedly emphasizing that the Muslims will get a truncated or mutilated, moth-eaten Pakistan. The Hindus have their homelands consisting of six vast provinces, which means, three-fourths of British India. Merely because a portion of the minorities in the Pakistan provinces have taken up this attitude, the British Government should not countenance it because the result will be, logically, that all other provinces will have to be cut up in a similar way*'. [Looks up] I suppose he means the Muslim minorities in other parts of India will also demand partitions?

Mountbatten: That is an empty threat.

Campbell-Johnson: He also says: '*If the Hindu minorities in Pakistan wish to emigrate to Hindustan, and vice versa, Muslims wish to go to Pakistan they will be at liberty to do so as sooner or later exchange of population will have to take place. It is quite obvious that the Congress has put up the Hindu Mahasabha in Bengal and the Sikhs in the Punjab, and its press is inciting the Sikhs and misleading them*'. I also have here a pamphlet issued by the Muslim League in Bengal.

[Mieville rushes in]

Mieville: I am getting a great number of reports of stabbing cases in Delhi—I think we should impose curfews in the affected areas.

Mountbatten: A fantastic communal madness seems to have seized everybody! It leaves me with no other option but partition. Ask the office to prepare the curfew orders, Eric.

[Mieville leaves]

Mountbatten: Now where were we, Ronnie? [Ronnie reads last line…] To give you one small horrifying example: my wife had Miss Jinnah to tea again last week. She told Miss Jinnah that she had spent a morning at Lady Irwin College, and was delighted to find how happily that institution was working and on what excellent terms the Hindu and Muslim girls were. In one class of fourteen Hindu and two Muslim girls, the class had elected a Muslim to be their Head Girl. To this, Miss Jinnah replied, '*Don't be misled by the apparent contentment of the Muslim girls there; we haven't been able to start our propaganda in that College yet*'. The Hindus are as bad. The determination from the highest to the lowest in the land to make out that the opposite religionists are devils incarnate, makes any sensible solution appear out of the question. The most we can hope to do, is to put the responsibility for these mad decisions fairly and squarely on the Indian shoulders in the eyes of the world, for one day they will bitterly regret the decision they are about to make.

Moving to a more hopeful note, my Reforms Commissioner V.P. Menon, Nehru's greatest friend Krishna Menon, and minority members such as Baldev Singh and Bhabha, have told me that the possibility of India remaining in the Commonwealth is a subject of heated discussion in the Congress at the moment. They now realize Jinnah's game and are beginning to be very frightened by its consequences on the rest of India. I feel that Congress should be given no inkling as to our attitude since this fear is the main hope of bringing them back into the fold. Lastly, my wife held an At Home for 600 students and staff of the women's medical and nursing colleges in Delhi. She has continued her visits to hospitals, medical and welfare centres, and had discussions with their heads. She also accompanied me on my tour of the Frontier Province and the Punjab and stayed for an additional two days to tour relief centres, refugee camps and hospitals in the most disturbed areas.

I am moving to Simla for a week with my staff and have asked Nehru to come as my guest, since I think he is nearing a breakdown from overwork. He will arrive on 8 May to spend four days with us. We have made real friends with him and whatever else happens I feel this friendship is sincere and will last.

SCENE 19

Viceroy's House—Simla. In the lounge, Nehru stands by open windows, looking out. Edwina Mountbatten enters, bright, cheerful, carrying an open book.

Edwina: Isn't this capital! What a lovely place!

Nehru: [Turns to face her, rubbing hands together] Yes! The clean, sharp air is a real tonic.

Edwina: Listen to this [sits down and reads from open book], '*Simla was variously called Mount Olympus, the Viceroy's shooting-box, the Indian Capua, the Abode of the Little Tin gods. It was a dream of coolness in a very hot land...a bitter-sweet memory of home-cuckoos and thrushes, pines in the mist, honey-suckle and roses in the rain*'. How romantic!

Nehru: You should see Kashmir—Simla can't compare with it!

Edwina: Listen, listen to this; Emily Eden, sister of Governor-General Lord Auckland, writes, '*Twenty years ago no European had ever been here, and there we were, with the band playing the 'Puritani' and the 'Masaniello', and eating salmon from Scotland and sardines from the Mediterranean, and observing that the 'chef's potage a la julienne' was perhaps better than his other soups.... We, 105 Europeans being surrounded by at least 3,000 mountain people, who, wrapped up in their hill-blankets, looked on at what we call our polite amusements. I sometimes wonder they do not cut all our heads off and say nothing more about it*'.

Nehru: You see? Your argument with me on Gandhi's non-violence is proved wrong. Our people have always been peaceable—the hill men especially are very gentle.

Edwina: [Finger on lips] Shh... Here's more; '*Victor Jacque Mont, a Frenchman, who stayed here in 1830, wrote to his father in Paris: 'Do you see Simla on your map: A little to the north of the 31st parallel of latitude and a little to the east of the 77th meridian of longitude, a few leagues from the Sutlej? Isn't it strange to dine in silk stockings in such a place, to drink a bottle of hock and another of champagne each evening, to have delicious Mocha coffee and receive the Calcutta papers every morning?*' [Pauses for breath]

Nehru: Stop that! I'm suddenly ravenous.

Edwina: [Ignoring interruption] And here's Captain Raleigh, a junior on Lord Amherst's staff, '*To describe the magnificence of this scene would be out of my power. You look downwards over the vale clothed with wood of the most gorgeous description. The stately, um... deodar*'.

Nehru: Deodar! That's a large oak. It can't compare with the Chinar of Kashmir.

Edwina: [Reading on] Hmm... '*Deodar and other majestic trees thickly interspersed with masses of wild, red, forty-foot high rhododendron trees in fruit and brilliant scarlet blossoms, a gaudy carpet of scarlet and green. Wild strawberries, raspberries, apricots and cherries—excellent for brandy—ripen along the hill paths, deer lurk among the pines, and when the aides-de-camp tire of playing cards round the log fires, they stroll through the woodlands taking potshots at mountain bears, leopards or golden eagles which chance their way*'.

[Nehru, who has been standing behind a grand armchair moves forward to a chair near Edwina, sinks into it and says indulgently]

Nehru: Go on...I'm transported to another world...

Edwina: [Looks at him for a moment, then switching from bright, loud voice, reads softly, gently] Colonel Chadwick writes, '*It is impossible to describe the delicious feeling of waking at Simla for the first time and looking out upon the purple and shadowy dells below, and the dark dense woods around, and the spotless Himalayas in the distance, and the moss and ivy on the trunks on the oak and pines about your path, and the dewy English wild flower and fern underfoot. The intensity... of such a moment... can neither be described, nor forgotten...*' [She looks at Nehru, leans over and places a hand on his arm] You are tired. You must sleep a while, Jawaha.

Nehru: [Looking lost]...and miles to go before I sleep...before I sleep...

[Mountbatten walks in briskly, smiling]

Mountbatten: Are we not having afternoon tea today? It's almost four and we [includes Nehru in a gesture] have a boxful of files to go through between tea and dinner.

[Mountbatten sits on sofa as Edwina goes to the door and rings a bell; she comes and sits down beside him on the sofa]

Edwina: Can't you delay your files to after dinner, Dickie? I'm afraid I've tired out Jawaha, I've been reading him the eulogies to Simla by Englishmen. And women!

Nehru: No, no! I am fine—we must get on with our work.

Mountbatten: I've reserved tomorrow for relaxation [to Nehru]—we'll take you to 'The Retreat' at Mashobra. Alan is staying there and has asked us over. You haven't been there, have you?

Nehru: No, I'm afraid no previous viceroy thought of inviting me.

[Laughs]

Chief Bearer: [Carrying tea-tray, followed by two bearers carrying cake and sandwiches] Good Afternoon *Sahibs*.

[He pours tea as the other two take food around]

SCENE 20

The retreat—Mashobra. A garden tea-party is in progress. Present: Campbell-Johnson, his wife and their son Keith, V.P. Menon, Krishna Menon, Nehru, Mountbatten and Edwina.

Mountbatten: 'The Retreat' is a fine place! Truly an escape from the despotism of dispatch boxes, is it not?

Campbell-Johnson: That's a famous quote from Viceroy Elgin, he's the one who purchased The Retreat when Mashobra was an unknown village.

Edwina: Quite glorious and completely remote.

Mrs Campbell-Johnson: I suppose the Vice Regal Lodge is too prepossessing for relaxation.

Krishna Menon: Viceroy's House is an oversized and pretentious medieval castle. Quite characteristic of the heavy-footed opulent flamboyance of the High Raj.

Mountbatten: Well, you are in good company in criticism of the Lodge. Lady Curzon is said to have quipped that only a Minneapolis millionaire would revel in it.

Edwina: Absolutely. It is bogus English Baronial—Hollywood's idea of a Viceroy's house. I can't bear to sit in the cavernous rooms, all chocolate brown paint and varnished wood. The roses and rhododendrons in the garden are nice though. [Looking around] From descriptions I've been reading in the Lodge library all the hill-slopes should be blossoming with wild flowers. I suppose too many roots were dug up by ladies trying to improve their herbaceous borders, so the flowers simply vanished.

Krishna Menon: More likely that too many blooms were heedlessly picked by servants for the vases of their mistresses' dining tables.

V.P. Menon: [Suddenly, loudly] It is beautiful weather for an outdoor party. So impossible in Delhi.

Campbell-Johnson: [Laughs] you know what an old resident of Simla told me? During the Dufferin's time here there were daily luncheons in the middle of forests, with all the tables, chairs, lace covers and silver laid on. Among Indians the practice was known as '*poggle-khana*'—the incomprehensible British habit of choosing to eat out of doors.

V.P. Menon: [Puzzled] *Poggle-khana*?

Nehru: *Are*, *pagal-khana*, Mr Menon. It means 'Dinner for madmen'.

[Campbell-Johnson's son gets up and tries to leave, Mountbatten pulls him back]

Mountbatten: [Putting an arm around him] Where are you leaving for sir? [Turning to Nehru] He's my godchild you know? He stands up so straight he will fall over backwards!

Nehru: Do you like exploring the hills, Keith?

Keith: Yes sir.

Nehru: I love climbing hills. Come, I'll show you a new technique of walking uphill backwards.

Edwina: Oh come, come Jawaha! Walking uphill backwards indeed.

[Nehru smiles, arm around the boy and walks off. Gradually, all drift out chatting. Only Edwina remains seated, smoking. Few moments later Nehru enters alone, sits beside her]

Edwina: How did the circus go? [Laughs] Seriously, why backwards?

Nehru: It's very scientific. It makes breathing easier at high altitudes and rests the calve muscles.

Edwina: Really! Have some more tea. [She pours tea] I've really, truly fallen in love with this place. You know, when Dickie was offered the Viceroyalty we got quite a shock, I thought it was a horror job. We never imagined we would find a friend such as you here.

Nehru: Dickie is a wonderful person—it's hard not to be his friend. When I first heard of Dickie's appointment someone told me the story of how during the 1945 election a Labour party canvasser arrived at your house and Dickie said 'oh you don't have to convince us. But you're going to have a devil of a time in the kitchen. The Butler and the staff are all out and out Tories.' So I thought it would be good to meet a straightforward English socialist again.

Edwina: He has an extraordinary facility for getting on with all kinds of people.

Nehru: And he has a very unusual wife—for a Vicerine! You are approachable and so human. Though I must say, when you made your entrance at the swearing-in, you looked so proud and distant.

Edwina: I suppose I might as well tell you, without my glasses I could hardly see anyone! And I had an awful attack of neuralgia. Besides, my first day at Viceroy's house was ghastly! The place is vast, the staff enormous. Behind handsome doors the state rooms are hung with cobwebs. Lady Wavell handed me a list of my personal servants, my bearer, *durzi*, *chaprassi* and *khidmatgar*! Phooey! Everything was too imposing, too theatrical.

But that's India I suppose…your family had quite a feudal lifestyle I believe?

Nehru: My father was a rather stylish person. But when he joined Gandhiji he slept on the floor in prison. Tell me about yourself. You belong to a very wealthy family?

Edwina: Yes, though we were always in and out of the kitchen and the housekeeper's room, and the stables and chatting with the farm boys. I shared a room with my sister, and our bedrooms and studies were simply furnished at home and at school. It didn't matter that I was going to inherit my grandfather's millions. I was sent to a Domestic Science Training Institute to learn competent housekeeping—it was cold—icy winds blew in from the Suffolk coast. It was during the war you know, and the house was run with minimum staff. We did our own cooking, cleaning and laundering. And the baths were in a separate annexe—we dressed in boots and fur-collared coats to go and bathe. You were at elite Harrow!

Nehru: Yes, but life was very serious for an Indian boy.

Edwina: Of course! And then prison awaited you back here. [A pause] I was taught at home initially, school was competition for the first time. Replying to questions in front of other people was a challenge. But I managed. I didn't shine at current events, though I did get 75 out of 100 for an essay on 'The Rights and Wrongs of Socialism', perhaps because of the Jewish blood from my grandfather. I am quite a mixed blood you know—my father's biological mother was a descendant of the American Indian princess, Pocahontas. And do you know that my mother's best friend was Sarojini Naidu? She was Chattopadhyaya then and they met during a holiday in Coblenz.

[Mountbatten and Campbell-Johnson passing by, stop for moment]

Mountbatten: Jawaharlal, has Edwina told you about her visit to the NWFP? She visited nine hospitals and seven refugee centres in areas devastated by communal disturbances.

Nehru: Oh? Why haven't you told me? I must know how bad things are….

Mountbatten: Well, she's the best person to tell you. She spoke with hundreds of refugees and in the hospitals with Hindu, Sikh and Muslim victims of the riots.

[Mountbatten and Campbell-Johnson leave]

Edwina: You look so tired. I didn't want to depress you further. It was such a sad tour—the devastation is like the Blitz at its worst—whole areas completely destroyed and burnt out willfully and the killed, maimed and homeless really tragic. The victims were largely Hindu and Sikh but also a good proportion of Muslims, it all seems so senseless and yet nothing seems to stop them….so harrowing. No words can describe the suffering and seeming hopelessness of the future of the victims.

Nehru: [Lifting his gaze from the ground] What about the relief agencies?

Edwina: The hospitals lack equipment and supplies on that scale, more camps are required to ease the overcrowding; the refugees need advice on hygiene; municipal committees are struggling to provide better drainage and clean water. I have drawn up a plan of action—I hope I can make a difference…. Why do you think there is so much hate between them?

Nehru: Much of the trouble between Hindu, Muslim and Sikh is artificially engineered and is the result of previous policies, missed opportunities and mistakes made on all sides. One thing is certain, India's problem is largely economic and social, far more than religious or political. Improvements are urgently needed in general living conditions, standards of education, employment and health. Look at the numbers of illiterate people, female and child mortality.

Edwina: The medical facilities are scandalous! For a population of four hundred million, there are fewer nurses than in London. Of course, ordinary Indian women are reluctant to take on professional or voluntary nursing—Amrit Kaur told me it's considered menial work. Understandably, I suppose, given the levels of pay and the bad accommodation in hospitals.

Nehru: [Bitterly] But nothing, nothing can excuse this barbarism of the people.

The members of the party come back from their walk and all begin taking leave of Campbell-Johnson and wife. Just then Gordon Mosley, BBC representative in Delhi arrives. Campbell-Johnson introduces him.

Campbell-Johnson: This is Gordon—I'm sure everyone knows him. He's come to stay with us for a few days.

[The party says goodbye and leave. Campbell-Johnson and Mosley sit down as Mrs Campbell-Johnson pours tea for them]

Mosley: What a fine place you're in Alan! A paradise at the top of the world. Who would believe you're here to say goodbye to the Raj.

Campbell-Johnson: It all seems cheerful—too cheerful! Actually, Gordon, we are in the heart of Sikh country here—in Simla and Mashobra. Sentries have been on round-the-clock guard here for the protection of our families and Muslim servants. The Sikhs feel they are being sacrificed on the altars of Muslim ambition and Hindu opportunism. Their leaders are becoming wilder-men like Master Tara Singh and some younger officers of the INA. As they feel hopelessly outmanoeuvred in the political struggle, they've begun invoking more primitive remedies. The outlook is rather stormy and unsettled, but you'll find out soon for yourself.

Ismay and two generals in uniform arrive.

Ismay: You've been holidaying all day, Alan, we just met the Vice regal party in a boisterous mood driving down the road.

Campbell-Johnson: Now that you are here with all the others I suppose hectic activity is forecast for tomorrow.

Ismay: Staff meeting at 9 a.m. tomorrow. You haven't met General Walker and General Willis—very old friends of mine. I thought I would use the one free evening Dickie's allowed me to look them up. [To the generals] As I mentioned, Alan is Lord Mountbatten's Press Attaché, the first and last time the Raj has appointed one. And this is his wife, Fay.

[Campbell-Johnson introduces Gordon Mosley, all sit. Fay goes into house, comes back after a minute followed by bearers with tea-trays.]

Campbell-Johnson: Gordon and I have been discussing the communal tangle here in the Punjab. Our Muslim servants are terrified.

Willis: The Hindus are dunderheads! When the Japanese were knocking at the gates of India, Gandhi sent a message to the British people expressing abhorrence of German Nazism and Italian fascism but hoping they would submit without fighting. Non-violence bunkum! The members of the Muslim League not only supported our war effort but encouraged Muslims to join the armed forces and fight.

Mosley: I was under the impression that it is the Sikhs who constitute the main support of the army

Willis: Let me give you the figures: 65 per cent of the Indian soldiers who fought in North Africa, Italy, Malaya and Burma were Muslims. This means, there were thirteen Muslims to every seven Hindus in the fighting forces, though there were only nine Muslims to every twenty-four Hindus in India. Do you think we can let down the Muslims now? They must have their own country—they can't live with the Hindu claptrap!

Walker: Muslims are certainly easier to get along with, less arrogant, more gregarious. You can visit a Muslim's home and take a meal without feeling that afterwards a whole ritual of 'purification' would be gone through because the house had been sullied. But in the Punjab, I must tell you that we don't have a Hindu–Muslim war—it is a Sikh–Muslim war. I have spent my entire career in this province and I can tell you the Sikhs spell trouble.

Mosley: The Congress have passed a resolution in favour of partitioning the Punjab and I was told in Lahore that the Sikhs had persuaded Nehru that such a move would call the League's bluff.

Willis: Precisely the man who is responsible for provoking Jinnah and the Muslims. I am told he gets on very well with the Mountbattens?

Ismay: Mountbatten thinks Nehru is very sincere and a fair man.

Willis: Did you hear that now? This ruddy Nehru will bowl Mountbatten over.

Campbell-Johnson: On the contrary, there are Indians who already blame Nehru for being too amenable to Mountbatten's charm.

Willis: I don't think Mountbatten should encourage Nehru too much. He is a leader of the Indian *babus*. And that beggar Gandhi as well, for all his Hindu mumbo-jumbo he only protects the moneylenders. The Jat is my man in the Punjab!

Walker: Speaking of *babus*—there was a joke about them in Calcutta when I was there as a young Subaltern. We used to refer to one as '*Babu Sillabub Thunder Gosht, BA*.'

Willis: I can tell you one better! When I was at Lhasa the Dalai Lama told me that a virtuous cow-hippopotamus by metempsychosis might, under unfavourable circumstances, become an undergraduate of Calcutta University, and that when patent leather shoes and English supervened, the thing was a *babu*. Ha-ha!

Walker: [Laughs] Ah! The language of Shakespeare: how it suffers in the mouths of Babus. One asked me if I had read 'Simpson and Delilah and Mr Monte Cristo'! He was a typical sample of patent leather shoes, silk umbrella, and the ten-thousand horse-power English words and phrases.

Ismay: Well, I'm not going to correct you on Nehru—you'll be giving him the salute soon enough. One thing is certain: if anyone can manage the Indians it's Mountbatten. Prime Minister Attlee told Mr Churchill in my hearing that Burma had shown that so-called experts were wrong about Aung San and Mountbatten had been right. He's the man for the job all right. [Stands] I better get back to Simla and prepare for tomorrow's meeting.

[Laughter all around as they say goodbye.]

SCENE 21

It is night in the study at Viceroy's Lodge, Simla. Mountbatten sits at the desk as Edwina enters.

Edwina: You're alone Dickie? I thought you would be having a nightcap with Jawaha. Has he gone to bed already? [Mountbatten frowning silently] Why—what is it Dickie? You look depressed.

Mountbatten: I've had a shattering day. On a hunch I showed Nehru the plan I've sent for Cabinet approval in London. Do you know he almost exploded! He was all heated up and his face went red with anger, then green in distress. He said it would balkanize India, and was a menace to the relations between Britain and India, and we were trying to endanger important, strategic areas of the country. He stood up and almost shouted at me: '*I will never accept a plan like this! Congress will never accept it! India will never accept it*'! My God, he can be egocentric and temperamental!

Edwina: Oh my poor Dickie. But you calmed him down?

Mountbatten: V.P. Menon soothed him with great difficulty. Now V.P. Menon's plan has been accepted by Nehru. I believe Krishna Menon has contributed to pacifying him too. So all is sorted out here. But Ismay and Abell are sweating in London—they've got approval for the plan Nehru has rejected. Now I have to ask them to get V.P. Menon's plan approved.

Edwina: Well, you should have consulted V.P. Menon earlier. He knows the Indian leaders and how to win them over.

Mountbatten: I thought I knew Nehru's mind. But the Hindus are strange, you can never tell with them. I talked to all of them and then I sat down and drafted a plan which I thought expressed their ideas. I was completely wrong. All my staff advised me not to show the draft to Nehru. Imagine! If I hadn't shown it to him what complete fools we would have looked with the government at home, having led them to believe that Nehru would accept it. Without that hunch Dickie Mountbatten would have been finished and sunk, and could have packed his bags.

Edwina: Dickie, I don't like to see you like this. You have to present a bold front. Do what you can to correct the situation and let's move on. And without Nehru there can be no progress in the solution.

Mountbatten: [Sighs] Yes. V.P. Menon said that your conversations with Nehru have helped greatly in making up his mind to go for Commonwealth membership. Thank you my pet.

[Edwina switches off lamps and holds out her hand to Mountbatten. They leave]

SCENE 22

Viceroy's study: Delhi. Mieville and Erskine-Crum seated. Campbell-Johnson puts papers together and moves towards exit.

Mieville: Where are you rushing off to Alan?

Campbell-Johnson: I have to arrange for Dickie to leave for London—he's taking the revised plan personally. Pity me, its sweltering heat outside—113 degrees in the shade! Moan. [Leaves]

Mountbatten: [Walks in and sits at desk and looks at watch] His Royal Highness is late. I'm going home Eric, you hold the fort while I'm away. Keep the gentlemen busy with all the nitty-gritty details of the plan.

Ronnie: [Enters] Mr Jinnah phoned to say he is delayed but Mr Bhabha is outside, says he just wants to see you for a minute.

[Mountbatten nods and Bhabha shown in]

Mountbatten: I congratulate you, Mr Bhabha on your efforts behind the scenes, you seem to have persuaded Mr Patel to accept dominion status.

Bhabha: [Smiling] I have indeed worked hard on this front—and I am really glad to see the Congress leaders are at last taking a realistic view. But I feel that you are making a mistake in dealing so much with the idealistic dreamers instead of realist men of action.

Mountbatten: Do you mean I should deal with Vallabhai Patel instead of Nehru?

Bhabha: I cannot say more, you may take it as you like. All responsible people in India are bound to take dominion status as the only solution. If we succeed in the first six months, no part of India would ever dream of leaving the Commonwealth.

Mountbatten: I sincerely hope so. Well, I'm off to London tomorrow.

Bhabha: I am delighted to hear that. Everybody in Bombay is saying: why doesn't the Viceroy go home? No one else can ever settle this.

[Jinnah and Liaquat Ali ushered in. Bhabha leaves.]

Mountbatten: So gentlemen, you have studied the draft plan. Are you satisfied?

Liaquat Ali: There are a few minor details, Your Excellency. Purnea used to be a part of Bengal—it has been removed. And,...

Mountbatten: I'm sorry, Mr Khan, I cannot tie myself down to any discussion of transfer of areas at the present stage. Sir Eric Mieville is to go into such questions and telegraph me in London—I'm going home tomorrow morning to settle things finally. All I ask of you is an acceptance of the general principles.

Jinnah: The general plan is acceptable to us.

Mountbatten: Very good. So, Sir Mieville will send the plan to the Indian leaders tomorrow. I intend to recommend to HMG that the transfer of power in India should take place as soon as possible. I have informed my prime minister of your desire that Pakistan should remain within the Commonwealth. Congress has now put forward a similar request—I shall pass both requests to HMG. [Leans back] So? You have got your Pakistan. What exactly does it mean by the way?

Jinnah: Well, Lord Mountbatten, P is for Punjab; A is for Afghan—that is the Pathan of the NWFP; K is Kashmir; as for—this letter does not exist in Urdu; S is for Sind and 'tan' for the last syllable of Balochistan.

Liaquat Ali: Your Excellency, the literal meaning of Pakistan is 'pure land'.

Mountbatten: I see. The question which now requires clarification is whether you, Mr Jinnah would prefer Pakistan to have its own Governor-General or to share a common one with India?

Jinnah: I cannot commit myself on this subject straight away but I have given some thought to it and I feel that it would be better to have two Governor-Generals. [Mountbatten's pleasant manner freezes] Of course, there should be a representative of the Crown who would be responsible for the division of assets between the two states. I am extremely keen that Your Excellency should fill that post, needless to say that I have complete faith in Your Excellency. And all your awards will be binding on me. I sincerely desire that you should stay on and be the supreme arbitrator.

Mountbatten: [Cold] I am honoured by your remarks, but I cannot consider taking on a post such as you suggest, nor would anybody else wish to. It would be an impossible position—the so-called arbitrator would be junior in rank to the Governor-General who is the King's representative.

Liaquat Ali: Excellency, if the two states wanted separate Governor-Generals, how would the division of assets take place?

Mountbatten: In that case they would both form an arbitration board. I should tell you that I am under extreme pressure from Congress who state that they will not continue in the Interim Government unless they are granted dominion status immediately after the announcement of the plan.

[Silence]

Mountbatten: Mr Jinnah, please send me a letter giving a full description of your scheme of a supreme arbitrator and two governor-generals by day after tomorrow. However, I wish to make it quite clear that if HMG finds your scheme impracticable, you will assure in writing your acceptance of the appointment of a common Governor-General.

Jinnah: No, no, no! That is impossible—I cannot give it in writing.

Mountbatten: If HMG decides that your suggestion is unworkable?

Liaquat Ali: I realize the point Your Excellency wants us to include in the letter is only accepting an alternative if HMG does not agree to the scheme.

Mountbatten: That's right. Please give the letter to Sir Mieville day after tomorrow and he will send a copy of it to the Congress. You see, Mr Jinnah, besides requiring the approval of HMG your suggestion would also require agreement by Congress.

Ronnie: [Peeping in from door] Mr Patel and Mr Nehru are outside, Your Excellency.

Mountbatten: Please show them in. [Stands up and moves to exit. Jinnah and Ali rise and follow. Patel and Nehru are brought in as Mountbatten returns]

Mountbatten: Well, does the Congress accept the plan?

Nehru: Yes, it is accepted.

Mountbatten: I would like to tell you that your point concerning the Hindu areas in Sind has been matched by Mr Jinnah's concern over Purnea district, he says it should go to Bengal. I have decided that questions of this kind should be referred to the Boundary commission—we will not take them up now. Is that agreed?

Nehru: Well, yes, we can leave it for now, but….

Mountbatten: So this will be the final plan for transfer of power. I leave for Britain tomorrow morning to present it to HMG.

Nehru: Yes, but I have to strongly stress upon one thing—once the announcement is made, the interim government should be treated by convention as a dominion government.

Mountbatten: That will be difficult—because of the Muslim League—but on my own part, I will give the government as much freedom as it wants in the day-to-day administration.

Nehru: Lord Mountbatten, if the Interim Government is treated as a dominion government it will have a great psychological effect. I am prepared to have you as our Governor-General, giving over-riding powers both in the protection of minorities and also on any matter affecting the separation of the Pakistan area. There ought to be no difficulty with the League then. You see, the present state of affairs is intolerable and I would be ready to resign if our request is not conceded.

Mountbatten: Can we not do this: we can have Muslim League members working in the Congress departments and vice versa....

Patel: Absolutely not acceptable—impossible!

Mountbatten: Mr Nehru?

Nehru: I am afraid not—I cannot accept that.

Mountbatten: Well, I will put forward your point of view to HMG—I think I can devise some means by which Congress will have a free hand so far as administration of India is concerned. What about Calcutta? In the event of partition, can Calcutta be declared a free port— you have to have an agreement on the jute trade?

Patel: I am strongly opposed to treating Calcutta as a free port.

Mountbatten: Perhaps you can go into the case for and against with Sir Eric Mieville while I'm away. Mr Nehru, Lady Edwina will be here shortly to give you a report on her trip to Multan, you must excuse me now, I have to prepare for my flight tomorrow.

[Patel and Mountbatten walk-out. Edwina enters]

Edwina: I am sorry Jawaha—I'm in no state to talk very much. Here are some of the papers that record what I saw and also what measures are being taken. As you know we leave for London tomorrow, 8.30 a.m.

Nehru: You look very tired—perhaps you are overworking.

Edwina: I visited all the hospitals and riot-wrecked villages. [Dead voice] There was a child with his hands chopped off. A pregnant mother had been disemboweled—whole families wiped out. I don't know how to describe it to you.

Nehru: I saw something like it in March—2,000 people died then. [Bitterly] India is becoming an unholy mess of bloodshed and hatred. I have such a sense of hopelessness...for the first time.

Edwina: I think Dickie and his advisors are right, partition appears to be the only way out.

[Nehru sits with head down in the fading light.]

[Outside the room, Christie and Abell are talking]

Christie: What's happening inside?

Abell: Mr Nehru and Lady Mountbatten grieving together for Mother India after her tour of riot-areas.

SCENE 23

A country house in England: An unshaven, obviously sick Winston S. Churchill sitting up in bed in a dressing gown with Mountbatten seated beside him.

Churchill: [Hands Mountbatten a paper] Read this letter Louis. Read it aloud.

Mountbatten: [Reads]: '*My dear Prime Minister, I am in a position to assure you that if an effective acceptance of dominion status for the several parts of a divided India are made good, the Conservative Party will agree to facilitate the legislation necessary to confer dominion status upon such several parts of India. Yours sincerely: Winston S. Churchill*'.

Churchill: If you can achieve dominion status for both Hindustan and Pakistan, the whole country will be behind you and the Conservative party will help to rush the legislation through. Do you foresee any difficulties with Mr Gandhi?

Mountbatten: Mr Gandhi is unpredictable but I doubt if he will create any difficulties which cannot be dealt with by Patel and Nehru.

Churchill: Have you received a letter from Nehru accepting dominion status?
He has given up the republic?

Mountbatten: He accepts dominion status—I have given a copy of his letter to the prime minister. But I have been unable to obtain a similar written assurance from Jinnah.

Churchill: By God, he is the one man who cannot do without British help.

Mountbatten: If he does not make up his mind soon and give me a letter I propose to inform him that we will go ahead with the transfer of power on a dominion status basis for Hindustan, with an option for it to be taken up at any time by Pakistan.

Churchill: The Conservative party will not agree to passing legislation under those terms. In fact, I may have to oppose that.

Mountbatten: Please advise me how then should I proceed if Jinnah is intransigent?

Churchill: [After some thought] To begin with, you must threaten. Take away all British officers. Give them military units without British officers. Make it clear to them how impossible it would be to run Pakistan without British help.

Mountbatten: I can try to follow some such policy—but ultimately I must be authorized not only to threaten but also to implement the threat of a transfer of power without dominion status for Pakistan. If I cannot do so Jinnah may hold out indefinitely and then we may lose both Hindustan and Pakistan.

Churchill: [Shaken] Take the Prime Minister's approval and meet the other Conservative Party leaders—meet Eden, Anderson, Macmillan and Simon and discuss this point with them.

Mountbatten: The Prime Minister will not agree—Mr Godfrey Nicholson wanted to see me but the Prime Minister said I was on no account to meet him. He added that Nicholson was a very unsound Conservative with sentimental ideas about India.

Churchill: Harrumph. Advise the Prime Minister to tell the other dominions to make Jinnah see reason. And give Jinnah a message from me—tell him, *This is a matter of life and death for Pakistan if you do not accept this offer with both hands.*

SCENE 24

In the reception adjoining Viceroy's study, Delhi: Full staff is present but not Mountbatten.

Abell: I thought Lord Mountbatten would be tired after his journey and the high-level discussions and would need a day's rest. Eh, Alan?

Campbell-Johnson: On the contrary, he looks more energetic than ever. Besides, there is just this weekend between us and the fateful conference. I need 48 hours in the day to deal with the publicity details for his momentous announcement on the transfer of power. Over and above the text of HMG's announcement, to be synchronized with London, the text of Dickie's broadcast will also have to be released. His voice will be heard over a world-wide network. He says provision also has to be made for broadcasts by Nehru, Jinnah and Baldev Singh.

V.P. Menon: Mr Gandhi will not press his opposition to partition to the point of sabotaging the plan, I'm certain Sardar Patel and Nehru will prevent that. They have accepted that the only way to eliminate Jinnah's nuisance value is by conceding Pakistan.

Colville: I have heard that Nehru put it privately to somebody that by cutting off the head they will get rid of the headache.

[Sniggers]

Campbell-Johnson: Besides the fatigue, I am also feeling depressed. You know I took a ride in Peter's Gray Rolls to visit my family in Simla for a few hours. On the way we saw lorries bringing out Muslims from the walled township. Muslim women were cowering against the wall. As we rushed past, the car radio was thundering out Bach's prelude and Fugue in F minor. It was as if by one strange apocalyptic flash all the grandeur and misery of the world had been revealed.

SCENE 25

At lunch in Christie's house: Present are Christie, H.M. Patel and Chaudhuri Mohammed Ali at the lunch table.

Christie: Thank heavens we are at the end of our labours. I am going to table the paper at tomorrow's staff meeting. The Viceroy would like to thank you personally for all your hard work and asked me to invite you to meet him in the evening.

H.M. Patel: What title have you thought of finally?

Christie: Nothing fancy, we tell it as it is. Let's say *The Administrative Consequences of Partition.*

Chaudhuri: It has been a very exhausting exercise in this weather, especially for you.

Christie: Yes, these are the stifling dog days before the onset of the rains. Though, I must admit both of you have done most of the hard work. Your tempers have borne up pretty well—despite the tough bargaining. I feared a walk-out by one of you each day!

Chaudhuri: Ha-ha. You need not have feared—H.M. Patel and I reached an understanding at the very outset to be completely frank with each other. We know each other well enough to realize that a walk-out would be pointless.

H.M. Patel: The advantage of being fellow civil servants is to have a sense of reality. Anyway, you did a superb job of reconciliation between us.

Christie: Ho-ho. Let's see how your compromises carry with the big chiefs—Sardar Patel has confidence in you, H.M. Patel, but how will Mr Jinnah react?

Chaudhuri: Jinnah Sahib has a facility for producing the incisive phrase—but Sardar Patel is blunt to the point of incivility—sparks will certainly fly.

H.M. Patel: Sardar is painfully honest but I don't think he can match Mr Jinnah's rudeness. What do you think Christie?

Christie: Dividing assets is never easy—but the Viceroy is most persuasive and he is determined not to let a deadlock develop.

[All leave table and walk to exit]

H.M. Patel: I better leave before we start another argument. I have an appointment with Sardar and he dislikes unpunctuality.

Christie: You are in no hurry are you, Muhammad Ali? Stay awhile.

[H.M. Patel leaves while the other two sit at low table and are served coffee while dining table is cleared]

Chaudhuri: You don't take anything stronger in the afternoon?

Christie: You are used to the old India hands—you know, gentlemen taking their ease on a long veranda, attended by a white-coated bearer, ice clinking in long glasses on lazy afternoons. We are modern day slaves and Lord Mountbatten is a ruthless slave driver.

Chaudhuri: We are going to miss you I think—all the English I mean. We never thought everything would happen so quickly.

Christie: We are rather unhappy that India will not remain one.

Chaudhuri: It was inevitable. Did you know Sir Syed Ahmad forecast it? In the Victorian era, the possibility of the English leaving India did not arise and yet he foresaw the ultimate conclusion. He said India was inhabited by two different nations and there would necessarily be a struggle for power between them if the English were to leave. 'His words had an intense influence on me—I remember them verbatim: *Is it possible that the Mohammedan and Hindu could sit on the same throne and remain equal in power? Most certainly not. It is necessary that one of them should conquer the other and thrust it down. To hope that both could remain equal is to desire the impossible and the inconceivable.'*

Christie: Clearly Mr Jinnah did not subscribe to this view when he was in the Congress party?

Chaudhuri: Oh yes. He hoped for very long that we could share the throne with our Hindu friends. But the idea of absorption, of gathering all the Muslims into the Congress fold, is typical of the Hindu mind and the past history of Hinduism. Nearly three centuries earlier the Mughal emperor, Aurangzeb, saw the danger of Islam losing its identity in India.

Christie: I think Mr Jinnah's fears are of more recent provenance. He appears to have a deep-seated dislike of Mr Gandhi. He referred to him as 'that Hindu revivalist' in one interview with the Viceroy.

Chaudhuri: Gandhi's ascetic personality appeals to the religious sentiments of the Hindu masses. All his fasts, his goat's milk, mud baths and days of silence make him pre-eminently a Hindu.

Christie: He always claims to be of all religions—a Muslim, a Hindu, a Buddhist, a Christian, a Jew and a Parsi.

Chaudhuri: Who but a Hindu can entertain such a preposterous hope of being all things to all men? Only Jinnah *Sahib* has the courage to say what he thinks of all this humbug. And we have no illusions about his non-violence. Do you know what Gandhi said at one of his prayer meetings? He declared 'even if the whole of India burns, we shall not concede Pakistan'. It is a sight to make angels weep.

Christie: The Nawab of Bhopal is on friendly terms with Mr Gandhi and he arranged a meeting between him and Mr Jinnah at which I believe a formula was worked out.

Chaudhuri: I know of that—Gandhi agreed to accept the Muslim League as the representative of the majority of Muslims but Nehru wrote to Jinnah *Sahib* that he and his colleagues rejected the formula. Actually, this is the first time they repudiated Gandhi's pledged word, no wonder he withdrew to Noakhali. It was freely said in Congress circles that the old man was suffering from the infirmity of wishing to go down in history as a second Buddha.

Christie: Do you think Gandhi was sincere in accepting the League?

Chaudhuri: Gandhi is head and shoulders above all other Congress leaders in intellectual power and political foresight. After trying his hardest not to let the Muslim League share power with the Congress, he realized that Lord Wavell was determined to bring the League into the interim government. Was it not better that the League should come in through the goodwill of the Congress and not through the favour of the Viceroy? Why not recognize the League and try to break down its guards of suspicion and mistrust? The other Congress leaders, however, lacked the suppleness of mind and the flexible strategy of the master. Now it's all over—I thank God. Well. Thank you for a fine lunch—time for me to go home now.

[Chaudhuri and Christie walk to the door as bell rings. Penderel Moon, V.P. Menon, and Major Short come in]

V.P. Menon: Are you leaving because of me, Muhammad Ali? Meet Mr Penderel Moon and Major Short.

[Chaudhuri greets them, excuses himself and leaves. The others sit as Christie calls for tea which is served after a few minutes during the conversation]

Christie: When did you return from England, Major?

Short: I received an SOS from Mr Baldev Singh. He is extremely worried since the March outrages when Muslim mobs attacked Sikhs and Hindus. He says the scale of murder, loot and arson was never before seen in the Punjab during a hundred years of British rule.

V.P. Menon: It is a foretaste of the blessings of Pakistan—the bazaars of Amritsar were burnt to the ground and murderous mobs of Muslims rampaged through Rawalpindi, Attock and Multan. The Sikhs were especial targets of attack and their houses and their beards alike were set on fire. The Muslim police looked away and there was no expression of regret by Muslim Leaguers.

Christie: I believe Master Tara Singh brandished a sword and raised provocative slogans in foolhardy bravado. Of course, the Muslim police did not take really strong measures against Muslim mobs.

V.P. Menon: Not a shot was fired, Christie. I have even heard that several British officers, who were appealed to for help by panic-stricken Hindus, told them to seek protection from Gandhi, Nehru and Patel.

Moon: That may be a stray occurrence Mr Menon—you can't generalize. In my state of Bahawalpur we have taken stern measures to suppress the disorders. To date there have been about one thousand casualties—even that is disgraceful and I don't want you to give publicity to them.

V.P. Menon: Don't worry Moon, these figures are not very bad. You don't realize what is going on elsewhere. Bahawalpur sounds like a paradise compared with East Punjab. There are no experienced officers there to cope with the mounting tide of refugees. You should come over there and help.

Moon: Thank you for the compliment Mr Menon, but my hands are full at the moment. I must admit some troops of the Bahawalpur army have targeted Sikh colonists who returned to fetch some more of their property after we had dispatched them safely to the other side. The killing of Sikhs has now become a more or less legitimate form of blood sport. I am sorry to say but a large number of troops in the regular army are infected by the communal virus—I have it on the authority of a young Sikh Major who travelled with me. But my Superintendent of Police Leghari and I are rapidly gaining full control.

V.P. Menon: As soon as Bahawalpur has calmed down you should consider coming and helping in East Punjab.

Short: The massacre of Muslims in East Punjab could have been avoided. My antennae told me that they would strike back when and where they felt themselves to be in the ascendancy. No one who knows the Sikhs like I do could believe that they would take lying down all the insults and injuries they had received. In the city of Amritsar the Sikhs were a small minority. The Muslim gangs had not come up against the hardcore Sikh community—the cultivators of central Punjab. Officials who should have known better began, after March, to say that the Sikhs had grown rich and fat in the Punjab colonies and lost their martial vigour, and the Muslims were hardier and not debauched by excessive prosperity. In their view the Sikhs, wherever they were, whether in India or Pakistan, would be a nuisance. They freely said that it was a good thing they would be split in two halves—it was better than having the whole hornets' nest.

Moon: I agree with you Short. A young Muslim *naib-tahsildar* told me that the Sikhs were getting ready to kill and drive out all the Muslims from Amritsar district. The earliest forecast known to me was made by the Senior Superintendent of Police in Delhi at the end of March. He said rather crudely that once a line of division is drawn in the Punjab, all Sikhs to the west of it and all Muslims to the east of it would be castrated.

Short: All I can plead for is that the line should be drawn sufficiently far to the west to bring some of the canal colony lands within India.

V.P. Menon: Do you think we can draw a line that will somehow lessen the danger of disturbances in the Punjab? What do you think, Moon?

Moon: After all that has happened to them in March, the Sikhs are bent on attacking the Muslims. No shift in the line will now deflect them.

V.P. Menon: You hold out no hope. Excuse me now, I must go. [Rushes out without another word]

Christie: He is very disturbed.

Moon: For the past month I have been surrounded by Muslim officials who are bitter at the rich *banias* laden with their belongings, who Bahawalpur is allowing to leave. They say: '*our people are being driven out of India empty-handed*'. I tried placating them and said they were not as barbarous as the Sikhs, or as mean as the Hindus and were expected to behave more chivalrously.

Christie: Menon doesn't have much sympathy with the Muslims—his boss Patel is an out and out communalist.

Moon: When Mr Menon visited me in Bahawalnagar from where we were evacuating Hindus after some horrible incidents, I introduced him to the Hindus there in Hindustani till I realized he couldn't follow. Being a South Indian he knows no Punjabi and hardly any Hindustani. I was in the curious position of acting as an interpreter between an Indian and his fellow countrymen. You know, Christie, most of the tribulations of the Punjab mean no more to the people of central and southern India than did the horrors of the Spanish civil war to the rest of Europe. To take a long view, most civilized societies have been liable to occasional pogroms. What is happening in the Punjab is not an uncommon phenomenon—what is unusual is its spread over such a wide area and the very heavy death toll.

Christie: It is, therefore, a good thing that Lord Mountbatten is driving ahead at top speed with his plan for Partition before the country and the armed forces are engulfed in universal strife. Perhaps the Punjab alone will have to pay in blood the price of freedom.

SCENE 26

Viceroy's study, Delhi, its dark panels now painted a pale green. Mountbatten seated with Mieville and Ismay, Vernon Erskine-Crum on either side. Patel, Nehru, Kripalani, Baldev Singh, Liaquat Ali, Abdur Rab Nishtar all enter one by one and sit. Jinnah last to come. Photographers snap them and leave]

Mountbatten: During the last five years, I have taken part in a number of momentous meetings at which the fate of the war had been decided, but I can remember no meeting at which decisions had been taken which would have such a profound influence on world history as those which are to be taken at the present meeting. The way in which power is transferred will affect not only India, but the whole world.

My brief when I came to India in March gave no indication of the necessity for speed for the transfer of power. However, from the moment of my arrival a terrific sense of urgency was impressed upon me by everybody I spoke to. I came to realize that the sooner power was transferred the better it would be.

Mr Jinnah has staked a claim for complete Pakistan. The Congress held that the partition of India was fundamentally contrary to its principles. But Congress has now accepted the principle that no area which contains a majority of Muslims should be coerced into joining the existing Constituent Assembly. In doing so, they have made it clear that they could accept the principle of partition so long as it was applied also to the non-Muslim majority areas which had been included in the original Pakistan plan.

During my recent visit to London, I had meetings with everyone in the Government and the Opposition and am happy to state that they are all broadly in agreement with the policy HMG intends to adopt. The most distressing question, discussed at the greatest length in London, was the position of the Sikhs. I have repeatedly asked the Sikhs whether they desire the partition of the Punjab and they have repeatedly replied that they did. But it became apparent that there would be frightful difficulties to work notional partition on any other principle other than division between the majority Muslim and majority non-Muslim areas. It has, therefore, been agreed that the Boundary Commission, on which Sikh interests would, of course, be represented, would have to work out the best long-term solution.

The question of Calcutta was also discussed in the cabinet—as to whether a referendum should be held in Calcutta as, according to Mr Mandal, the vote of the Scheduled Castes might result in a decision in favour of Calcutta joining Eastern Bengal. But there were indications that the number of Scheduled Castes was not large enough to affect the issue. Many of the poorer Hindus in Calcutta come from Bihar, UP, etc., and a proportion of these are Scheduled Castes, but there is nothing to suggest that they would prefer Muslim to Hindu rule. During the disturbances in Calcutta, the Scheduled Castes have contributed their full share of the casualties on the Hindu side. In any case, it would be impossible to hold a referendum of the Scheduled Castes in Calcutta at short notice as there is no separate Scheduled Caste electoral roll.

Before leaving for London, I was asked by both parties to consider the transfer of contiguous areas in which there was a majority of the opposite community, from one side to the other—particularly Purnea and Sind. HMG's announcement will not mention this and it will have to be dealt with separately through the Boundary Commission.

It has always been impressed upon me by all of you present here that you want the partition and the transfer of power to take place with the utmost speed. Therefore, I have asked for legislation to be rushed through during the present parliamentary session, to give dominion status to the successor authorities that will emerge. Mr Churchill has given a written assurance to the Prime Minister that the opposition will facilitate the passage of this bill. It is hoped that it will create an all time world-wide legislative record. Power will, therefore, be remitted on a dominion status basis in the first instance. Thereafter, the new governments will be free to withdraw from the Commonwealth whenever they so wish. Of course, British assistance will not be withdrawn prematurely, I consider it the duty of the British to continue to help, not to rule, India. We will stay at your disposal for as long as you wish.

However, it is very difficult to persuade British officers to serve on at the present time, the principal reason for this is the increase in communal warfare and strife. We are examining how it will be possible to make available the greatest possible number of British officers for the armed forces that you would want to keep.

HMG's statement, which is to be released tomorrow, is the plan drafted by me in association with Mr Jinnah, Mr Liaquat Ali Khan, Pandit Nehru, Sardar Patel and Sardar Baldev Singh and I am gratified to feel that their support will continue.

[All five leaders signify assent. Copies of the statement are handed around]

Please take these copies of the statement to your Working Committees and let me know by midnight how things stand. I do not ask you to fully agree to the terms of the statement. I am, however, asking you all to accept this statement in a peaceful spirit and to make it work without bloodshed, which would be the consequence if you do not accept it.

Nehru: Lord Mountbatten, can you give us a further definition of the difference between agreement and acceptance.

Mountbatten: Agreement would imply belief that the right principles were being employed. I have had to violate the principles of both sides, so I cannot ask for complete agreement. I ask for acceptance, in order to denote belief that the plan is a fair and sincere solution for the good of the country.

Nehru: There can never be complete approval of the plan from Congress, but on the balance, we accept it.

Jinnah: It is perfectly true that neither side agrees with certain points in the plan. Its formal acceptance by the Muslim League will have to come later. The decision cannot be left to the leaders and the working committee alone. We have to bring the people round. Much explanation will be necessary.

Mountbatten: I am willing to take the risk of accepting the words of the leaders and the backing of their Working Committees. I have to ask for the preliminary agreement of the working committees to support the plan.

Jinnah: I can only speak for myself. I would like Your Excellency to consider, that in order to give a definite answer, it is necessary to make the people understand. The Muslim League is a democratic organization. I and my working committee will have to go before our masters, the people, for a final decision.

Mountbatten: There are times, Mr Jinnah when leaders have to make vital decisions without consulting their followers and trust to carrying them along at a later stage. In democratic countries, parliaments could always disagree with the decisions taken by prime ministers and cabinets.

Jinnah: If a ready-made decision is put before the Muslim League they would be upset. They would ask why they had been called if they had no opportunity to express their views before having been committed. In the meanwhile, I will make every effort to see that the people remain calm. I emphasize, that I will go to my masters, the people, with no intent of wrecking the plan but with the sincere desire to persuade them to accept it. The Viceroy wants me to do it and I will do my best.

Mountbatten: Mr Nehru, are you also confronted by the same problem as that stated by Mr Jinnah?

Nehru: Sardar Patel and I have been committing ourselves, step by step, to the present plan in consultation with our colleagues, including the Congress President. The working committee has also considered the broad outlines of the plan. The All-India Congress Committee, the larger body might feel hurt that they had not been consulted earlier. But owing to the peculiar nature of the case, we have had to ourselves make decisions and we have to take the responsibility on our own shoulders. The difficulty lies in the circumstances. I and my colleagues have been caught in the tempo of events. The urgency of the situation makes it difficult for us to be vague.

Kripalani: I agree with what Pandit Nehru has said. We have to take responsibility. A letter will be sent to Your Excellency this evening giving the Congress Working Committee's reaction to the statement.

Jinnah: I am afraid I will be unable to report the opinions of the Muslim League Working Committee in writing. I will, however, come and see Your Excellency tonight and make a verbal report.

Mountbatten: Very well, I shall be satisfied with that. I must thank you all for your loyalty and honesty. I much appreciate the support you are all giving me. And I understand your difficulties. Now, on a brighter note, I intend to make a broadcast over All-India Radio at 7 p.m. tomorrow evening. This will be recorded in London and relayed by a hook-up system all over the world. I would be most grateful if Pandit Nehru and Mr Jinnah will follow me by broadcasting immediately after the announcement. You might give your personal assurances of support for the plan and say that you would use your best endeavours to ensure a full and peaceful acceptance of it by your respective parties. Mr Jinnah—do you agree?

Jinnah: Yes, I can make such a broadcast, although it will be difficult for me.

Nehru: I agree, and I will be definite in my broadcast. May I suggest that Sardar Baldev Singh also make a broadcast?

Mountbatten: Certainly, that would be ideal.

Baldev Singh: No, no, I will not know what to say—I cannot make up my mind to support the plan until I know that the Congress and Muslim League are going to support it.

Mountbatten: Please make an appeal for peace and for all bloodshed to cease.

Baldev Singh: Yes, I can make that appeal.

Mountbatten: I am prepared to let you have the text of what I am going to say in my broadcast—perhaps you could also do the same? It will be advisable to rehearse it once.

Patel: [Smiling] I must point out, Your Excellency, that the general rule is for the scripts of broadcast speeches to be submitted to the Honourable Member for Information and Broadcasting before they are used.

Mountbatten: In this case, I think we should bring our scripts to the meeting tomorrow and read them out here.

[Nehru and Baldev Singh nod assent]

Jinnah: I will say in my broadcast what comes from my heart—without any script.

SCENE 27

Viceroy's study. Mountbatten pacing around, Ismay seated.

Ismay: When did Mr Jinnah say he would come? It's midnight, and I am no longer as young and energetic as you, Dickie.

Mountbatten: I don't trust him at all—I need you as a witness to whatever he has to say....

[Voices outside] ah! He's here. [Mountbatten quickly takes his chair]

Jinnah: [Walking in] I am extremely sorry Lord Mountbatten to keep you up so late, but it was unavoidable. [Sits down]

Mountbatten: Well?

Jinnah: I must reiterate the remarks I made in the morning. I really cannot do more than try my level best to persuade my Working Committee to support the plan. You see, the constitutional process has to be followed, and....

Mountbatten: I have to warn you, Mr Jinnah, that the Congress party are terribly suspicious of this tactic of yours—you wait till they have made a firm decision and then leave yourself the right to decide what suits the Muslim League several days later. I warn you that Nehru, Kripalani and Patel made an absolute point of rejecting the plan unless the Muslim League accepts it simultaneously.

Jinnah: But you see, Lord Mountbatten, the League's Council meeting cannot be called for several days. There has to be enough notice given, you know.

Mountbatten: Well, in that case the Congress and the Sikhs will pull out in tomorrow's, in fact this morning's meeting. Chaos will follow, and you will lose Pakistan for good.

Jinnah: [Shrugs, waits a moment] What must be, must be.

Mountbatten: Mr Jinnah, I do not intend to let you wreck all the work that has gone into this settlement. Since you will not accept for the Muslim League, I will speak for them myself. I will take the risk of saying that I am satisfied with the assurances you have given me. I have only one condition—you will under no circumstances contradict me and when I look towards you, you will nod your head.

[Jinnah nods]

SCENE 28

Viceroy's study. All the Leaders of the previous meeting are present.

Mountbatten: Well, that is final then. I have one last request to make of you—please ask your subordinate leaders to refrain from speeches of recrimination which are likely to produce violent reactions. Bury the past and the prospect of building a fine future will open up.

Liaquat Ali: Your Excellency, it may be possible to control the speeches of subordinate leaders—but there should be a request for restraint on the part of super leaders such as Mr Gandhi at his prayer meetings. It is true that he preaches non-violence but many of his speeches can be taken as an incitement to violence.

Mountbatten: I saw Mr Gandhi yesterday, and his emotions are those of a man who has lived, worked and prayed for the unity of India and I understand his feelings. But I made clear to him the immense effect the speeches at his prayer meetings have. It was his day of silence but he wrote a very friendly note to me at the meeting and I hope he will help the situation. Of course, he always makes it clear that he is not even a 4-*Anna* member of the Congress party.

Kripalani: I am surprised at Mr Liaquat Ali Khan's complaint. All that Gandhiji says is in advocacy of non-violence. And all members of Congress hold to the idea of a united India.

Mountbatten: But surely the emotion engendered, particularly in the more unintelligent people, is to think: this partition is wrong; we must resist it, we must not give in.

Patel: I am certain that once the decision is taken, Gandhiji will accept it loyally.

Liaquat Ali: But you see, Mr Gandhi recently used words to the effect that people should not look to the Viceroy and the leaders for a decision. They were told to do as they felt. That kind of statement is bound to encourage the people to go ahead on their own lines.

Patel: I disagree. No such inference can be drawn.

Jinnah: If Mr Gandhi goes on with his present line, the impression will be created that the people should not submit to what is being decided by the present conference. I myself do not think that his intentions are bad, but the language he has adopted recently has insinuated that the Muslim League is going to get Pakistan by force. I, of course, have refrained from criticizing him in public.

Mountbatten: Well, I think this subject has been ventilated sufficiently. [Dramatically lifts 34 page booklet above his head and bangs it down on table, startling leaders] This is a paper titled 'The Administrative Consequences of Partition', it is a masterpiece of compression. I would think it can be studied by you with great profit.

[Mountbatten gets up and thanks them and they leave. The rest of Mountbatten's staff troops in]

Mountbatten: I have to brief you on the developments of the last two meetings. Ismay and I saw Jinnah for an hour last night. Though he could give me nothing in writing, he promised to get the plan accepted. I must say his delight was unconcealed.

Congress and the Sikhs handed in their letters also during the night. The Congress did try a sleight of hand over the NWFP—they wanted the referendum there to decide not only between India and Pakistan but also whether it could remain independent. However, V.P. Menon spoke with Patel and I pointed out to Nehru that I had dropped the clause of independence at his own insistence.

Jinnah made a feint too—he wanted a referendum for independence in Bengal for he believes the untouchables would vote with the Muslims rather than the Hindus. Well, I talked him out of that. Finally, I gave them copies of John Christie's excellent paper on the administrative consequences of partition. They all looked like goldfish out of water. It was clear from their reactions that none of them had even begun to think of the complications with which we are all going to be faced. Perhaps this is lucky, since it will enable us to hold the initiative in Viceroy's House during the coming difficult period.

One of the points I raised with them was how undesirable it was that the magnificent Indian army would have to be divided. As you know, I did my best to keep it intact to serve both states but both Nehru and Jinnah were firm that the army must be divided. Jinnah insisted rather comically that he had to have his own army even if it consisted of one sergeant and one private.

I told them that they would have to answer Field Marshal Auchinleck on points such as whether the army was to be divided on a geographical or a communal basis, and whether a Muslim soldier living in Bombay would serve in the Hindustan or Pakistan Army, and if the latter, whether he would have to transfer his domicile. Ismay, can you tell us now of your discussions with Auchinleck.

Ismay: [Wears glasses, clearing throat] Well, Claude Auchinleck is being very obdurate. He says to split an instrument like the Indian army would be to ruin it—it would mean a drastic breakdown of morale and that he has no intention of doing it. He seems also to be convinced that Indian independence will be followed by a massacre of the British in India. I have a letter from him here: [reads] '*As the Viceroy's advisor on all military matters I suggest that the British forces should be retained in India until at least 1948, longer if necessary. I realize that the Viceroy has every right to disregard my advice for over-riding political considerations. That is solely his responsibility and it is not my business to comment on his decision. Moreover, I cannot state with any certainty that during the period of reconstituting the army it will retain cohesion or remain reliable for use in the event of widespread disturbances*'. [Takes off glasses] I explained to Claude that both countries were insistent that they should have their own national armies by independence and did not care what chaos or confusion was caused in the process. For them the Indian army does not have the same mystique as it does for British officers. The Indian leaders have always looked with distaste upon it as a mercenary organization which was all too often used against the Indians. The politicians will certainly not be sorry to see it disbanded and truly national armies—Muslim and Hindu—born in its place.

Mountbatten: You better get him to come and see me. I want no bloody nonsense from Claude. When I put forward the idea of retaining British forces once, Liaquat Ali Khan was favourably inclined. But Nehru remarked he would sooner have every village in India put to the flames than keep the British army beyond independence.

Mieville: I have to report a conversation V.P. Menon had with me recently. He maintains that British forces will be no help at all in any real conflict between Hindus, Muslims and Sikhs as most soldiers are already busy swapping with each other and scrabbling for jobs to bother about communal riots.

Mountbatten: [Looks at watch] It's almost time for my meeting with the States Negotiating Committee. The Princely States are going to be a headache.

Ismay: It's going to be tricky. I suppose they will react just like many old Muslim friends of mine. One of them—a senior officer and a close friend for a quarter of a century—cut me to the quick by saying *'We soldiers have trusted you for forty years, and now you are going to betray us'*.

Mountbatten: The Princes of India are in a pathetic situation. They belong to a remote past. And most of them have no idea of how to conduct themselves towards the people who are going to be India's new rulers. At my first official reception, one of them was described as 'wandering around like a letter without a stamp'.

Ismay: We cannot acquit ourselves of all blame. We ought long ago to have used our Paramount Power to reform the system of government in the more backward or reactionary states.

Mountbatten: Very true. I have a special duty towards them as they are all in treaty relations with His Majesty. Fortunately, I know a number of them well—some of them have been friends since 1921. Ten of them were ADCs with me to the Prince of Wales. They really lived in great style—many of them were immensely rich; they had their own armies, and one of them even had his own air force.

SCENE 29

Princes Council Chamber, Viceroy's House, New Delhi. Photographic circus with much posing and laughter, the Princes in flashing jewels and costumes, perspiring and mopping faces in the heat [108.4 F]. Mountbatten in full vice regal uniform, all decorations, medals in place, not showing any discomfort while Princes take turns to stand under the fans.

Photographers leave with all those royals who are not part of the Committee below.

Viceroy's meeting with States Negotiating Committee begins.

Mountbatten, Ismay, Mieville, Vernon and Corfield face galaxy of States representatives: Nawab of Bhopal, Maharaja of Patiala, Maharaja of Dungarpur, Jam Sahib of Nawanagar, Raja of Bilaspur, Sir Mirza Ismail, Prime Minister of Hyderabad, Sir Mitter, Baroda, Sir Mudaliar, Mysore, Rai Bahadur Kak, Prime Minister of J&K, Diwan of Gwalior, Sir C.P. Ramaswami Diwan of Travancore, Sir Krishnamachari, Jaipur, Sardar Panikkar, Bikaner, Sir Sultan Ahmed and Sardar D.K. Sen, Chamber of Princes, Mir Maqbool Mahmood, Secretary-States Negotiating Committee.

Mountbatten: As you are aware, I have been holding negotiations with the political leaders of British India and the outcome of these negotiations cannot but have a certain effect on the position of the states. The plan that has now been devised has been broadly accepted by the Indian leaders and I am going to make a broadcast this evening, followed by Mr Nehru, Mr Jinnah, and Sardar Baldev Singh.

Both the Congress and the Muslim League expressed their desire for the transfer of power to take place as soon as possible. The only way that power could be handed over in the immediate future was on the basis of the 1935 Act with Dominion Status. This solved many problems. For example, the British would be enabled to remain as the servants of India for so long as they were wanted. I have today put forward the proposal that power should be remitted on 15th August. This is, of course, a secret and the date should not be repeated outside this room.

The main consequences of the new plan on the states would be two-fold. First, it is improbable that the two new dominions would have such loose centres as exist at present.

Secondly, the fact that two separate dominions are voluntarily entering the Commonwealth will, I hope, represent a measure of compensation to the states who are the old allies and friends of Britain.

Sir C.P. Ramaswami: I wish to appeal to Your Excellency that Paramountcy should be loosened or allowed to lapse before the date of the transfer of power. This will enable the states to negotiate on equal terms with the two prospective dominions. I feel that there may be states which are not likely to join up with either dominion. It is even more essential for their bargaining powers to be improved.

Mountbatten: In my opinion, even at the present time, negotiations by the states are possible on a basis of complete freedom. In any case, my instructions are that Paramountcy should lapse on the transfer of power.

Sir Mitter: Your Excellency, what will happen to economic and commercial agreements when Paramountcy lapses?

Mountbatten: Interim arrangements will be required for the period between the lapse of Paramountcy and the conclusion of fresh agreements. These arrangements can best be made on a stand-still basis, and in negotiating them, I and the political department will give all the assistance we can during the remaining period. Sir Conrad Corfield will explain this now.

Corfield: I can give some examples of how arrangements on a stand-still basis can be made. When Paramountcy lapses the states will be free, for example, to imprison the Postmaster of an Imperial Post Office. If you do so, however, you will run the risk of cutting yourselves off from all-India communications, so you will presumably agree to treat Post Offices with consideration to ensure their continued functioning. Another example is railways and cantonments in Indian States, where the Crown representative has at present the powers of jurisdiction. These powers will revert to the States on the lapse of Paramountcy. Arrangements will be made whereby this will not affect the working of the railway and the accommodation of the Indian army till the conclusion of fresh agreements.

Nawab (Bhopal): Apart from agreements, there are also certain claims which will have to be settled in advance of the lapse of Paramountcy.

Corfield: I am not clear what claims your highness is referring to. Claims arising out of the end of British Paramountcy will be a matter of negotiation with the new governments.

Sir C.P. Ramaswami: There are a certain number of agreements into which the states have entered which are not with the Crown representative.

Corfield: Efforts were made to establish a committee for such purposes but the interim government did not agree to this. Existing contractual agreements will be a matter for discussion with the new governments.

Raja (Bilaspur): Is the entry of states into either dominion a matter of free choice?

Mountbatten: Most certainly, yes.

Raja (Bilaspur): What is likely to happen to states which decide to not join either Dominion? Does His Majesty's Government envisage further relations with such states?

Mountbatten: That is a hypothetical question. At the present stage, your first step should be to enter into practical negotiations with one or other or perhaps both of the successor dominion governments. Whereas I do not wish to give any official advice, I will be willing to give personal advice to anybody who comes and asks me for it. At this moment I have one suggestion to make: in coming to your decisions, please cast your minds forward ten years and consider what the situation in the country and in the world as a whole is likely to be at that time. Thank you, Gentlemen.

SCENE 30

Ismay is in his drawing room. Jinnah is ushered in by the bearer who then brings in and serves the drinks.

Ismay: I'm really glad that you could come—I'm very disturbed about the relationship between you and Lord Mountbatten. I want to have a most serious and frank talk with you, if I may.

Jinnah: Of course, we have always welcomed each other's frankness, have we not?

Ismay: You must give me a patient hearing and then you may tell me what you think has gone wrong. First of all, your announcement that you intend to assume the appointment of Governor-General yourself came at the eleventh hour and this put the viceroy in an extremely awkward position. I may tell you it has lost you a lot of ground in England amongst all shades of political opinion.

Secondly, the Viceroy had particularly asked you to restrain your press but your paper has been chortling over the fact that Congress is going to have a European Governor-General, while Pakistan is to have one of its own nationals.

Then there is the question of the flag. You had given a provisional agreement to a Pakistan flag with the Union Jack in the corner, but subsequently said that you could not accept it.

Finally, you are now refusing to fly the customary flag for a dominion Governor-General on your official residence and not willing to allow the Pakistan navy to fly the White Ensign. Lord Mountbatten is a naval man and the last refusal is the unkindest cut of all. He feels the rebuff so deeply that he is thinking of sending the Prime Minister a telegram saying that it seems hopeless to try to cooperate with you.

Jinnah: I am being completely misunderstood. From the start I dissented with the idea of a joint Governor-General. I was sure, I'm still certain, that it would never work

Ismay: Our grievance is not about your decision, but the fact that you waited until the eleventh hour to announce it. I may remind you that Sir Eric Mieville and I had asked Mr Liaquat Ali Khan in the very early days of June to persuade you to nominate the Governor-General of Pakistan as soon as possible. If you had only said frankly that you proposed to be Governor-General yourself, a great deal of misunderstanding and trouble would have been saved.

Jinnah: I must reiterate that I never gave the Viceroy the slightest grounds for believing that I would agree to a common Governor-General. As for the Muslim press, they did no chortling until the Congress attacked me for having first agreed to a common Governor-General and then breaking my word. This was an intolerable and untrue accusation and had to be countered.

Ismay: What happened to the Viceroy's original design for the flag?

Jinnah: I admit that when I first saw it I did not see any objection to it but my colleagues pointed out that it would be impossible to have the cross and crescent on the same flag. All the old hatreds and rivalries would be revived.

Ismay: But you even object to flying the dominion flag over your residence.

Jinnah: I think it is a mistake for the king to continue signing himself 'George R.I.' after the 15th August. He will no longer be Emperor of India and it will be resented.

Ismay: What does that have to do with the dominion flag, you will be part of the Commonwealth and all dominions fly it.

Jinnah: Surely, I am entitled to fly any flag I like over my own personal residence?

Ismay: Your residence will, in a sense, not be a personal one. It would be the residence of the King's representative and it seems only right that the King's emblem should be flown.

Jinnah: But look at the position of Ireland—India and Pakistan will have the same constitution as Ireland has. Unlike the other dominions we will be able to secede from the Commonwealth without an act of British Parliament. I am therefore in favour of the Irish model.

Ismay: I am not aware that if Canada or Australia desired secession it would require an act of [British] Parliament. In any case, I am not concerned with constitutions but with the practical applications. Do you really wish the relations between Pakistan and the UK to be the same as those which now obtain between Eire and the UK? We do not help them with officers, or supply them with the latest equipment. Nor do we admit them to our staff colleges. In fact, they enjoy none of the benefits of a dominion. You, on the hand, appear anxious to have a very large number of British officers and officials to help you. You have insisted that Pakistan wanted to be at once and always a member of the British Commonwealth.

Jinnah: [Resigned manner] You know, Lord Ismay, I have acquired the reputation of having complete authority over my people merely because I always study their views and wishes and faithfully express them.

Ismay: That was precisely what Mr Churchill had claimed to do for the British people in 1940.

Jinnah: [Smiles, nods] Although I personally would not object to flying the dominion flag, I have a feeling that my people would resent it. It would be a thousand pities if it is flown and then removed as the result of agitation.

Ismay: I do not agree. If you start off by flying your own flag, British public opinion will attribute this lack of customary and friendly courtesy to you. But if the dominion flag had to be given up owing to pressure from your parliament, public opinion in England will not take it so badly.

Jinnah: Well, I will have another talk with my colleagues on this and let you know the result. You mentioned something about the navy—there must be some misunderstanding. The Pakistan navy will certainly fly the White Ensign—it is an emblem of comradeship between all the navies of the dominions. I will ensure that it is flown.

Ismay: Thank God—it really upset the Viceroy.

Jinnah: [Rising] I must leave….

[Ismay walks him to door where Jinnah stops and puts his hand on Ismay's shoulder and speaks]: I beg you to assure the Viceroy that I am his friend and yours for now and always. I beg that he should judge me by my deeds and not by words.

SCENE 31

Evening in private sitting, Viceroy's House. Mountbatten with Edwina, a bearer serves drinks and leaves. Mozart plays softly.

Mountbatten: I've finally landed myself in a position from which I must extricate myself with honour.

Edwina: Jinnah's done something? He came to see you in the morning.

Mountbatten: Yes. He had been promising to send me a letter on who he wanted as the first Governor-General of Pakistan. The moment he entered, he dropped his bomb, '*Your Excellency I have to ask you to recommend to London that I be appointed as the Governor-General of independent Pakistan*'.

Edwina: The Congress has informally asked you to be the GG of India, has it not?

Mountbatten: I'm sure he knows that—and he wants to be contrary. I must say I was upset. I pointed out that his powers as a Prime Minister would be far greater than as a GG—which is merely a titular head. He gave me an arrogant smile and said, 'in my position it is I who will give advice and others will act on it'.

Edwina: Doesn't he realize that only with a common GG, will Pakistan stand any chance of securing its fair share of the national assets?

Mountbatten: Precisely. I asked him if he realized what it might cost him. He just shrugged and said it may cost him several crores of rupees in assets, to his great regret. He looked triumphant rather than regretful as he said that. I'm afraid I rather lost my temper and told him it might just cost him the future of Pakistan, and left Ronnie to show him out.

Edwina: That's no good. You can't allow him to get under your skin.

Mountbatten: What do you think I should do? If I stay with India I'll be forever accused of taking sides. If I go home I let down the Congress leaders.

Edwina: It's very straightforward, Dickie. We must leave on the transfer of power. That is the only way you can preserve your reputation for impartiality.

Mountbatten: I'm just whacked and worn out and would really like to go. But Krishna tells me I cannot let Nehru down. To refuse to stay because Pakistan doesn't want me would be to cause unmerited offence. In both cases I'm in the wrong. [Pause] I'm so depressed because until this stupid mishandling of the Jinnah situation I'd done so well. It has certainly taken me down many pegs.

Edwina: No one is indispensable, you always say. You can explain this to Nehru. He will surely understand you're exhausted. You've been looking rather worn out.

Mountbatten: I feel haggard. And the job is getting more and more difficult. Dear old V.P. Menon told me a few days ago that all the leaders have gone neurotic and Nehru is heading for a breakdown. He said that the only man who can hold India now is me, and if I break down too, all will be lost. Everyone on both sides hangs on to me. I get so harassed by the scenes and squabbles about partition—it's only by a show of optimism that I keep them all together. The one saving grace is the monstrous burden of the Punjab and Bengal partitions will be off my back—I direct everyone to Radcliffe from 8th July.

Edwina: I forgot to ask—Alan said you declared the 15th August as D-Day?

Mountbatten: [Perks up] The date came to me as if by inspiration—it is the anniversary of my appointment as Supreme Naval commander. You remember?

Edwina: [Stands beside his chair with hand on his shoulder] Of course I do. There is another anniversary coming up, our silver-wedding on the 17th. We'll throw a party and invite both Nehru and Jinnah and ease the tension. Cheer up Dickie.

Mountbatten: I can just see them doing a jig together. [Smiles up at her]

SCENE 32

Staff meeting: Viceroy's study.

Mountbatten: First, I am going to read out a note I have written on the Princes. [Reads from a paper] '*Shortly before I came to India the King summoned me and expressed great worry about the position of the princes. He urged me as his cousin to persuade the princes to come to some arrangement with the new regime. Whether to join up or a federation was not clear. So my interpretation of the mission is to get them somehow into one dominion or another. Frankly, I have no patience or time for semi-enlightened autocrats at best and squalid degenerates at worst.*

They are really a bunch of nitwits—they could have democratized their administrations when they saw Congress power rising. They did not even join the Indian federation when they had the chance in 1935. Bhopal particularly, has been trying to organize a bold front against Congress power but his forces are in disarray and deteriorating rapidly. As Chancellor of the Chamber of Princes, Bhopal was given a look at the Independence bill even before Congress and Muslim leaders saw it. His first question was: Would HMG grant dominion status to individual Princely States in the same way as to India and Pakistan? When I said that was impossible he began complaining bitterly that the British were once more letting the princes down and he as a Muslim prince of a Hindu state would be put at the mercy of Congress. Three days later he resigned as chancellor and announced that he would consider himself free and independent the moment the British departed. He abhors Congress and will have nothing to do with Congress dominated India. He doesn't realize that the partition means that a scurry for shelter has already begun. The maharaja of Bikaner has already gathered considerable number of princes in a group willing to join the Indian federation before independence. They will automatically become part of India after TOP. They hope to safeguard their rights and privileges by this move. Of course, I doubt Congress will allow them to get away with much'.

[Puts paper down] And now for your comments and suggestions.

Mieville: Perhaps we can persuade them to join by pointing out that if they don't they will be outside the Commonwealth and become ineligible for future decorations from the King. The King already has decided to sweeten them by extending the style of 'His Highness' to all of them with a 9 gun salute to them, their wives and widows.

Abell: I don't think we should mention this concession to them as yet—not in the presence of all of them. It would make minor princes more amenable but it won't please the more important princes who already have this privilege. For example, the Nizam looks slightly mollified by the grant of the title of 'His Highness' to his second son— but this will be nullified if Faridkot was to get it too.

Mieville: Sir Conrad Corfield has been trying to get them to liberalize their administrations but he's also pushing them to form a solid block to resist politicians. He's a convinced royalist himself and thinks that the Viceroy, as a member of the royal family, will back him to keep the Princes out of the Congress' clutches.

Abell: Actually he's dismayed that you [to Mountbatten] pulled him up—he says you are extremely unsympathetic and not worried about the future of the princes.

Mountbatten: They have vast incomes, all the customs and taxes and mineral wealth they control. They've enjoyed almost godlike privileges and how many have shown themselves worthy of that? A few wisely employed professional premiers but the bulk of them are profligate—dancing girls and wild living. And Corfield hasn't done much to prevent political persecution in their states. It was his duty to see that they reformed. He's spending all his time to prop up the Nizam by waving the Instrument of Paramountcy. He told me that the treaty with the British Crown does not include any sort of allegiance to British India. In other words, even the smallest of the princes can become independent states. Nehru and his colleagues will never allow that.

Ismay: Corfield has been corresponding with Lord Listowell who, for a Labour minister, has shown surprising sympathy for his views. Both of them have the attitude that they need not make things easier for India.

Mountbatten: [To Ismay] When you and Abell went with the draft plan to London, Corfield also went and got Listowell and the SOS to support the Paramountcy clause. I had to face Nehru's screams about Balkanization. When I went with the final plan that s.o.b. Corfield sneaked back to India without telling me and got to work. He cancelled British troops stationed in the states, and all the arrangements with railways, P&T, customs etc. He also ordered removal of confidential reports and letters between his department and the princes and got them burnt. In all four tons of papers concerning the Princes were destroyed.

[Pushes chair back violently and leaves the room]

Ismay: He is terribly upset.

Campbell-Johnson: He has taken a calculated risk and is personally undertaking to get all the Princes into the bag of the Instrument of Accession. V.P. Menon has sold the whole thing to the Congress—of course, he has Patel's support.

Mieville: Lord Mountbatten's assessment is probably correct—I heard the Diwan of Travancore attacking Nehru as 'unstable' and Patel as 'ruthless' but he told him not to be a fool. Travancore is the strongest breeding ground of Communists and if suddenly they revolt after 15th August, India would not come to his help.

Abell: Patel himself can call on and off an agitation whenever he pleases.

Mountbatten: [Returns] I am glad to say that Nehru has not been put in charge of the States Department which would have wrecked everything. I have just learnt that Patel is going to take over. He is essentially a realist and very sensible and completely influenced by V.P. Menon. It is V.P. Menon who has been invaluable in getting Congressmen to give fair play to the princes—which they little realize.

[V.P. Menon is announced]

Mountbatten: Talk of the devil—[as V.P. Menon walks in] I was just saying how you are invaluable in getting the princes a fair deal.

V.P. Menon: Nothing can succeed without you, Lord Mountbatten. We desperately need your help in getting the states to accede to India. It needs great statesmanship to bring it about and nobody but you can perform this role. Lord Mountbatten, the wounds of partition might to some extent be healed by the states entering the Indian dominion. You will secure the gratitude of generations of Indians if you can assist in achieving the basic unity of the country.

SCENE 33

Patel's house: Patel is gently swaying in a Gujarati swing and V.P. Menon is in an armchair.

V.P. Menon: Corfield is destroying all evidence against the Princes which might give Congress a stick to beat them with or establish authority over them. The Travancore Maharaja has got so encouraged he's declaring he will become an independent sovereign on 15th August and is appointing a trade agent with Pakistan. So has Hyderabad. Many a prince whose private armies have built up to great strength during the war is flexing his muscles and waiting for the British nanny to sail away.

Patel: The Nizam has a very large and well run army and Corfield has made repeated requests to Sardar Baldev Singh to remove the Indian army division from Hyderabad. He has been saying that if it stays it will be an army of occupation.

V.P. Menon: I've been told that the army commander Auchinleck has privately assured the Nizam that as long as he is directing the army there is no need for the Nizam to worry.

Patel: I am to head the new states ministry, V.P. Menon and I want you to be the secretary of the department. You have to immediately suggest what we can do with the princes.

V.P. Menon: There are less than eight weeks to go before independence. Why not approach each prince individually and negotiate on a simple formula. Ask them simply to accede to the Indian union under three subjects only—Defence, External affairs and Communication.

Patel: But what if they refuse?

V.P. Menon: How can they refuse? Until now the British protected them from unrest. But if now people rise up and begin to demand their freedom and the right to join India—that is, if popular agitation threatens their rule and even the safety of their lives, where can they look for protection except to us?

Patel: Yes… I see what you mean. The Congress underground movements in Princely States must become active. But you think we should not show our anger openly against the British for the unfriendly action of cancelling Paramountcy? I can't stomach this insult.

V.P. Menon: The cancellation of all British treaties with the princes is a blessing in disguise, Sardar. They had given them all sorts of privileges. If they had passed on Paramountcy to us we would have had to go on treating the princes as demigods in their own states. But not now: Paramountcy lapses. So do the privileges. We start with a clean slate. It is our turn now to say how the princes will behave. I think the smoothest channel through which we can achieve our goal will be the viceroy. His relationship to the British Royal family is bound to influence the rulers. I propose that the active cooperation of Mountbatten should be secured.

Patel: And can we achieve that?

V.P. Menon: I undertake to put forward my proposal to him. With your blessings Sardar I will succeed.

SCENE 34

Viceroy's study: Mountbatten, Ismay, Mieville, Nehru, Patel and Kripalani are present. A tear-off calendar showing in bold letters the caption ***'66 days for transfer of power'*** *is on the wall behind the Viceroy's chair. The number of days go on reducing at each scene in the study.*

Mountbatten: The Diwan of Bahawalpur has raised the question of the legal validity, after the transfer of power, of contractual agreements with the states. Mr Jinnah has expressed the view that it would be legally binding upon the successor authorities to continue these contractual agreements.

Patel: One of the first agreements which will have to put on a standstill basis is that of supply of arms by the Defence department—the states should not be allowed to bring in arms from abroad.

Nehru: I entirely disagree with the idea of complete independence for the states. They never had an independent existence before. I advise you to read Edward Thompson's *History of the Indian States*. Hyderabad, for example, has grown up through treachery and had always been in the wake of the victors to gather the spoils.

Mountbatten: From conversations with representatives of the states I have got the impression that the reason why some of them have not yet joined the Constituent Assembly is that they fear a much tighter centre under the new plan.

Patel: So far as the states are concerned, the centre will only be strengthened with their consent. And as for your opinion that the states are moving towards more representative government, I think you are greatly mistaken.

Mountbatten: Well, we disagree on this—I have spoken with them on this score and have been assured by them.

Nehru: [Flaring up] I challenge from the highest Constitutional basis, the idea that any ruler can decide himself whether or not to join the Constituent Assembly. I will encourage rebellion in all states that go against us.

Kripalani: [Quietly] The people must have some say in the matter.

Mountbatten: I myself have no doubt what will happen in the end. Some rulers I have spoken to are already seeing sense and some are fast beginning to. Next, I suggest we discuss the boundary commissions for Bengal and Punjab. There is a suggestion that we have one Muslim representative from western Punjab; one Hindu representative from eastern Punjab; one Sikh representative, one from Pakistan as a whole and one from Hindustan as a whole. The same composition for Bengal, save a Bengali instead of a Sikh. You could send me the Congress suggestions. The difficulties regarding the Sikhs are great—they represent only 13 per cent of the population....

Patel: I think the correct figure is 18 per cent.

Mountbatten: In any case, an enormous transfer of population would be required to build up even one district into a Sikh majority area. I think Mr Jinnah will agree to the basis of transfer of population....

Nehru: I am opposed to the principle of population transfers—it is impossible to transfer holy places. The canal regions are another important consideration. The Sikhs built up this area largely by their own labour. I discussed this with the Punjab Governor and we agreed it would be essential to have a joint irrigation board.

Mountbatten: I agree—both sides would gain from that. As for religious places, Mr Jinnah has promised he would guarantee freedom of access to them.

Patel: I very much doubt such an undertaking by him.

Mountbatten: Incidentally, I hear Mr Jinnah has sold his house in Bombay?

Nehru: Yes, to Mr Dalmia for 21 lakh.

[All of them move to door, Nehru and Kripalani exit. Patel turns to Mountbatten]

Patel: Don't worry too much about the Princes, Lord Mountbatten. The Princes are ours and we shall deal with them. The problem is unimportant; after transfer of power, the people will rise, overthrow their rulers and rally to independent India. [Bows out]

SCENE 35

Viceroy's study: Mountbatten, Mieville and Jinnah seated.

Mountbatten: Mr Jinnah, I am not raising the matter on personal grounds, but you must give me your decision as to whom you would wish as the first Governor-General of Pakistan. I have already stressed the advantages of having a common Governor-General during the period of partition—mind you, I am not seeking the appointment myself—it is an entirely free choice of the two dominions. All I want is an early decision because it affects a clause in the bill that is to be laid before parliament.

Jinnah: I hope that I will be allowed to see the bill and comment upon it?

Mountbatten: I had a great tussle with HMG about it and fought hard so I am glad to say that you will be able to see the bill, though I cannot allow you to take a copy. About the Governor-General....

Jinnah: Yes, I am thinking about that, let me put it like this. Whatever decision I reach, it will not be on the grounds of not wanting you as the Governor-General. I have implicit trust and confidence in Your Excellency. But the rule of my life is that I must always consider the interests of my people. At various times of my career, I have had to pass over those nearest and dearest to me. I will be ready to convey my decision to you in about a day or two.

Mountbatten: Perhaps you could also let me have the names of your nominees for both Boundary Commissions at the same time?

Jinnah: Certainly, I shall do so. But, I feel that it would be impossible for the Congress and my party to agree upon the chairmen for the Commissions. I suggest an independent chairman for both commissions should come from England. He should, in fact, act as an umpire.

Mountbatten: I can tell you in confidence that the man who has been suggested as chairman is Sir Cyril Radcliffe.

Jinnah: I will also let you know in a day or two whether I consider him to be a suitable chairman. Of course, I have heard of him and of his high reputation at the bar. There is one matter that I cannot emphasize enough, Lord Mountbatten—I must have a Pakistan army ready by 15th August. There must be an operational commander-in-chief in Pakistan by that date who would take his orders from the Pakistan Government.

Mountbatten: That can be done, but for administrative matters both armies should continue to be under Field Marshal Auchinleck.

Jinnah: But the Muslims no longer have faith in the Field Marshal. They would much prefer to see someone else in his place.

Mountbatten: I must disagree absolutely—there is no more reliable or respected officer in India than Field Marshal Auchinleck!

Jinnah: Please think it over—and now I must take my leave.

[Jinnah leaves]

Mountbatten: Phew. A very hard nut to crack!

Mieville: I suspect he doesn't trust you either. And he is also going to do a check on poor Cyril Radcliffe who has never been to India and has no connection with any Congress person.

Ronnie: [Looking in] Giani Kartar Singh and Sardar Baldev Singh, Your Excellency. [Ushers them in]

Mountbatten: Giani Kartar Singh, I received your letter. I am very interested in your welfare—but you see after the 15th of August I will have no special powers at all, and even if I am the Governor-General, it would be a purely constitutional position. Of course, I promise to use whatever influence I have with the major parties on putting forward your point of view.

Baldev: Your Excellency, we are certain that neither of the major parties will give us any safeguards or weightage.

Kartar: Sir, the time for action is now, while you still have your powers.

Mountbatten: I have already talked to both sides about the minorities and both have given assurances. I think the presence of so many members of the world press in India will provide you with an important safeguard if you use it properly.

Kartar: We have two main points: first we should have weightage in the legislature of the East Punjab, or the Hindi-speaking parts should be separated off and there should be a province only of Punjabi-speaking areas. Patel told us that he prefers the separation of the province. Second thing we want is more representation in the Constituent Assembly immediately. We have only two representatives and they cannot be in every committee. Then there are three points I did not mention in my letter: 1) the boundary should be drawn more favourably to us 2) the transfer of population should be arranged 3) Your Excellency's broadcast should give the Boundary Commission as part of the plan of 3rd June.

Mountbatten: But the Boundary Commission will have to deal with a large number of documents—the Muslim League will put in opposing ones. I cannot include it in my broadcast—but I'm sure you will have greater bargaining power than you imagine because of your military importance in the new union of India.

SCENE 36

Mountbatten's study, Delhi. [5th July] Mountbatten and Jinnah are speaking in very formal tones.

Mountbatten: I have received a letter from Dr Ingram asking if you will be prepared to denounce the Poona pact as far as Pakistan is concerned.

Jinnah: Certainly, the Poona pact will not operate in Pakistan. I intend to see that the Scheduled Castes in Pakistan receive really fair treatment. Of course, I cannot give you any details about their position till the Pakistan Constituent Assembly discusses it.

Mountbatten: Mr Jinnah, it is customary for the king to bestow the GCMG on Governor-Generals when they are appointed—would you like me to submit your name for the honour as you will be appointed GG of Pakistan by the King?

Jinnah: Thank you for the offer—I will consider it and let you know.

Mountbatten: Do you still wish me to be the Chairman of the Joint Defence Committee if I remain as the Governor-General of India?

Jinnah: Of course, I would wish you to continue as chairman.

Mountbatten: Perhaps you could let me have a letter to that effect soon. Have you seen the design I sent you for the new flag of your country? [Jinnah shakes head, murmurs 'no'] The Union Jack in the upper canton is only one-ninth of the whole instead of one quarter as is the case in the other dominions—you must have seen that in the Australian flag. The Congress is likely to agree to a similar flag.

Jinnah: I will look at it and let you know my opinion soon.

Mountbatten: And would you like me to come down on the 14th of August for a farewell ceremony at Karachi, since the Pakistan areas will pass out of my control on the 15th?

Jinnah: It would give me the greatest pleasure to welcome you there.

Mountbatten: Good! We can discuss the details later. The last thing I have to ask you about is the names of suitable candidates to be Heads of the Defence services in Pakistan. Have you given any thought to it?

Jinnah: I would like very much that all three heads should be British, and in fact, I was going to request you to let me have the particulars of the candidates. And possibly, you can also give me the opportunity of meeting them?

Mountbatten: Very well, I will be happy to send you the names of the alternative candidates.

Jinnah: I have a telegram here for your Prime Minister and the leader of the opposition—would you kindly have it sent on? It contains a protest on there being no adequate machinery to ensure that the assets are fairly divided and their transfer correctly implemented. I have also protested against the exclusion of the Andamans from the bill.

Mountbatten: [takes the paper] I have been informed that recently you sent a letter to the Maharaja of Kashmir urging him to join Pakistan and promised him every sort of favourable treatment—including the freedom to carry on his autocratic government. Am I misinformed?

Jinnah: I have never written any letter to the Kashmir Maharaja—it is an absolute fabrication. I have no intention of doing so either. I would, though, like to discuss matters with Mr Kak—the Prime Minister of Kashmir—if I could.

Mountbatten: I can ask the political department to put you in touch with him when he is here—he's due on the 25th July.

[Jinnah leaves after a cordial handshake]

Ismay: [Enters the room] I saw him leave. Any new demands?

Mountbatten: He wants to meet Kak, the Kashmir Prime Minister.

Ismay: Patel wants him removed because he is said to be pro-independence for the Kashmiris.

SCENE 37

Viceroy's study: 12th July. Mountbatten seated. Jinnah is shown in. Mountbatten stands silent till he sits, then sits himself without a word

Jinnah: Lord Mountbatten, I believe Congress is exerting intense pressure on the Nizam of Hyderabad. I must in all fairness tell you that every Muslim throughout the whole of India, yes, all the hundred million Muslims, would rise as one man to defend the oldest Muslim dynasty in India.

Mountbatten: Mr Jinnah, if the Nizam will not play at all with Congress, all they have to do is not to play with him; that can only end in the quiet disruption of the dynasty from within, without any opportunity being given to the hundred million Muslims to rise.

Jinnah: [After long pause] Excellency, it is a matter of great personal regret for me but I have been unable to find a single supporter for the idea of a Union Jack on the Pakistan flag.

Mountbatten: Flags are an important outward and visible symbol of close relations within the Commonwealth, Mr Jinnah—a small Union Jack on your flag would bind you closer to the other British Dominions.

Jinnah: I personally regret it very much, but it is repugnant to the religious feelings of the Muslims to have a flag with a Christian cross alongside the Crescent. About the GCMG as well, I'm afraid to report that my party is strongly opposed to my accepting this honour. You see, the Muslim League has only recently passed a resolution rejecting all British honours and my people feel I will be in an impossible position if I now accept a British honour.

Mountbatten: I hope you will at least adopt the custom of hoisting the Union Jack alongside the dominion flag on all special occasions such as the birthdays of the royal family and the dominion days of the other dominions?

Jinnah: Certainly—if you will give a list of the days on which the Union Jack should be hoisted throughout Pakistan, I will see that it is done.

Mountbatten: I am rather unhappy about your ungracious action in opposing the suggestion I made on the King's signature—it had been privately agreed to by the Congress leaders. The King would only continue to sign 'George R.I.' after he dropped the title 'Emperor of India'.

Jinnah: I am the last person to dictate to His Majesty how he should sign his name. If the king continues to sign his name with a 'Rex India' no one in Pakistan would object. But I could not agree *to inviting* the King to continue with a legally incorrect signature. I hope you will not press me on this.

Mountbatten: Right—we shall say no more about it. I would like to make a suggestion to you about the Sikhs—I urge you to try for a settlement of the boundary difficulties out of court—do not let them fester in the commission.

Jinnah: I am not very hopeful of getting an agreement from them—but I am willing to meet Giani Kartar Singh as I promised. I would be grateful if you could facilitate such a meeting. I have some excellent news to give you about the NWFP. Dr Khan Sahib has been saying to the press that anything over 31 per cent would be regarded as a Muslim League victory. I now believe that we may be getting as much as 75 per cent. Would you be prepared to put a Muslim League ministry in power in that event?

Mountbatten: Constitutionally, I can do that only on the advice of the Executive Council for Pakistan—it is very fortunate for you that I am forming the Council in six days time, otherwise you might have had Dr Khan's ministry in power until the 15th August. I am also reconstituting the government on the 19th—here is a copy of the Order.

Jinnah: Thank you, I will have to give it due consideration and….

Mountbatten: It will not be necessary for you to spend any time considering it—it is an Order from the Governor-General, that is, myself, which is legal and binding under clause 9 of the Bill passed by the British parliament.

Jinnah: [Seeing Mountbatten is upset] Lord Mountbatten, please believe me that I intend to be a loyal and permanent member of the Commonwealth. I am hopeful of a change of heart among my people in the not too distant future. Their friendly relations with the rest of the British dominions will improve year by year, until all feeling of bitterness has passed and they can regard themselves as truly a member of the British family.

Mountbatten: I sincerely hope so, Mr Jinnah. [Stands up, pushing his chair back] And now if you would excuse me….

Jinnah: [Rises slowly] I am sorry to mention a trifling matter—but it is of importance to us. I would like the Governor of West Punjab to leave Government House soon as I would be moving in there myself. And yes, General Gracey should also vacate Flagstaff House as soon as possible. I understand he is leaving Karachi before the 15th August anyway—so perhaps he could move into another house temporarily with his luggage. I regret the inconvenience, of course.

Mountbatten: Of course. I will let General Gracey know this immediately.

[Jinnah leaves. Liaquat Ali shown in moments later]

Liaquat Ali: Good day, Your Excellency. Has Jinnah *Sahib* left? I received a message you would like to see me and I thought you wanted me to join him.

Mountbatten: I wanted to see you alone, Mr Khan. I want to make it quite clear that I cannot make the Orders for Pakistan on the advice of Mr Jinnah. Since he is going to become its Constitutional Governor-General he should no longer give me advice on this matter. All advice should, henceforth, be submitted through the Pakistan Council.

Liaquat Ali: I understand Your Excellency. I will explain it to Jinnah *Sahib*. Err…may I mention something that has been on our mind—unrelated, of course, to any Constitutional matter.

Mountbatten: [nodding] Yes, yes, please go ahead.

Liquat: Is it possible that you can use your famous powers of persuasion to make the Congress agree to let the Pakistan High Commissioner and his staff be housed in the Red Fort?

Mountbatten: [Amazed look] What's that? The Red Fort did you say? [Shrugs] Well, I can ask them.

Liaquat Ali: Thank you very much, Your Excellency.

SCENE 38

Viceroy's study: Mountbatten, Gandhi, Patel and Nehru are conversing.

Mountbatten: I called this meeting to consider Mr Nehru's wish to go to Kashmir. I know the history of this affair from the time I arrived and I am sympathetic to his mental distress at having been unable to visit his friends in Kashmir and endeavour to get Sheikh Abdullah released. But I sincerely feel that Mr Gandhi should visit Kashmir in place of Mr Nehru. I admit I am to blame for the delay in this affair—but I did think I could speak to the Maharaja more effectively. Unfortunately, I was unable to discuss the release of Sheikh Abdullah with the Maharaja because he was indisposed. However, whatever Mr Nehru's personal emotions might be, I will be failing in my duty if I allow him to go there now.

Gandhi: Mr Kak, the Prime Minister of Kashmir did not want me to visit Kashmir. What is wrong if Jawaharlal goes?

Mountbatten: This is hardly the time for the Vice-President of the Interim Government and the Prime Minister of the Dominion

Government which is to take over power in 17 days, to leave the capital. Such a visit will be extremely difficult to explain away to world opinion. A visit by any Congress leader cannot fail to be badly received in the world press at a time when Kashmir has the choice of Pakistan or India before its ruler.

Nehru: I am very disturbed emotionally with things there—and what could be more natural than the Congress sending a high-level emissary to lay the advantages of joining India before the ruler. Everyone knows I am over-worked and would like to go away for a few days rest somewhere, and Kashmir would be the best place to have some rest.

Mountbatten: If you go Mr Nehru, it will be regarded as a piece of straightforward political lobbying. The effect would be somewhat mitigated if Mr Gandhi went because in the mind of the world he is a man of religion. Mr Patel?

Patel: I am of the view that neither Pandit Nehru nor Gandhiji should go. But if it is a choice between two evils then I consider that Gandhiji's visit would be the lesser evil.

Gandhi: As Lord Mountbatten seriously regards Jawaharlal's going objectionable, I am prepared to go in his place.

Mountbatten: I will send telegrams immediately to the resident in Kashmir and the Governor of the Punjab then about Mr Gandhi's visit.

SCENE 39

Mountbatten's study: Mountbatten and Nehru.

Mountbatten: Sir Stafford and Lady Cripps are going to Burma next month, and if you have no objection, I intend to invite them to stay with me in Delhi.

Nehru: It will be a great pleasure to have them here. And of course, they must stay with you.

Mountbatten: Lord and Lady Addison are also going to be in Calcutta for one night on their way to Canberra. Perhaps the BOAC can put them up there.

Nehru: I think you should write to the new Governor—it will probably be Mr Rajagopalachari—and ask him to put them up. I am sure he will be glad to do so.

Mountbatten: What is this confusion over the Commander-in-Chief? I have complete faith in Field Marshal Auchinleck's integrity. The best proof of his impartiality is to be found in the fact that the Muslim League, your Congress and the Services Clubs in London, are all equally convinced that he is not adequately looking after the interests of Muslims, Hindus and the British element. Sir Chandu Lal Trivedi will come up and visit you—I'm sure he can convince you of the genuine misunderstanding between you and the C-in-C. And I've been meaning to ask you, to avoid a similar misunderstanding between us you know, if you would object to my writing a fortnightly letter to the king and if I might make these letters personal and not show them to you as Prime Minister?

Nehru: I trust you Dickie—you can do as you wish.

Mountbatten: Jahawa—I am very concerned about the success of your government. Unless you get a really sound cabinet in which young, talented and enthusiastic members are dominant, you will lose a great opportunity of gripping the imagination of the country. Frankly, I think your greatest weakness is your personal loyalty to old friends and colleagues. Unless you get rid of a lot of top-weights like Rajagopalachari, you will be greatly hampered. You should get a crowd of really good young men.

Nehru: In principle I agree with you but there is a remarkable dearth of good young men between the ages of 30 and 45.

Mountbatten: Well, Bhabha and Matthai should both be kept in important positions. They are extremely able and fearless. On the other hand, Baldev Singh appears to me to be unsatisfactory as Defence Minister. Rajendra Prasad, of course, is a dear old man—he can always be made the speaker in the house. I hope you don't mind the friendly advice I'm giving you as the constitutional Governor-General? With a good cabinet the Congress can remain in power for the next few years at least.

Nehru: Not at all—I will always look to you for advice on such matters, Dickie. I intend to pick unknown young men and put them in as deputy secretaries or parliamentary secretaries to get experience. And as soon as the new government is set up, I want to take up the whole question of planning. I'm going to appoint a strong planning commission and produce a series of plans on the Russian model—a one, five, and ten-year plan.

Mountbatten: For that you need Mr Patel's cooperation! [Shakes a finger at Nehru as latter prepares to leave. Nehru walks out, smiling]

Ronnie [Walking in]: Have you spoken to Nehru about Krishna Menon, Dickie? Lord Ismay has just been telling me that Menon made a very unfavourable impression in home circles when he was in England. With the opposition leaders at home he is very much *persona non grata*. And now his selection as High Commissioner to Britain is upsetting the Secretary of State as well.

Mountbatten: I have written to the Secretary—Menon's services have been of great assistance to me in the difficult negotiations here in recent weeks. I came to know him some years ago in England when he was very much of an outcast because of his left-wing views and activities. He has never forgotten this and I have found him a valuable contact between Nehru and myself. He has Nehru's complete confidence and through him I have been able to keep well informed about the trend of Congress opinion. In fact, with V.P. Menon's close contact with Patel, I know all that is going on in both camps in the Congress through the two Menons. I must say, the realistic attitude of Patel is a great asset to the Congress party, as opposed to the emotionalism of Nehru. Though one cannot suppose an open clash between such differing temperaments can be prevented for all time.

Ismay: [Walking in] Punjab CID has sent me very incriminating evidence of Tara Singh's involvement in the Sikh plans to make bombs and attack all the headworks. They plan to wreck the trains carrying Pakistan government staff from Delhi to Karachi and to assassinate Jinnah during independence celebrations there. And Vernon's just bringing in the latest lists of refugees and casualties. [Vernon enters] Here he is.

Vernon: [Reads] As of today, there are 70,000 refugees at the Purana Qila in Delhi. UP and other neighbouring states have large numbers also. About 60,000 Muslims from East Punjab have gathered in Kanpur. The lists of columns of refugees, both Hindu and Muslim, are enormous. They are moving on specified routes in both directions. Rukhanwala to Khem Karan—column number 12 of 30,000 persons; column 13 of 30,000; column 14 of 40,000; column 15 of 30,000. Muslims escorted from Moga to Ganda Singhwala—20,000; from Sri Gobindpur over Dera Baba Nanak bridge—2,500; Muslim evacuees: 12,000 in Garha; 114,000 in Dasuya; 47,000 in Hoshiarpur; 62,000 in Nasrala—the compiler says Nasrala is not on the map. The Hindu and Sikh columns exiting daily from Lahore and Lyallpur and Kasur and Rajganj have no figures—we haven't received any count from West Punjab. Those counted coming in on this side are: Lohar to Khurla—

10,000 on foot and 300 carts; Kartarpur to Beas—4,500 and 300 carts; Beas to Gindhiala—3,000 and 555 carts. From Jaranwala, Jhelum–Chakwal, Chiniot, Jhang Maghiana, Arifwala, and so on and so on—no figures available.

Ismay: Punjab Governor telephoned that despite acute floods with the bridges over the Sutlej connecting Kasur, Ferozepur, Moga and Fazilka destroyed, the murders and massacres haven't let up. The venality of it—they are coming into their own Dickie! You wouldn't believe it—in the partition sub-committees, the division of spoils has descended to the sublimely ridiculous. Apart from tables and chairs, with the chairs described as officers, revolving, armless and cushioned, they are fighting over hat stands—do they wear hats for God's sake! Every tray and jug, pisspot, spittoon and chamberpot, every doormat and peon's bench, the Lord save us, even waste paper baskets and name boards are a bone of contention. The Muslim and non-Muslim members submit separate reports. The *coup de grace* was when they argued about the beds to be reserved at the Ranchi Mental Hospital for the areas to fall in Pakistan! A very sad business. Well—I'm off to lunch now. [Leaves]

Vernon: Dickie, I'm not coming in after lunch today, I have to collect those papers from the Military Department.

Mountbatten: Right. I'll just dictate a letter to Ronnie before you leave as well. [Vernon leaves] [Begins dictation]: '*Dear Krishna, I cannot let you leave India without giving you my warmest personal thanks for the way you have helped me in all these difficult negotiations. I feel that history will show that you have helped the future of India very much by the advice that you gave me. I am glad to think that I shall have a personal friend as the first High Commissioner in London. Your letters to me from London should be sent to Lord Listowel's private secretary and you can ask him to put them in the Viceroy's bag. I enclose letters for the Prime Minister and Secretary of State which are unsealed. Please read them and then seal them down and deliver them on arrival. I hope they will be helpful to you. Edwina asks me to say that she will also miss you very much. Yours etc: Dickie Mountbatten.*'

Ronnie: I'll send this straightaway. So tomorrow is D-Day.

Mountbatten: A great day Ronnie—a day of historic achievement.

SCENE 40

It is night in the Viceroy's study. Mountbatten and Campbell-Johnson are at the desk with one lamp burning, putting papers in order and drinking coffee. Mountbatten pours cognac into their cups and as the clock strikes midnight he takes off his reading glasses while Campbell-Johnson fiddles with the radio impatiently. Finally an uproarious assembly is heard with voices shouting 'Jai Hind' and sounds of clapping followed by ringing of chimes and blowing of conchshells. The radio is switched off.

Campbell-Johnson: It is done. The assembly has proclaimed independence. The leaders will be here at 12.45.

Mountbatten: Time to lock up the dispatch boxes Alan. Come— [Begins putting them into almirahs and clears the desk of all papers with Alan's help]

Campbell-Johnson: All clear now. I'll call in help to make room for the press—they will come in full force.

[Goes out and returns with two peons who push back chairs and tables. Correspondents and cameramen start coming in]

Campbell-Johnson: Neville, Donald, are the leaders behind you?

Neville: They are going to be delayed with all the tremendous throngs outside the assembly. Immense crowds have gathered on the route to this place.

[Pressmen are asked to flank the room, photographers stand on the circular table. Nehru and Rajendra Prasad arrive. Mountbatten stands at his desk to receive them as Prasad faces him.
Nehru half sits on the table between them]

Prasad: Lord Mountbatten, the Constituent Assembly has taken charge and…. [Stops and looks at Nehru]

Nehru: And endorsed the request….

Prasad: And endorsed our request that you should become the first Governor-General.

Nehru: The first Governor-General of independent India.

Mountbatten: [Smiling] I am proud of the honour, and I will do my best to carry out your advice in a constitutional manner.

Nehru [Hands Mountbatten a large envelope]: May I submit to you the portfolios of the new cabinet?

Mountbatten: Thank you very much. [Prasad and Nehru leave, the press follows them out. Mountbatten alone with Campbell-Johnson, sits down and opens the envelope] Good God! It is empty!

Neville [Sticks his head in at door]: Alan, will Nehru's coronation be on time tomorrow?

Campbell-Johnson: On the dot – 8.30 a.m., the Durbar Hall.

SCENE 41

Leaders seated flanking the red and gold thrones in the Durbar Hall. Red velvet canopies lit with hidden lights above the thrones and carpets of gold. Audience is in place. Trumpets sound as Mountbatten and Edwina enter, led by stiff procession of ADCs to thrones. A Chopin Polonaise is playing throughout the scene.

As Mountbattens sit, whole Durbar Hall resounds with the explosion of one of the photographers' flash bulbs. A few people in audience look startled. Music becomes louder as ceremony conducted with Indian Chief Justice administering oath to Mountbatten and an Indian Secretary of Home Department swears in ministers of new government.

The ceremony ends, the music fades away, and a band plays 'God Save the King' followed by 'Jana Gana Mana'.

SCENE 42

Mountbatten's study: Mountbatten, Nehru and Patel.

Mountbatten: At the Pakistan Independence Day Dinner in Karachi, Jinnah leaned across the table and told me: '*The only wrong act which I think you have committed since you came to India has been your stampeding the Princes into acceding to the Dominion of India. What does it matter if they are independent*?'

Patel: You see! His only idea was to weaken India by leaving our territory thoroughly balkanized. If you had not succeeded in getting the states to join us, we would now be in a terrible mess. Lord Mountbatten, I am most grateful to you for having carried out all the negotiations and I hope you will continue with the Hyderabad delegation.

[Patel leaves]

Nehru: The Sikhs are driving me crazy. Liaquat Ali and I met Master Tara Singh and Giani Kartar Singh and both candidly admitted that they had been openly inciting followers to violence—of course, they insisted it was only in self-defence. Now, things have gone too far and are becoming dangerous for the Sikh population itself. Tara Singh and others are now prepared to use full influence and stop the fighting. The middle classes of all communities in both east and west Punjab are now thoroughly frightened. I think they will really make an effort to end the warfare.

Mountbatten: I am deeply concerned about the Sikhs and would like to monitor them continuously. You are going to be away from Delhi for a few days—who will be your deputy in the cabinet with whom I can discuss this?

Nehru: Sardar Patel.

Mountbatten: I suggest you give him the title of deputy Prime Minister—he will be officially bound to inform me of everything then.

Nehru: I will think it over…[Baldev Singh enters]

Baldev: Lord Mountbatten, we have to change the Punjab Boundary Force. People are saying everywhere that it is deliberately not stopping the massacres.

Mountbatten: Out of the question. There can be no change till the leaders—especially Sikh leaders—stop their followers from organized murders, riots and arson. I don't want a breakdown in the morale of the army.

Baldev: I assure you that Master Tara Singh and Giani are going around the villages preaching peace—of course, the *goonda* elements take advantage but it will be controlled. Real problem is the Muslims will not call off the troubles in West Punjab—they stand to gain so much by looting rich Hindus and Sikhs there. Now see, looting has started in Lahore but Amritsar is quiet.

Nehru: If I may intervene—the argument against the Boundary Force is not so much a military question, I would like a change from the psychological point of view. The force is being blamed for the killings so some compromise on military reorganization should be made.

Mountbatten: I'll have to discuss this with the Commander-in-Chief. Mr Singh, I'll fix a meeting with the generals and let you know the time. [Baldev leaves]

Nehru: I am coming to the conclusion that it will now be best for the minorities to leave both the new provinces of Punjab. There are so many cases of West Punjab refusing to release Hindus and Sikhs. People are getting increasingly angry with us. I am very worried about what will happen to the 45,000 Muslims in India if Pakistan becomes an all-Muslim state and India in consequence becomes an all-Hindu and Sikh state.

[Ronnie walks in]

Ronnie: There is an urgent message from Mr Asaf Ali that the Jamia Millia College is going to be attacked and police arrangements are very poor. I have informed Police Headquarters.

Mountbatten: Ali—isn't he the Indian ambassador to the USA?

Nehru: He has come home for a few days.

[Amrit Kaur rushes in]

Amrit: The Lady Hardinge Nursing College is expecting an attack. Please ensure protection—there are so many young Muslim girls there.

Nehru: [Jumping up and ushering her out] Come with me—let's go to Sardar Patel.

[They leave] [Ismay and V.P. Menon enter]

Ronnie: The Prime Minister has been with you for the last three hours—is it a big problem?

Mountbatten: He's been discussing the communal situation. The interesting thing is that he really came simply and solely for company, to unburden his soul, and to obtain what comfort I had to give him. He has lately written me two or three letters beginning: *'I don't know why I'm writing this letter except that I feel I must write to someone to get my troubles off my chest.'*

[Field Marshal Auchinleck, Generals Lockhart and Bucher knock on door]

Mountbatten: Come in Field Marshal. You have to solve the trouble in Delhi. We've just had two panic calls.

Auchinleck: I know the solution—deal mercilessly with the Sikhs. Arrest all those seen on the streets and shoot those found carrying a weapon of any sort. My intelligence organization has been watching the Sikhs carefully for a month now and had foreseen the trouble—but not in such a serious form. I think it is very important that the government should take very drastic action. Arrested Sikhs should be kept for 48 hours without anything to eat or drink. General Lockhart has just had a meeting with Sardar Patel—he can tell you the latest situation.

Lockhart: Patel has already announced his intention of dealing strongly with Sikh trouble makers. He has given me a free hand. He has given orders that the primary object of the exercise is to go after the Sikhs as they are responsible for the reign of terror—as he put it. A new regiment of *Madrassis* is arriving in Delhi—it is a first class unit with a good reputation for complete impartiality.

Mountbatten: General Bucher?

Bucher: Sir, In my view, action only against the Sikhs would make them coalesce both in the Punjab and in the Sikh states and they would become even more dangerous. In Calcutta, in fact, Sikhs have been even more responsible for the trouble than at Delhi but no orders specifically against them were passed. General orders will be better—anybody armed, regardless of community, should be shot on sight and martial law can be declared in some areas of the city.

Mountbatten: So we agree that the primary object must be to round up the Sikhs but there should be no apparent discrimination.

Auchinleck: The object will have been achieved if in 48 hours time the local graves and detention centres are more fully occupied by men with long beards than those without.

Ismay: Field Marshal, any blatant action against the Sikhs will have disastrous effects on the Sikh troops in the army.

Auchinleck: Lord Ismay, I have seen Major General Pert this morning. He tells me that the Sikhs are working to a detailed plan and the next development will be the eviction of all the Hindus from East Punjab. He suggested this plan might be Communist in origin—having got rid of the Muslim landowners, they now plan to oust the Hindu merchants. Sikhs as a whole are more arrogant than he has ever seen them. In his view, Sikhistan has already been established. And as for the army officers, they are mainly partial to their own communities anyway.

Mountbatten: Field Marshal, I suggest your men should handle the situation as best as they can but in constant cooperation with Sardar Patel's department.

[Auchinleck and Generals leave]

Ismay: Jinnah made exactly the same complaints about the Sikhs at my meeting with him in Lahore. He sees the bloody scenes being enacted on this side as the result of plans prepared in detail over many months. Muslims were marked out, arms collected and duties apportioned for the butchery. Along with the Sikhs he also implicates the Hindus – particularly the RSS and the members of the Congress party. He doubts the good faith and honesty of the Indian Government as it had proscribed the *kirpan* and then cancelled the order two days later. He accuses the police of being fully implicated in the disorders. The Pakistani High Commissioner was present in Karachi and asserted that whatever orders may be given by ministers, he had met with complete obstruction at the lower levels. Of course, I vigorously defended the Government of India's intentions and efforts. But Jinnah was absolutely fatalistic—India will never keep faith, he said, there is nothing for it but to fight it out.

[Ronnie announces Shyama Prasad Mukherji. Ismay walks out]

Mountbatten: What a pleasure to see you, Mr Mukherji—you can help me to make sense of the communal situation more than anyone else. You are the leading light of the Hindu Mahasabha and control the RSS do you not?

Mukherji: Oh no—I don't control the RSS—but its leaders love me and trust me.

Mountbatten: They will do whatever you ask them to do, I'm sure. Can they establish peace in Delhi?

Mukherji: They have already started participating in the rehabilitation of Delhi on my request. In fact, it is the RSS which is going around burying dead bodies.

Mountbatten: There should not be any bodies to be buried, Mr Mukherji. Tell me what line do you take on the transfer of populations?

Mukherji: Lord Mountbatten, I am prepared to fully back Nehru's policy—no Muslim should be forced to go to Pakistan and no Hindu forced to come here. The inevitable consequence of this will be a pan-Hindu/Sikh state here which will have no Muslims.

Mountbatten: Unless vast, additional territory is given to Pakistan how can there be any question of transferring 45 million Muslims who are still in India?

Mukherji: That, Sir, is entirely their lookout. They have brought this upon themselves. If the ultimate policy is to make the populations of both dominions strictly communal, then Jinnah will have to take the 45 millions and fit them into his existing area.

Mountbatten: How do you reconcile this statement with allowing people to choose where they are to live?

Mukherji: Let me be clear—I am in favour of free choice as long as possible but, the time may come when Jinnah's behaviour will leave us no alternative but to insist on a clean sweep of Muslims.

Mountbatten: That is a disturbing thought. Please do keep in touch with me—we must meet again soon.

[Mukherji leaves. Maulana Azad enters]

Azad: Lord Mountbatten, I can turn to no one but you in this hour of trouble. You cut short your holiday in Simla and rushed back to Delhi—you have saved the situation. I must pay tribute to the impartiality of British officers.

Mountbatten: India and Pakistan must sort this out Mr Azad—how long can the British officers remain? In any case, they are being attacked by both.

Azad: I really deplore the communalism of both sides—especially of the leaders. I want to meet Mr Jinnah and come to some understanding with him on behalf of the 45 million Muslims left in India.

Mountbatten: Mr Azad, I am aware that Mr Jinnah has refused to shake hands with you as he regards you as a traitor to the Muslims. If there is to be some agreement then Nehru and Liaquat Ali will have to work on it. Suhrawardy came to see me and insisted that all the massacres were the fault of the Sikhs. He even accused Nehru of hiding the truth and refusing Liaquat Ali's suggestion, that UN observers should tour the affected areas.

Azad: Nehru is not considered sufficiently communal on the Hindu-Sikh side.

Mountbatten: Mr Gandhi told me that even his remarks are becoming more and more obnoxious to the Hindus and Sikhs. Actually, they are under intense pressure from Patel. When I suggested appealing to the UN on the issue of Junagadh, Patel gave me a curt 'No'! He said as possession is nine points of the law, even a discussion by the Indian and Pakistani representatives in the UN would give a false impression of a dispute when none existed. And Nehru, who had agreed with me, now said he was also not in favour of going to the UN.

Azad: I have heard that Sardar Patel is also giving sympathy to the communalism of the Sikhs in the navy. The situation is very serious—there are only 4 per cent Sikhs who are demanding the removal of *Halal* and replacement by *Jhatka* meat. The Muslims are ten times as numerous—if imposed on them they will be forced to leave.

Mountbatten: The cabinet must resist any move to concede Sikh demands. The largest part of the chief petty officers and petty officer rates are Muslim and their flight will leave the navy with insufficient officers.

Azad: I don't see how the cabinet will resist the Sikhs....

[Interruption by Ronnie: informs V.P. Menon waiting to see Mountbatten urgently. Azad leaves]

V.P. Menon: [Rushing in, in a panic] Lord Mountbatten, we are in a serious crisis—there is a complete split between the Prime Minister and Deputy Prime Minister over the policy towards Junagadh. Both are threatening to resign.

Mountbatten: If Nehru resigns, Patel's extreme communalism will soon plunge India into an untenable position. Nehru's reputation stands higher than ever in the eyes of the world—he is admired for his courageous, unbiased policy in the face of communal sentiments of the Hindus and Sikhs.

V.P. Menon: Sir, he is very unpopular in India at the moment—he has lost all his following. He may not even get elected if there is a fresh election. Sardar Patel is the embodiment of the feelings of the Hindu/Sikh majority at present. His stock is higher than it has ever been—he alone can really hold the cabinet. Nehru alone will be unable to do so—and the government will fall.

Mountbatten: Therefore, everything must be done to avoid a split between them. But how does one do that when Patel announces rebuilding a temple and restoring idols as his first priority?

V.P. Menon: Sardar Patel is right on Junagadh, Sir. Though I am not a Gujarati, I also feel emotional about this issue. We will be letting down the small states which have acceded to us by allowing Junagadh to attack them. I feel like resigning and going to fight with a *lathi* as a volunteer on behalf of the wronged states.

Mountbatten: What exactly does Patel want?

V.P. Menon: His minimum demand for staying in government is that we should take a strong line in Kathiawar to show that India is not afraid of Pakistan and does not intend to be bluffed by Jinnah.

Mountbatten: Does he not see that entering Junagadh would get us into Jinnah's trap—he could haul us before the UNO for attacking Pakistani territory. All our international prestige will be lost.

V.P. Menon: Sardar says that the country that has lost its national position need not bother about its international position. He thinks the government will be forever dishonest if it lets down its own nationals in Kathiawar.

Mountbatten: V.P. Menon, Patel is in a very dangerous mood. He is not only dissatisfied with the army as now organized and officered by the British, he even questions whether it is possible to make anything of the existing Indian officers. He contemplates raising a special army from patriotic Indian youths. In his military ignorance he seems to think that he can produce an army worth its name within a few years. He does not seem to realize that even the Russians had to keep senior Tsarist officers for close to twenty years to prepare their army. But of course, it isn't the Russian army he wishes to copy, he wishes to copy Hitler's army, the SS. We all know what happened with the SS when it got up against the regular German army, and how in the end the downfall of Germany was brought about. No, I'm sorry to say this is a fascist mood. Patel says he will not provoke war—but his bellicose line over Junagadh is designed to prove that might is right. He may get away with his Junagadh like Hitler got away with Austria, but he will meet his Poland if he goes on like this. He sat here and described Nehru as '*my leader who is carried away by his lofty ideals into the skies*'. I see this as a danger signal. At the present moment, the man who has his feet on firm ground is Nehru.

V.P. Menon: As long as you are here you can hold the position, Lord Mountbatten. Sardar Patel has unbounded faith in you.

Mountbatten: God knows why, since I'm thwarting all his warlike designs. Mr Gandhi will be here any moment now—I'm going to raise the matter with him.

[Mountbatten walks out with V.P. Menon, re-enters with Gandhi and seats him before going to own chair]

Mountbatten: I have been following your admirable advice to all on establishing peace in the country but, you will forgive me for saying, it is no good preaching to people until you keep the leaders straight on the communal outlook. I am referring, particularly, to Mr Patel.

Gandhi: I agree. You have summed up the position correctly. I tried to solve the matter in my own way by requesting the British Prime Minister to withdraw all British officers from Kashmir. Even if the Indian troops were to be driven back and Sheikh Abdullah and his men stood side by side with them in defence of their hearth and homes, it would have a wonderful effect throughout India, whatever the outcome of the battle. The fact that Muslims, Sikhs and Hindus had fought together for a common cause would be a turning point in history—a beacon of hope.

Mountbatten: How is a solution possible when Mr Patel is so warlike? He mobilized the entire cabinet against Nehru accompanying me to Lahore for talks with Jinnah. Why are they opposed to it so violently?

Gandhi: Jawaharlal is very ill. He is advised total rest. The cabinet is naturally worried about his health.

Mountbatten: Please don't cover up the issue—I know that their opposition started much before his illness. In fact, it caused his illness—he is really sick at heart with the situation. I offered to postpone the trip till he was well again but the cabinet flatly refused to allow him to go. I would go and see anyone, anywhere, anytime, if it would help the public interest.

Gandhi: I feel exactly the same.

Mountbatten: You are, of course, a great man.

Gandhi: I prefer to be called a good man.

Mountbatten: Tell me in your heart you must know why Patel and the others are so against the visit to Lahore?

Gandhi: It is sad but true—Sardar and the cabinet can never forget that they had been underdogs of the Muslims for so long. They feel the visit will lower their prestige. It will increase the prestige of Jinnah. They are convinced that Field Marshal Auchinleck and Lord Ismay are anti-Hindu and pro-Muslim and are encouraging Jinnah. I am very anxious about the future. I feel it has been a great mistake to make two co-equal dominions. Mutual hatred has bitten deep into men's hearts and it is impossible to see how the tragedy will ever end.

SCENE 43

The Imperial Hotel: Journalists at the bar.

Neville: Stephens, have you seen the *Times* centre-spread on Kashmir? It reports that in one area 237,000 Muslims were systematically exterminated by the forces of the Dogra State, headed by the Maharaja in person.

Stephens: [Pulling out a file from briefcase] Let me give you the latest figures from my editorial: '*Within a period of eleven weeks starting in August systematic savageries practically eliminated the entire Muslim element in the population, amounting to 500,000 people.*' You know Richard Symonds don't you? I introduced him to you last year in the office of *The Statesman* when you visited Calcutta. He says the Dogras have burnt whole villages in the districts of Poonch and Mirpur. But most of the adult men of Poonch were ex-servicemen in the Indian army with close connections with the people in Jhelum and Rawalpindi in Pakistan. They evacuated their women and children, crossed the frontier, and returned with arms supplied to them by willing people. The present position is that the Kashmir state forces have been forced to withdraw in certain areas.

Neville: No wonder the tribal *lashkar* has given a call for *jihad* in Kashmir. I suppose the Pakistan government can do nothing about that. [*Sotto voce*] I heard this morning that Mountbatten has dispatched V.P. Menon to get Kashmir's accession to India signed by the Maharajah. One of the best informed of the Delhi political correspondents, Sri Krishna let out that the airlift of Indian troops to Srinagar is on the ready.

Stephens: So Mountbatten is going to drop the cloak of Governor-General and assume the role of supreme commander. It is a travesty of justice. I was called to dinner by the Mountbattens last evening and was startled by their one-sided verdicts on affairs. They seem to have become wholly pro-Hindu. Kashmir is technically an independent country—the Maharaja entered into a standstill agreement with the Pakistan government.

Neville: Poor Jinnah! Because of its Muslim population and geographical situation he always claimed that it would fall into his lap like a ripe fruit. Now this great state that is mainly Muslim will be legally lost to him.

Stephens: If Junagadh, despite its Muslim ruler's accession to Pakistan, belonged to India because of its Hindu majority, how can Kashmir, with its Muslim majority, be a part of India simply by virtue of its Hindu ruler signing away accession to India?

Neville: My source tells me that Sardar Patel feels the problems can be solved peacefully and to mutual advantage by letting Kashmir go to Pakistan in return for Hyderabad coming to India. Nehru is the obstacle to any agreement. And Nehru has convinced Sheikh Abdullah that he will grant virtual independence to Kashmir.

Stephens: My problem is Mountbatten. Why is he making himself the instrument of Indian ambitions?

Neville: The threat that India will leave the Commonwealth and Britain will lose its influence. He has worked very hard to achieve that. I suppose that is crucial—in the long run influence is a very much finer and more durable and eternal thing than power.

Stephens: Mountbatten's personal influence has been rather destructive. Look at the way he has dealt with the princes. In his book *friendly advice, moral pressure* and *command* mean much the same thing. The ICS men call it *doing a Wylie.* It was Francis Wylie who first put the screw on the Indian Princes.

Neville: My knowledge of the Maharajahs comes from Jarmani Dass' account of Kapurthala and Patiala Raj—rather juicy tidbits of royal scandal. I haven't had the time to see *The Pathology of Princes* yet, though I have a copy. The Congress party paints a rather grim picture of starving peasants in the Princely States.

Stephens: Peasants do not take easily to controls as even the government found out during the Calcutta famine. They are very particular about their food, mainly on religious grounds. Hindu widows in some parts would sooner die than eat milled rice—for them it must be hand-pounded. Some eat nothing but parboiled grain, barley excoriates the stomachs of some while millet reduces the social status of others. Don't buy the canard that portrays the rajas as 'tyrannical despots and unsavoury creations of British imperialism'. I doubt if any group has had such a bad press as they except the Jews in Germany! For example, Holkar is very well disposed towards the notion of democracy. Of course, he has a consuming passion for all things American.

Neville: I remember a couple of years ago, the rulers had a meeting at the Taj Mahal Hotel in Bombay committing their kingdoms to democratic principles or some such thing.

Stephens: Bhopal called on all Princely States to adopt written constitutions providing for popular institutions with elected majorities. These initiatives promised to transform them into Western-type monarchies. But Mountbatten has handed them over to the Congress party.

[An English businessman—Russell—approaches and greets Stephens]

Russell: Hello Stephens – I'm really glad to see a familiar face after Delhi's faceless bureaucrats.

Stephens: Russell—what are you doing so far from Bombay? Come join us for a drink. This is Neville—he is the Delhi correspondent of

Time and *Life*. Russell has been with Killick Nixon and Company since 1935—a *pucca* Bombay businessman.

Russell: You newspapermen have a good place going here—though I'd rather have the Byculla club or the Bombay Yacht club any day.

Stephens: Still doing the idle pleasures, Russell? He was a real gadfly—flitting from dinner parties on Malabar Hill to boating parties at Juhu beach in the moonlight. A great hit with the girls.

Russell: Ah—the days of youth. The war put a stop to all that. I had a life change during the Naval Mutiny—when a ship's main four-inch guns were trained in the direction of the yacht club's veranda while I was having drinks before lunch.

Stephens: Come to Calcutta—the grand Tollygunge club will soothe you of all fears. Mind you, it has a six-year waiting list—but editors of *The Statesman* can perform miracles.

Russell: Calcutta never! Your city is like an eighteenth-century colony which has been cut off from the rest of modern India. Actually—that's the reason I'm in this city—I am wondering if I should transfer to Pakistan. Many of my friends are making their home in the new country. I too have no wish to stay on in the emasculating and exasperating atmosphere of a Hindu republic.

Neville: Strange—you are the fourth person who has raised this question today. One ICS and two IP officers have mentioned it to me—for them the reasons are not hard to find. Pakistan has a dearth of civil administrators and it is an age old feeling among British officers that the Muslim races are upright, uncomplicated and conservative in outlook—much preferable to work with. Moreover, they are tired of dealing with the Congress party. But business and commerce, I would think, would prefer to hang on here.

Russell: I was in Karachi on the great day surrounded by a cross-section of Muslims watching the Independence Parade and I felt the tears coming to my eyes. It was so friendly with real comradeship on both sides. The next day I was overcome with sentiment when Jinnah attended a Dominion Day service in Karachi's Anglican cathedral.

Stephens: It is a very difficult choice. Especially for those still young enough to look forward to further employment—will they receive adequate compensation and proportionate pensions? An ICS friend in Bihar has sent me a most depressing letter—he is spending all his time haggling over the correct rate of compensation for his return to Britain. What he fears most is landing a mediocre job in the

Home Civil Service, living in some backstreet in London and tooling off to a stuffy office everyday.

Neville: It's probably worse or equally bad for the older men. My uncle is in the final lap of service and has grown accustomed to a life of relative ease and comfort. The prospect of living in semi-detached suburbia is a poor exchange for a spacious bungalow and a clan of servants at one's beck and call. He says he would die in the 8.45 train from Seven Oaks everyday!

Russell: I got a severe dressing down once from Morarji Desai when I was a member of the Bombay Legislative Assembly. I made the mistake of asking why he had moved that Ministerial salaries should be reduced by 90 per cent. He called us the new Mughals.

Neville: On my recent trip home I realized the trauma they apprehend. My aunt burst into tears at the rationing—the weekly allowance of 13 ounces of meat and one egg hit her hardest.

Stephens: The army is worst off—and it is not just personal. The regimental officers have a great deal of anguish and bitterness. Men who have seen Sikh serve with Punjabi Muslim, Meo Jat with Hindu have to come to terms with the fact that the one institution which provided racial and religious solidarity in India is to be disbanded. A great tradition that took two hundred years to build was dismembered in three months.

Neville: I've attended some final parades and farewells in Delhi and the final hugs of affection and tearful farewells to brothers in arms going to Pakistan have been very moving.

Russell: I came to Delhi to meet John Christie who is trying to convince me to stay on here. He himself has decided to take the job of representing the considerable British business interests in India—mainly the Association whose membership is predominantly British. His familiarity with the politicians will stand him in good stead. For my part, I can't bear the politicians!

Stephens: I too think you should stay on, Russell. The air services are mushrooming and visits home will no longer be the slow and tedious voyages of old. Of course, nothing as fast and modern as Mountbatten's Avro York!

Russell: Oh, the BOAC is operating a prestigious flying-boat service from Poole—I came back in it from England last month. A fantastic experience: having a luxurious lunch flying over France at about 13,000 feet. They put us up at an excellent hotel at Marseilles for the night, gave us lunch at Sicily and then on to Cairo for another overnight stay. It took five days in all and the BOAC staff pampered us thoroughly.

Stephens: I'm tempted to go home just for that! My friends in Calcutta have been complaining that the aircraft which fly on the India routes are converted bombers or developed from surplus RAF planes. [Sees a Clergyman who has just come to other end of bar and calls out] Dr Bailey—what is a man of God doing in this den of iniquity?

Bailey: [Approaching] Hello Stephens. I've been meeting my superior who is staying with his son here. The son is in the modern Church—the Press—ha, ha.

Stephens: Are you staying on or going home?

Bailey: I can't think what to do. My servants asked me for references because they assumed I would go back. They don't really differentiate between us men of the cassock and the British Raj, you know.

SCENE 44

Government House, Lahore: Jinnah speaking on telephone.

Jinnah: General Auchinleck—you are responsible for partitioning the army. I order you to send the Pakistani forces immediately to Kashmir to protect the Muslims there.

Auchinleck: [Voice on air] Sir, Pakistan does not have an army at this stage. We have partitioned barely half the army so far.

Jinnah: How can you tell me that! The Indian army is already in Kashmir. It has illegally occupied Kashmir.

Auchinleck: No Sir. The presence of Indian troops in Kashmir is due to the fact that the Maharaja has acceded to India. Any action by the Pakistani army would be interpreted as hostile, enemy action.

Jinnah: What nonsense. They are trying to massacre the Muslims there—we are fully entitled to go to their support.

Auchinleck: Sir, I'm afraid I will be compelled to withdraw all British officers in those circumstances.

[Jinnah bangs the phone down. He paces the room then sits down with frozen face]

[After a moment Mountbatten and Ismay are announced and ushered in and seated]

Jinnah: Welcome to Lahore. [Lashes out] I am astounded at the speed with which your Indians have been able to send troops to

Srinagar. They should have communicated with Pakistan on a matter of such intimate concern to us as the accession of Kashmir.

Mountbatten: We had no news till the evening of the 24th and on the 25th we sent up reconnaissance parties to verify the situation. It was only on the 26th that we decided to send in the troops since the Maharaja had announced his intention of acceding on that date.

Jinnah: We should have been informed on the 25th.

Mountbatten: I really could not credit you, Mr Jinnah, with allowing an armed incursion of the tribes to take place and wanted to verify it before making so serious an accusation.

Jinnah: The accession of Kashmir was not bona fides! It rests on fraud and violence and can never be accepted by Pakistan.

Mountbatten: The Maharaja was fully entitled to make such an accession and it is perfectly legal and valid.

Jinnah: No, it has come at the end of a long intrigue and has been brought about by violence. His premier had advised the Maharaja to remain independent. India has committed violence by sending her troops into Srinagar.

Mountbatten: The Maharaja was most anxious to remain independent. Nothing but the terror of the invasion which Pakistan sent in would have made him accede to India.

Jinnah: [Angry] The Government of India encouraged the Kashmir government to massacre Muslims in Poonch and Mirpur—the tribes were furious.

Mountbatten: I am the head of the Government of India—and it is obvious nonsense to say that we encouraged any massacres.

Jinnah: Very well, it was the Congress party that did it. It encouraged the Maharaja who incited his Dogras against innocent Muslims. Even today there are 90,000 Muslims in Jammu who are in danger of being massacred.

Mountbatten: Mr Nehru has expressed horror at the massacres and issued stringent orders to the army to stop them. I myself have supplemented his instructions. We already have a brigade of 2,000 men in Srinagar; a 4th battalion will be flown in today and a 5th battalion within the next two days. There will be no difficulty in holding the place—the prospect of the tribes entering Srinagar is remote. So how do you propose to stop the fighting?

Jinnah: Both sides should call off their forces simultaneously and should withdraw at once. I would like to fly up to Srinagar with you. The two of us can settle this in one day.

Mountbatten: I am rather astonished at the degree of control you appear to have over the raiders.

Jinnah: I will threaten them that if they do not stop fighting the forces of Pakistan will join the Indian forces in crushing them.

Ismay: The Indian forces are on the outskirts of Srinagar in a defensive role—they have nowhere to withdraw to. All the tribes have to do is to stop attacking.

Mountbatten: Mr Jinnah, why do you object so strongly to a plebiscite?

Jinnah: With Indian troops in military occupation of Kashmir and Sheikh Abdullah in power, such propaganda and pressure will be brought to bear that the average Muslim will never have the courage to vote for Pakistan.

Mountbatten: We can invite the UNO to undertake the plebiscite—it will be free and impartial.

Jinnah: You and I are the only two persons who can organize a plebiscite—we should do it together.

Ismay: Lord Mountbatten is a constitutional Governor-General and a Britisher, and even if the Indian Government trusts him to do that, I am sure the British Prime Minister would not approve as it would compromise the British position.

Jinnah: I am really bitter about the cancellation of the Indian delegation's visit to Lahore for discussions. How soon will Mr Nehru be well enough to come to Lahore?

Mountbatten: He is unwell. Now it is your turn to come to Delhi since I have come to Lahore as the representative of India. Come and stay with me as my guest in Delhi and I will take you to see Nehru in his bedroom.

Jinnah: That is impossible. I am so busy that I simply cannot leave Lahore.

Mountbatten: Is there any problem more serious or urgent than Kashmir? If you admit that Kashmir is top priority then all other work should stand aside for it and you should come to Delhi at once.

Jinnah: I regret that is impossible—the whole burden is on my shoulders here. My Prime Minister is also ill.

Mountbatten: Then come as soon as he is well.

Jinnah: We shall have to see.

Ismay: It would stand well in world opinion if you return Lord Mountbatten's visit and discuss Kashmir with Mr Nehru.

Jinnah: I have lost interest in what the world thinks of me since the British Commonwealth let me down when I asked them to come to the rescue of Pakistan. It is quite clear that India is out to throttle and choke Pakistan at birth. If they continue with their oppression there will be consequences. I am not afraid of them. The situation is so bad that there is little which can make it worse.

Mountbatten: Mr Jinnah, war is admittedly very harmful for India but it would be completely disastrous for Pakistan and yourself.

SCENE 45

Government House, Lahore. Meeting: Nehru, Baldev Singh, G. Ayyangar, Liaquat Ali, Ghulam Mohammad, presided by Mountbatten.

Liaquat Ali: I am very happy that Prime Minister Nehru is fully recovered and could visit us here in Lahore.

Mountbatten: We have a bad situation confronting us—large scale massacres and looting and the abduction of women. My plea to you, gentlemen, is to establish peace and discuss all differences in a spirit of dialogue and compromise.

Nehru: Atrocities have been committed on both sides. But, for the last month, after Indian troops moved into Kashmir, it is the raiders who are responsible for the massacres and abductions.

Liaquat Ali: The raiders? Muslim women of good families have been abducted, taken to Jammu, stripped naked and raped!

Nehru: The Indian forces have controlled the situation completely—since that incident, very few Muslims have been killed after the accession. The abducted women are being recovered—Lady Mountbatten herself is leading the women's group to monitor it. The Sikh troops will be removed absolutely.

Mountbatten: I suggest this meeting set up two teams of high-ranking representatives of both dominions to tour the areas and investigate fully.

Liaquat Ali: You, Prime Minister Nehru, talk of the sanctity of Indian territory—how did you respect the 'sanctity' of Junagadh territory? The so-called provisional government of Junagadh was set up in India, it was provided arms by India, and it then invaded and captured territory belonging to Junagadh. The head of this provisional government made a public statement that its success was due to assistance provided by the Deputy Prime Minister of India!

Nehru: In some ways India may have been in the wrong but no parallel with Kashmir is tenable. There is a vast difference of scale. The Pakistani army is openly involved.

Mountbatten: General Messervy has categorically assured me that he gave orders forbidding the Pakistan army to issue arms to raiders.

Liaquat Ali: Look, the ex-supreme commander put on record that there were 30,000 armed people on the frontier. They had arms factories of their own which produced first class weapons. Some Pakistan soldiers on leave may have their rifles and may be taking part in the fighting. But the raiders got arms from Afghanistan and Russia.

Nehru: Pakistan territory is being used as a major base for operations.

Ghulam Mohammad: Many stories circulating are not true. But the feelings of the Pakistani people on Kashmir are certainly very strong.

Ayyangar: The raiders passed through Pakistani territory. Recognize your duty! Following the international code, was it your duty to stop them or not? Own up responsibility.

Liaquat Ali: I cannot stop them. It would mean going to war with the tribes. As it is we are under continual attack by people for our leniency over Kashmir. We have not recognized the accession of Kashmir to India. Just as you don't recognize Junagadh's accession to Pakistan!

Ghulam Mohammad: The murder of Muslims in Kashmir was the cause of the attack by tribesmen. It all started with incursions of Akali Sikhs and RSS bands into Kashmir.

Baldev: That is far fetched! It is like the rumour about Naranjan Singh Gill who was about to invade Lahore with 10,000 men. The truth was he did not have more than five followers from his own village.

Ayyangar: Pakistan must declare it will influence the raiders to withdraw; it must prevent any more from coming into Kashmir.

Ghulam Mohammad: India must declare withdrawal of its troops, an impartial administration and a plebiscite.

Nehru: Out of the question!

Ghulam Mohammad: The only way of getting the raiders out is a change of administration in Kashmir. Then Pakistan would do everything to withdraw them.

Nehru: India has already gone further than it need have. We went out of our way to offer a plebiscite—there was no necessity for us to do it. Now we are told we must change our administration.

Ayyangar: Is it realized how unpopular the government of India is because we pledged a free and impartial plebiscite? Now they order the administration to be changed. There is no such precedent!

Liaquat Ali: There is. Governors in the North-West Frontier Province were changed before a plebiscite.

Mountbatten: Now hold on—there were political agitations and violence in the Frontier....

Ghulam Mohammad: Pardon me! The final position is immediate promise of an impartial plebiscite.

Nehru: Plebiscites take time to prepare... and the present administration is the first fully responsible government which has been set up in Kashmir after overthrowing the Maharaja's autocratic rule.

Liaquat Ali: The people of Kashmir are illiterate and oppressed—they are bound to vote in favour of whatever administration is in power. If an Englishman went as administrator, they would vote to join the United Kingdom.

Mountbatten: Liaquat, I am sure the call of Islam has greater influence upon Kashmiris—after all, religion is a factor of great importance among the illiterate.... Well, at least make some joint statement to stop the massacres....

[Silence, shuffling, silence]

Mountbatten: I think the Government of India should put out a unilateral statement promising plebiscite. India's policy, at least, will be clear to the world. It might induce Pakistan to effect a withdrawal of the raiders.

Nehru: I will never make such a statement! The question of plebiscite in Kashmir does not arise till the raiders are thrown out. If necessary, I will throw up my prime ministership and take the sword myself to lead the men of India against the invasion! Even if it takes five or ten years!

Mountbatten: Then may I suggest we go to the UN. Will you all agree to a joint approach to the UN?

Liaquat Ali: Yes, I will agree if the UN advises an impartial administration before the plebiscite.

Nehru: I entirely reject this idea. The plebiscite comes into the picture only when hostilities cease and there is peace in Kashmir.

Mountbatten: If we do not find any way out of this impasse it will not be the political leaders who would suffer in the fighting but the humble people of Kashmir. Misery will result not only in Kashmir, but also throughout the subcontinent. You people should be now settling down to formulate plans for the betterment of the lot of your people… history will judge you harshly.

[Meeting breaks up into groups, whispering, raised voices sometimes. Dinner is announced and all move out. Mountbatten and Liaquat return]

Liaquat Ali: You know there are 40 million Muslims left in India—they made great sacrifices in the cause of Pakistan and earned the enmity of the Hindu majority in whose midst they will have to live. We have to save the Kashmiri people from Indian vengeance.

Mountbatten: You cannot achieve that by pushing in tribal invasions!

Liaquat Ali: It is fully within my power to call upon the tribes to withdraw straightaway. But I have to make some concrete offer in return—or my appeal will be ignored.

Mountbatten: But you agree to the proposal that the UN be brought in?

Liaquat Ali: Yes, I will support it.

[They move out. Mountbatten returns holding Nehru's arm]

Nehru: No! I cannot agree to the UN. I can only request the Security Council to verify Pakistan's role in promoting and assisting the raids in Kashmir. The most important thing for us now is the military action in defending our territory. We have to push them back.

SCENE 46

Mountbatten's study: Mountbatten and V.P. Menon are conversing.

V.P. Menon: Yesterday, Nehru called a meeting which Sardar Patel, Gopalaswami Ayyangar, and Gandhiji attended. All agreed that the fighting must be stopped but were bitterly opposed to any step which could be taken to mean surrender. Ayyangar remarked that Your Excellency did not fully appreciate India's point of view but Gandhiji insisted it only appeared so because you were trying to emphasize Pakistan's point of view, because you wanted to be fair.

Mountbatten: Gandhi is a very fair man himself. What is the inside story in Kashmir?

V.P. Menon: There are difficulties inside Kashmir. Nehru is backing Sheikh Abdullah fully while Sardar Patel, on my advice, is backing the Maharaja who is willing to concede responsible government on the Mysore pattern. But the Sheikh is demanding much more. The home department is convinced that RSS activities in Kashmir have now completely ceased—they are no problem.

Mountbatten: I had an hour's discussion with Baldev Singh and he claimed to have the most simple and straightforward view: either India wants Kashmir and should go ahead and take it regardless of any other consideration, or, it wants a plebiscite and should hold it immediately. He feels the two objects are hopelessly confused at the moment and Indian troops are fighting largely against the people of Kashmir in order to create conditions for a plebiscite. He has no doubt at all that the plebiscite would go in favour of Pakistan. He assured me that there would be no trouble from the Sikhs in that event.

Ronnie [Enters]: Malcolm MacDonald, Arthur Henderson, High Commissioner Sir Terence Shone and Mr Symon are waiting to see you.

Mountbatten: Bring them in and ask Vernon to come as well.

[V.P. Menon leaves and the others enter and settle down]

Mountbatten: So, Henderson, did you see Jinnah in Lahore?

Henderson: Yes, and he was fulminating on India's attitude on Kashmir. Calls it completely bogus and dishonest.

Mountbatten: You dropped in at Calcutta on the way—what did Rajagopalachari have to say?

Henderson: He was very pessimistic—he considers the only satisfactory solution for Kashmir is partition. In fact, he says it is inevitable and therefore Poonch district should be immediately transferred to Pakistan and the rest should continue under the Maharaja with accession held in abeyance. Of course, he emphasized all these were his personal views, not of the government.

Mountbatten: Nehru openly admitted that if he had not acted immediately and sent in the troops, his government would have fallen and an extremist government would have replaced him and declared war against Pakistan without a moment's delay. And of course, the 200 British inhabitants in Srinagar would have been murdered by the raiders.

Shone: Jinnah, as you know, had ordered troops to occupy the Banihal pass cutting off Indian troops at Srinagar. When General Gracey insisted on phoning Field Marshal Auchinleck to inform him, Sir Francis Mudie abused him violently on the telephone.

Mountbatten: Yes, Auchinleck rescinded Jinnah's orders as Kashmir had already acceded to India before the Indian troops landed. Jinnah's tactics continue to be never to agree to anything and never to accept a compromise!

MacDonald: But Nehru is rather unbalanced over Kashmir!

Mountbatten: I have no doubt that the final answer is partition of Kashmir. I cannot, of course, advocate this—I'll be hounded out of India immediately.

Symon: India has been gracious in offering that a plebiscite be held.

Mountbatten: I have also persuaded them that it should be held under the UN.

Shone: Why not under the Commonwealth?

Mountbatten: I've considered that very carefully. Whatever the solution suggested by the Commonwealth, those who suggest it would be hated by both sides. Look at the example of Cyril Radcliffe—he did a magnificent job on the Boundary Commission and now is loathed by both India and Pakistan. Both consider him a crook. Jinnah, by the way, wants to join the Commonwealth. He believes they will look upon Pakistan as a bastion which they would maintain whatever it costs.

Henderson: In Greece, despite UN observers, the fighting between Greek troops and the raiders who were nourished from outside Greece still goes on.

Mountbatten: They are not exactly parallels—a clash of ideologies between communism and democracy is involved in Greece. In Kashmir the dispute is on pseudo-religious grounds which the rest of the world hardly understands.

[The visitors, except Henderson, leave]

Mountbatten: Ronnie, Vernon—we are just going to have a personal chat. Can you ask for some whisky to be sent in please?

[Ronnie and Vernon leave the room. Drinks served after few moments]

Henderson: Stories about the war between the Pandit and the Sardar are doing the rounds in the civil service, are they true or just wishful thinking?

Mountbatten: They have such an uneasy partnership, very strained. I told them both clearly that they could not hope to do without each other. I do hope a split will not occur. The Patel faction accuses Nehru of riding roughshod over cabinet and passing orders without reference to the ministries concerned. Recently, Sheikh Abdullah asked for 20 lakh rupees and several lorries. Nehru arranged it out of the Ministry of Communications' funds without consulting any of the ministers. On the other hand, Patel has appointed his own men to high commissions and embassies abroad and moves them around without even informing Nehru who heads the external affairs and Commonwealth relations. Both make speeches without referring to each other and say things the other does not agree with.

Henderson: I must say, you are very well informed about your ministers.

Mountbatten: And how do I know all this? My main informant is Gandhi. He is very depressed and doubts the two can carry on together for long. When I forecast disaster from a split—Gandhi was really frightened. If Patel resigns he will form a right-wing party for which he won't lack many rich supporters. Nehru will be attacked, and the communists, who are well organized, may step in for all we know.

Henderson: No, not seriously? The Civil Service opinion is unanimous on this score—the Indian communists are no threat as of now.

Mountbatten: It's really funny—Patel is a Gujarati and he made absolutely no sense whatever on the Junagadh issue. He wanted to send troops in from the start. This really distressed Nehru. On the other hand, Nehru has shown very little sense about Kashmir and Patel is in real despair about what is going on there. The meeting between Nehru and Liaquat Ali was equally confusing. Nehru paid him compliments on acquiring a sylph-like, rejuvenated appearance and Liaquat Ali spent half-an-hour explaining his new diet and then they went at each other with hammer and tongs. Oh well. Time for dinner—Edwina is probably wondering what's keeping us.

[Mountbatten and Henderson leave]

SCENE 47

Study: Mountbatten and Ronnie are reading files. Vernon brings Amrit Kaur into the room.

Amrit: I'm sorry Lord Mountbatten for coming without an appointment. There is an urgent message from Gandhiji. He asks you to please phone Jinnah Sahib to stop the massacres in Karachi and allow the refugees to leave for Bombay by steamer.

Mountbatten: My dear, I have no value any more with Mr Jinnah. Since the last meeting in Lahore he has taken a violent dislike to me. He made a number of accusations against me to the BBC correspondent. But I'm meeting Liaquat Ali at Lahore tomorrow morning—I'll take it up with him.

Amrit: Gandhiji thinks all this looting of refugees leaving Karachi for India is because they are very angry by India's refusal to hand over their 55 crores.

Mountbatten: Very likely. I consider this refusal to be unwise. Really, its unstatesmanlike and the only dishonourable thing the Government of India has done to my knowledge.

Amrit: Can't you influence them—you are the Governor-General? Make them cancel their order.

Mountbatten: I have already spoken so strongly—there is nothing left to say. [Patel is announced] Just the man who can solve this—I shall plead with him again.

[Walks Amrit out and comes back with Patel speaking agitatedly]

Patel: I am resentful that Mahatmaji decided on a fast without consulting the Prime Minister or me. A week ago it would have been alright, now after the massacres in Karachi and in the refugee train from the frontier the Hindus and Sikhs will say his fast is directed against them. The only way to establish any decent relationship between the communities now is to remove every Hindu and Sikh from Pakistan and drive out the Muslims from East Punjab and the neighbouring areas.

Mountbatten: And what about the four crores of Muslims in the rest of India?

Patel: Their situation has remained unchanged throughout all the troubles. Their greatest safety lies in the complete removal of such incidents.

Mountbatten: I agree with Gandhiji that Muslims should at least be safe in the capital of India, it is essential for communal harmony.

Patel: If necessary, we can achieve it by the police and military until we stamp out the disorder. But I don't see how Gandhiji's do or die method can work. He has put me in an impossible position. And you, you have been goading them, Amrit Kaurji and Gandhiji. They are attacking me for withholding the 55 crores and pressing me to hand them over. I'm pained and surprised to hear that you characterized my action as dishonourable.

Mountbatten: I have repeatedly said so to you, separately and in the presence of others….

Patel: How can you use that word 'dishonourable'? It is not dishonourable! You were not at the Partition council meeting at which I made it clear that this was only one agreement that had to be negotiated. H.M. Patel informed Mohammad Ali again and again that the agreements would not be implemented until all outstanding matters including Kashmir had been settled satisfactorily. Do you suppose we would have given 75 out of 400 crores when the Hindus owned 90 per cent of the wealth of India? Do you suppose we would have given them 50 years to pay back, with a four years moratorium at the beginning? Do you suppose we would have gone out of our way to give them all these, far more generous terms than they could ever hope to get from the Arbitral tribunal, unless it was in the hope that all issues including Kashmir would be settled once and for all?

Mountbatten: Well, alright, in the light of all you are telling me, and specially as I was not present at the meetings and could only go on hearsay—I am prepared to withdraw the epithet 'dishonourable'. But, I still consider it a most unwise and unstatesmanlike action. It will ultimately boomerang.

Patel: We must disagree [walking off] I have a meeting now….

[Mountbatten accompanies him to door. Nehru appears with another person]

Nehru: This is our new minister for food and agriculture. He wanted to be introduced to you.

Mountbatten: Excellent. Come in. Let's have some tea.

Minister: Thank you Sir, but I must rush off to the department. I am meeting the visiting British Agriculture Minister.

Mountbatten: You must come in and tell me what your policy requirements are—I could help you get the machinery.

[Minister leaves]

Nehru: I'm glad you encouraged Gandhiji on his fast. I hope it will bring our people to their senses. You know [places hand on Mountbatten's arm], I have known Gandhiji for 32 years… last evening before the prayer meeting I was with him for one hour, and also just before he came to see you, but he did not tell me of his decision. You were the first person he told. [Pauses] May I raise a delicate, personal matter? How long have you decided to stay with us?

Mountbatten: About the 15th of April I think.

Nehru: Can't you stay longer? The Constituent Assembly will meet for the final constitution making process in April and they will finish their work within two months. We would like you to not leave before mid-June….

Mountbatten: Look, I won't press the mid-April date—can't we leave it open for some time? Actually, [laughing] I wish to avoid entering a new period after the scheduled interim period is over. For then, I might as well stay for five or ten years as for a year.

Nehru: All right, we'll talk again [stands to leave].

Mountbatten: Why don't you stay—Krishna is coming to see me now.

Nehru: Meeting with Sardar Patel.

Mountbatten: Then come for dinner tonight. Edwina asked me to ask both you and Krishna together.

[Nehru leaves. Krishna Menon enters]

Mountbatten: Has your visit back in India been as profitable as we expected?

Krishna: Useful, specially to collect additional staff for the high commission and to renew contact with secretaries of government departments. But I've drawn a zero with ministerial contacts. Although I'm living in the prime minister's house it's been impossible to have a heart to heart with him. Not even on my policy in London. He is so over-worked. And then there's Kashmir and his troubles with Sardar Patel. The only talk I insisted on having at an early breakfast was on your future. I made it quite clear to him that he can't afford to do without you. I'm sure he'll invite you to stay for as long as possible.

[Coffee is served]

Krishna: He is really feeling very sentimental over Kashmir. I tried not to laugh when he struck a dramatic pose and said: '*In the same way that Calais was written on Mary's heart, Kashmir is written on mine.*' You must not desert him at this time, Dickie, he's in a very difficult position. [Lowers voice] I can tell you, in strictest confidence, the rift between Patel and Nehru for the last ten years has widened to a very dangerous point. In the past, Nehru always gave way for the sake of a united front against the British. That reason no longer remains and it is inevitable that they will drift apart. They represent absolutely different points of view.

Mountbatten: I think, at the present time it is more important than in the past that they remain together. Can you imagine the consequences of a split in government, the formation of a separate Patel party attacking Nehru with all the inside knowledge he has? While the Kashmir case is heard at the UN? I also think Patel should continue his policy with the Indian princes. He alone can—if anyone—settle the question of mergers and new constitutions in the states in a satisfactory manner.

Krishna: I disagree totally. It is a disaster that Sardar Patel has got the ministry of states. Nehru should have retained it. To top it all, that extremely dangerous and double-dealing V.P. Menon is Patel's Secretary!

Mountbatten: You can't expect me to agree. I have the greatest regard for V.P. Menon—he is competent, loyal and statesmanlike.

Krishna: You are known for your loyalty to friends, even those rotten princes. But keep an open mind and appreciate what others think. Let me tell you, Patel is running a sort of underground organization within the government which ensures he has virtual control. He has his spies in every ministry, every embassy and every high commissioner's office. He is ruthless and powerful and everyone is afraid of him. He can exercise most improper pressure on governmental affairs. Nehru is not given the position due to him as Prime Minister and is unable to control the cabinet the way a Prime Minister should.

Mountbatten: Look Krishna, both the PM and Deputy PM frequently behave in an unconstitutional manner. I think that is largely due to inexperience. [Krishna shakes head] Anyway, a split would be disastrous. I trust you will do all you can to heal the breach. I am working with Gandhi towards this objective myself.

Krishna: Patel knows he can't run the government alone as only Nehru has an international reputation and prestige. He only wants to exercise backroom control.

Mountbatten: Neither can Nehru carry on without Patel, my friend.

Krishna: Anyway, your friendship really gives Nehru much support. Don't desert him now.

Mountbatten: You may be surprised to know that Sardar Patel is just as keen to retain my services. But I don't think I should stay more than a few weeks beyond the interim period.

Ronnie: [Peeps in] Mr K.M. Panikkar is here.

Krishna: [Leaving] You must discuss it with Nehru….

Mountbatten: He's also coming to dinner tonight, we'll talk then. Edwina has to be consulted on this. Come early.

[Krishna and K.M. Panikkar meet briefly at door]

Mountbatten: So? Rajkumari Amrit Kaur tells me that Gandhi is coming around to India remaining in the Commonwealth.

K.M. Panikkar: I have known his mind as well as most, I have no doubt that has been his view all along. But Nehru alone can carry the people with him on this score.

Mountbatten: I'm thinking of suggesting to Nehru that you should act as special envoy to negotiate the Commonwealth structure. Perhaps you can go with Nehru to London in February?

K.M. Panikkar: A special envoy will be necessary. Krishna Menon has grown in stature since he became high commissioner but he is still a very controversial figure.

Mountbatten: What do you think of Gandhi's fast, is it essential?

K.M. Panikkar: You know, Gandhiji fasts against people he loves and hopes to change. Once he fasted against Ba, his wife, because she had stolen a piece of handmade silk to give to her grandchild. It is a custom to give newborn children pieces of cloth….

Mountbatten: What do you mean 'stolen'?

K.M. Panikkar: People would hand-spin cloth and send it to Gandhiji with their addresses and he would have a list of these… so he knew if one was missing. Actually, Gandhiji is very unhappy with Sardar Patel's Lucknow speech. You know, where he said India would reply to Pakistan in Lahore and Rawalpindi. It was not reported in the newspapers but Gandhiji came to know of it. All Sardar Patel's actions are known to him, such as ordering Muslims out of Gurgaon half-an-hour after Ayyangar had persuaded them to return to their homes. He called Patel and said: '*We have been one for thirty years, but now I see that we are two*.' At this Patel wept and promised to behave, but he hasn't changed. I myself had a stand-up row with him on the issue of marching into West Punjab. Very few people speak to him frankly these days, it is a dangerous sign. And that Shankar—his Secretary, is a bad influence on him.

Mountbatten: I'm sure Gandhiji's fast will tip the scales and Nehru and Patel will come together again.

K.M. Panikkar: Between them I would give Patel a ten to one chance. The Indians always flatter those in power, and he is very powerful. But eventually they support those who are right, and Nehru is right against him.

Mountbatten: I am glad to hear that—but I hope with Gandhiji's help to reunite them.

[K.M. Panikkar leaves. Baldev Singh arrives]

Baldev: Wherever I go people are puzzled about Gandhiji's fast. Why did he choose this moment and on what grounds did he break the fast?

Mountbatten: It seems quite clear to me. He was trying to restore communal peace and when those concerned gave written undertakings he was satisfied and broke his fast.

Baldev: This is not the general view. People think the sole reason for the fast was to force the government to hand over the 55 crores to Pakistan. This is the greatest slap in the face the government has received. If there had been an opposition party, they would have brought down the government

Mountbatten: Not at all—Gandhiji raised the matter of the 55 crores after he had already decided on the fast.

Baldev: But I was present at Birla House when the decision to pay the money to Pakistan was announced and I had a bet with Mr Birla that Gandhiji would break the fast within 48 hours—and he did!

Mountbatten: There is no connection....

Baldev: Lord Mountbatten, it is deplorable. After Sardar Patel declared in the house that not a paisa would be paid till Kashmir was settled—even Nehruji said no military stores would be sent to them and both of them gave a press interview, then one old man's fast made a mockery of the unanimous cabinet decision.

Mountbatten: No, no, the last joint defence council meeting was before the fast....

Baldev: [Shaking head vigorously]: Our government has received a very severe blow to its prestige. (Leaves with crestfallen look)

SCENE 48

Patel's drawing room. Patel is reclining in chaise longue. Manibehn is giving him medicines. Gordon Walker and a young woman knock on door.

Patel: Come, come Gordon, sit down. Do you never rest?

Walker: Good morning, Sir. May I introduce Mr Kingsley Martin's daughter—she has been asking me to bring her along for months.

Patel: Welcome, welcome. Have you met my daughter, Miss Kingsley?

Manibehn: I am Manibehn. Come with me—I'll show you the garden with the typical Gujarati swing. Have you tried it?

[Both leave while talking]

Patel: Have you come to bother me on Kashmir again? The British view is very different from ours. You want to put India and Pakistan around a table—but that means a compromise. India has always given way to get some settlement—why should we continue to do so? I was bitterly against taking the case to the UN. At the UN, things are settled by power politics.

Walker: What do you mean by power politics?

Patel: It is the USA, they regard us as pro-Russian because we refuse to become a dependent of America's. Their attitude is also because of the personality of Asaf Ali, our Ambassador to Washington. His appointment has been a mistake.

Walker: Krishna Menon in London is very sincere and honest, but he is a little difficult isn't he?

Patel: Oh yes, really. His appointment was a great mistake also.

Walker: Are you worried about the Communists?

Patel: Not at all. They are growing in Hyderabad and Madras because of the factions in the Congress. Once the communal question is dealt with, the Communists will be no problem.

Walker: And the Socialists? They are weakening the Congress?

Patel: Oh no! [Laughs] They will be wiped out. They are in no way different from the Communists, they fight each other to control the unions but when in control they are just as bad.

SCENE 49

Prime Minister's office: Nehru and Gordon Walker are talking.

Nehru: The only motive of the United States, Mr Walker....
Walker: Call me Gordon, please...
Nehru: Gordon, their only motive is to secure positions for the next war and to weaken Russia. For that they want military and economic concessions in Pakistan, and they are convinced that it will prostitute itself to America to secure its ends in Kashmir. Pakistan wants Kashmir to sell it to the USA!
Walker: Deputy Prime Minister Patel tells me that the Americans think India is pro-Russian.
Nehru: Rubbish! India is not pro-Russian and if the US state department read their own ambassador's reports they would know it. The American Ambassador is Grady, by the way. He is a good man though rather nineteenth century in his economics. Do you know that the Americans are also behind the way the Palestine vote has been lined up? The Zionists tried hard to bribe us with the promise of millions.
Walker: Really! Do tell me more.
Nehru: I cannot say more. My sister receives daily warnings that her life is in danger unless she votes right. In any case, if the USA thinks of bases in the Frontier Province it is stupid. India's defence interests extend to the Middle East. Anyone invading the Middle East must regard India as its zero of defence in depth. We have just sent our Ambassador to Persia. His first task is to counteract local propaganda about India becoming a Hindu state!

SCENE 50

Gandhi is assassinated. At the funeral there are huge crowds, pyre burning high, surrounded by Congress leaders, Mountbatten, Edwina and daughter, all seated on ground with Indian leaders; cries of 'Mahatma Gandhi amar rahen' and general keening in the air; suddenly crowds surge towards pyre. Mountbatten and his staff linked together in a human chain leave the funeral.

SCENE 51

Mountbatten and Nehru are in Mountbatten's study.

Mountbatten: Please, I beg of you to take precautions. If there is a widespread plot, you will be the next person on the list for assassination. Come and stay with us at Government House.

Nehru: Thank you, I know you speak out of concern, but that would send a wrong message to the plotters. I don't mind if you speak to the home ministry about increasing my protection. The RSS has penetrated the government services very widely. Secrecy is non-existent. Immediately after the cabinet decision to ban them, the news leaked and all the RSS records were sent to Alwar—you know its ruler is with them. An airplane from the disposals department was sold to the RSS for two thousand pounds while exactly the same airplane is sold to commercial bodies for fifteen thousand. Many government servants are pulling strings for the RSS.

Mountbatten: It is a sad time. We can postpone discussion of all items by a week—but the UN....

Nehru: I always felt it was a mistake to go to UN, though not as strongly as my colleagues. Now, I know it was a grave mistake. I bitterly regret it.

Mountbatten: Come on now, you have always stood for arbitration. Don't let the tragedy disorient you.

Nehru: I stand by arbitration in principle but the UN has been a great disillusionment to me. It is clearly an American racket. They are wholeheartedly with Pakistan, the whole thing has been a racket against India in New York.

Mountbatten: I can't agree. I freely admit that I pressed you to go to the UN and I am convinced now as much as ever that I was right. Trouble is, Pakistan had the classy Mohammad Ali working behind the scenes, he' a great diplomat. You sent Ayyangar, he is not a good social mixer and his voice is harsh and inaudible. Completely the wrong type of person, he cannot persuade anyone. Sardar Patel is coming in a few minutes, why don't we discuss sending a new man?

Nehru: You discuss it with him, I'm feeling unwell. I'll go home and rest. [Leaves]

[Abell brings some files and places them before Mountbatten]

Mountbatten: I'll look at these after Patel's appointment—he should be here soon. He has quite a communal attitude, doesn't he Abell?

Abell: Oh yes, when the parliamentary delegation from Britain was here, before your arrival, he informed them rather pompously that creating Pakistan was not in the hands of the British government. His exact words were: '*If Pakistan is to be achieved Hindus and Muslims will have to fight. There will be a civil war*.' [He leaves]

V.P. Menon: [Enters] Lord Mountbatten, Sardar Patel sent a message that he will be here soon.

Mountbatten: I have been waiting for him. Tell me V.P., is Nehru right to worry about Mr Patel's communal attitude?

V.P. Menon: He is not communal at all, just because his ideas are different the Socialists are attacking him. Sardar thinks that striving for equality, uniformity and homogeneity in social, cultural and economic spheres is a fantasy, a fiction. Political unity is the nearest one can come to by way of national consensus. Any other kind of unity sought by Nehru is unreal and unachievable. As far as religion is concerned, he is disdainful and indifferent to any excessive preoccupation with it. You know his father's religiosity turned him completely away from any ritualism.

[Patel arrives. V.P. Menon excuses himself and leaves]

Mountbatten: [Very warm handshake, hand on arm] Gandhiji's loss has been very great to you personally... you know he and I were of one mind that any split between you and Nehru would be disastrous. I hope things are better between you now?

Patel: [Slowly] Gandhiji told me of his talks with you—[emotional]—just an hour before he was killed. He told me all your criticism of both of us, Nehru and myself. He told me we must remain together. He was going to call Nehru and tell him similarly. He was going to state in that very prayer meeting that people were wrong in thinking I had acted improperly or that I could be blamed for my attitude towards communal disturbances. [Pause] The position in the country is very serious now. I admire Pandit Nehru, respect him and love him, but he has never understood the Hindu mind.

Mountbatten: Interesting that you should say that. Just this morning Mrs Naidu was telling me how much Nehru values his friendship with my family because he had a completely English education, outlook and mind.

Patel: Yes, that is true. I don't think he has such a relationship with any Indian family. He is very good at addressing large crowds and swaying their emotions temporarily, he inspires them. But he cannot hold the Hindu masses. Hindus are a simple people, they are feeling bullied by Pakistan. Before Gandhiji's fast our government was beginning to gain Hindu confidence by its firm handling of Pakistan over Kashmir. Since the fast and the lamentable climb-down over the 55 crores most of that confidence has disappeared.

Mountbatten: V.P. Menon told me that Gandhiji was seen as instrumental in paying the 55 crores to Pakistan and that led to his assassination. Tell me, how did your differences with Nehru become so well known?

Patel: Unfortunately, things reached such a pitch that I had to tell the whole Cabinet I was unable to continue... but Gandhiji pressed me to stay. Have you seen the news today? Jayaprakash Narayan is Nehru's friend, he has made a monstrous attack on me implying that, as Home Minister, I am responsible for Gandhiji's death. And the saddest part is that the Prime Minister condemned Narayan at the Congress parliamentary party meeting but denied condemning him to the press and in his broadcast.

Mountbatten: That is absurd, of course.

Patel: I can give you the details of all the security arrangements that I made. Of course, Gandhiji refused to let us search people at his prayer meetings—can I be blamed for that? Do you know that 80 per cent of the Intelligence staff was of Muslims who have all left for Pakistan? Your predecessors appointed only Muslims. We don't even have enough intelligence staff.

Mountbatten: What about the Hindu Mahasabha? The socialists want a ban on their organization—even Nehru is very worried about them.

Patel: I am not in favour of going against democratic principles. India's draft constitution has recognized Muslims as a separate entity Lord Mountbatten, surely you don't advise that we ignore the Hindus? We cannot suppress the Hindus. Act firmly, yes, but with fairness and justice.

Mountbatten: But your economic policies are the real bone of contention, are they not?

Patel: Look, the credit of India is at the lowest ebb now. When we tried to float a small public loan it remained completely unsubscribed. Who would believe that the government of free India asking their people for a small loan would fail to get any support? This gives an idea of how the internal credit of the government has sunk.

Mountbatten: Nehru, we know is anti-capitalist, is that the problem?

Patel: Lord Mountbatten, as a complete disciple of Gandhiji I renounced private property and stand to gain nothing from capitalism. I'm not against nationalization and high taxes. But India, at this time, is not sufficiently advanced for socialism to work. The only way to raise the standards of living is to industrialize the country and for that we would have to depend on private enterprise. Gandhiji agreed with me that controls on sugar, cereals, petrol should be relaxed because they encourage corruption. Of course, we must curb the activities of private capital so that it can't exploit the people but we have to restore the confidence of private enterprise in their future. You know, [stands up, heated manner] two days before Gandhiji's assassination, four ministers informed me that they were going to resign because Pandit Nehru appoints committees concerning their departments without consulting them. He passes orders over their heads. Their resignations are held up only because of Gandhiji's demise. I am prepared to work loyally with him only if some agreement is made to keep the cabinet together as a happy team.

Mountbatten: Please sit down—I propose to speak to Nehru about this tomorrow.

Patel: [Sitting down] Please don't say I came to you with all these troubles, I beg you.

Mountbatten: Don't worry, I know most of the history from Gandhiji. I will quote him as my source. But I must say Nehru is not the only sinner on constitutional procedure. It appears you have so much influence in the Public Service Commission that the civil servants look towards you rather than to the Prime Minister.

Patel: No, no actually, the Prime Minister is under too much influence of the Socialists. But they are totally unreliable. They were offered seats in the Congress Working Committee, but they refused to cooperate. Then the Prime Minister offered them seats in the central government but they again refused. I personally offered to hand over one entire province for them to carry out their experiments without hindrance. Again they refused. They are thoroughly irresponsible and are exploiting the great calamity of Gandhiji's death for party ends.

Mountbatten: Anyway, I can be a peace-maker only when both sides admit their mistakes and join together to put matters right. But there is another important matter I have to discuss with you… about the UN.

Patel: [Agitated] I was always against reference to the UN because we had no friends there. India voted against Anglo-American interests at practically every opportunity whereas Pakistan very brilliantly sided with them—particularly British interests—on every occasion except on Palestine. Even with Russia we had no good position owing to the lamentable dispute on whether Ukraine or India should be given a seat on the Security Council. I received letters from civil servants who were attached to our delegation and all know this.

Mountbatten: I am sorry that you did not tell me about this earlier.

Patel: Because I realize that once an application is made to the UN it can't be withdrawn. It is a very difficult position now.

Mountbatten: Do you think we sent a good team led by G. Ayyangar?

Patel: No, he has many difficulties....

Mountbatten: He has a hoarse, inarticulate way of speaking. And he is a teetotaller! He misses all the get togethers for drinks.

Patel: He goes to bed very early you see, about 9 p.m.

Mountbatten: Pakistan's men, Sir Zafrullah Khan and Mr Ali must have done brilliant work behind the scenes. They meet the delegates socially at cocktails and meals and after-dinner gatherings. India, I'm afraid, completely missed the bus. Sir C.P. Ramaswami would be the best leader.

Patel: If we could get Nehru to agree to that! H.M. Patel would partner him very well.

Mountbatten: Yes, H.M. Patel and General Chowdhry would be ideal persons to work behind the scenes. My experience of international conferences shows that most of the work and progress is at meals and after dinner. A teetotaller and a man who goes to bed at 9 can't do much good outside the conference room.

Patel: To tell you frankly, we are reaping the fruits of three blunders: Appointment of Krishna Menon, a well-known Communist sympathizer in London, Asaf Ali in America, his wife is practically a Communist, and Mrs Pandit at the UN. She went out of her way to vote with Russia. This is the basic reason for American hostility.

Mountbatten: Well, I must act fast now to stop this slide... I'll let you know what I can do.

[Both walk-out together]

SCENE 52

Viceroy's House, private lounge: Mountbatten and Nehru.

Mountbatten: Are you pleased now at the way things are going at the UN? [Nehru nods] I claim the whole credit for this change. I've been working very hard to obtain it.

Nehru: I suspected as much. But I've come about Hyderabad. Kasim Razvi and the Razakars are carrying out a campaign of terror across the border into India. I've received several hundred letters and telegrams that they are committing brutal murders and are following a scorched earth policy in the border areas. The provinces surrounding Hyderabad are very angry that our government is doing nothing to protect the people.

Mountbatten: I have asked the Nizam's constitutional adviser to join us and discuss the situation, you know, Sir Walter Monckton….

[Abell ushers in Monckton]

Mountbatten: Ah! Here you are. What is this I hear about Razakars?

Monckton: I saw Mir Laik Ali this morning—he's prepared to ban the Razakars and introduce a new government on the basis of parity immediately.

Nehru: I will meet him myself. I want to encourage Hyderabad as an Islamic cultural centre within India.

Monckton: Excellent, Mr Nehru! Such a policy would appeal greatly to moderate Muslims in Hyderabad and to the Nizam himself.

Mountbatten: I am seeing him at luncheon today. [To Nehru] Why don't you invite him tomorrow?

Monckton: The problem is that Mr Munshi has given instructions to Hindus not to join any new government of the Nizam's.

Nehru: That is not true. Hindu leaders did not want to join till they were sure that a genuine step forward was being taken.

Mountbatten: [To Nehru] I'm sure you can iron out such misconceptions when you meet tomorrow. I have to visit Mr Patel now—is he feeling better?

Nehru: [Rising] It was a big heart attack, but he is better now. Right—I'll see you tomorrow.

SCENE 53

Patel is reclining in chaise longue. Manibehn and Dr Sushila Nayar are sitting beside him. Mountbatten enters. Patel tries to sit up.

Mountbatten: Please, lie down Mr Patel, don't over exert yourself.

Patel: [Semi-reclining] I am very anxious about Hyderabad.

Mountbatten: That is what I have come to reassure you about. Monckton was here to see me and says that….

Patel: Monckton has no power. The Nizam is not going to arrest Kasim Razvi.

Mountbatten: The Nizam is in a very difficult position, the chiefs of police and army and Hyderabad's home minister are all Ittehads.

Patel: You demand high ethical standards from us, they are not imposed on Pakistan or Hyderabad. Look at what Pakistan has done in Kalat, oppressed it fully.

Mountbatten: Kalat hasn't got an adviser of the calibre of Monckton who can expose such behaviour in the world press. The fact is we have to handle this carefully. If the Nizam is pressurized too much the Ittehadis will start massacring Hindus. That will cause communal bitterness throughout south India and Mahatma Gandhi will have died in vain.

Patel: If Gandhiji had not pursued his method so violently he might be alive today! We could have brought in his policy slowly and carefully. People are dazed and bewildered by his death at the moment, but I warn you there will be a violent reaction if men like Razvi incite Muslims in India and there is no Gandhi now to hold it in check.

Mountbatten: The Prime Minister is in favour of handling the Nizam delicately….

Patel: [Sitting up with a jerk] I am afraid Nehru's own life will be in danger if he tries to force Gandhiji's doctrines on an unwilling India in the face of Razvi's menace. Public opinion is vociferously asking for action.

[Manibehn and Sushila hover over Patel and force him to lie back]

Patel: [Slow, weak] The Nizam plans to give a loan of twenty crores to Pakistan, the people of India will never accept that. If we don't stop the Nizam we will be overthrown.

Mountbatten: Please don't worry so much, V.P. Menon is working out the strategy to deal with Hyderabad. You must rest and get better soon. I will leave now.

Patel: You have not had even a cup of tea—let them give you some of our famous *chaach*.

Mountbatten: I will come again—and Edwina would also like to accompany me. You can feed us whatever you like then.

SCENE 54

Mountbatten's study: Mountbatten and Rajagopalachari are talking.

Mountbatten: Your party and you personally, have suffered a great loss in the death of Gandhiji. Now Nehru needs your support.

Rajaji: Of course. Nehru has lost his principal supporter and friend with Gandhiji gone. I think it is vital that you should stay and be his guide. I am very worried about Kashmir... it has one per cent of the total population of India and we are imperilling the future of the whole country for it. It is not worth it.

Mountbatten: Nehru is not willing to give up Sheikh Abdullah....

Rajaji: Yes, he is more influenced by him than any other aspect of the Kashmir problem. You must advise him to change his stand.

Mountbatten: Well, I shall try my best.

[Rajaji leaves. A moment later Nehru arrives and sits down]

Mountbatten: I saw Mr Baldev Singh this morning—he is very happy that Gen. Bucher has agreed to stay on as c-in-c and he wants him to stay on as long as possible. He thinks General Cariappa is not sufficiently stable or balanced to succeed Bucher. Why don't you send Cariappa off as ambassador somewhere?

Nehru: I'll discuss that with Sardar Baldev Singh soon. But what did he feel about the merger of the Sikh princes?

Mountbatten: Oh, he's very pleased, but he doesn't think that will solve the problem of the Sikhs.

Nehru: In what way?

Mountbatten: At present Sikhs form only 38 per cent of East Punjab, he thinks if Gurgaon is included in Delhi province then it would improve the Sikhs ratio to about 42 per cent.

Nehru [Irritated]: Does that matter so much to him?

Mountbatten: He's most anxious about this. He said there is a great difference between being above or below the 40 per cent mark.

Nehru: Nothing will induce me to take out Gurgaon from the Punjab and include it in Delhi. Frankly, this is merely another move on the part of the Sikhs to establish their right as a noisy and determined minority to rule the remaining 60 per cent in East Punjab. There are so many inter-provincial boundary questions, for e.g. in Bengal and Bihar. Once you allow such a matter to be raised I don't know where it will stop. As it is, I stopped Andhra from breaking away from Madras.

Mountbatten: Sir Chandu Lal, the governor of East Punjab considers the conciliation of the Sikhs very important because they have suffered more than anybody else. They want an effective share in the power of the province. Sir Chandu Lal says there is parity between Sikhs and Hindus in present East Punjab, and hopes a system of parity can be made permanent.

Nehru: We cannot agree to introduce such a system of weightage on the basis of religion under the new constitution!

Mountbatten: Think about it, Jawaha. I'm really gratified that you have decided to declare a national holiday and hoist the Union Jack on the King's birthday this year. I propose to give a large party for the Diplomatic Corps that evening, it will also be our farewell to them. I hope you'll come to it.

Nehru: I certainly will, if I can.

Mountbatten: And do you give your permission to present a dominion flag to the Bishop Cotton School at Simla at a Christian religious ceremony?

Nehru: Of course, why not?

Mountbatten: Oh! I forgot to tell you something. Edwina had quite a brainwave, she suggested that Patel should become the first Indian Governor-General after I leave. He is seventy-two and after his recent heart attack he needs to relax. She herself spoke with his daughter who agreed it would be good for his health. But he laughed and refused when I brought it up.

Nehru: Of course, he would never agree. Your schemes for all of us are endless.

Mountbatten: That reminds me. The various governors and chief ministers should have some sort of uniform or designed clothes that they can wear on ceremonial occasions. For instance, Mr Rajagopalachari would look fantastically ludicrous in a *dhoti* surrounded by his staff and bodyguard in full uniform and all the servants in red livery when an ambassador in a tailcoat presents his credentials. He should, at the very least, wear an *achkan*-coat like yours.

Nehru: [Laughs] Oh, come, come.

Mountbatten: Seriously, I don't think it in keeping with the dignity of India!

Nehru: I don't think Rajaji has ever worn anything but a *dhoti* in his life. I doubt you can change his mode of dressing. Why don't you take up this sartorial question with him next time you meet?

Mountbatten: I will, I will. I am also going to propose to him that the Ashoka wheel should take the place of my cipher on the servants livery when I leave.

Nehru: Excellent. Take it up directly with him. I have to rush off to a meeting now. [Leaves]

[Agent-General for Hyderabad is announced]

Agent-General: Your Excellency, I have a letter from the Nizam to be delivered to you.

Mountbatten: [Reads] I'm most disappointed. He refuses to come to Delhi. We could have reached a settlement here.

Agent-General: Your Excellency, I was shocked on my visit to Hyderabad to see how much the situation has deteriorated. Half of the moderate Muslims have now joined the Ittehad. Even Kasim Razvi appears moderate to many now. The extremists in the Congress refuse to join any parity government but moderate Congressmen are now inclined to join and have gone to Mussoorie where Mr Patel is convalescing to seek advice from him.

Mountbatten: Let me tell you the story of the Kashmir Maharaja. In mid '47, I told him that he had three courses open to him. He should accede to India or to Pakistan before the 15th August. If he acceded to India, I pointed out that Indian troops would support him as the Pakistan government and army would not be set up before the 15th. I impressed upon him that the only fatal course of action was to do nothing; yet, that is what the Maharaja chose. The dire consequences of this were obvious for the whole world. Now, I say that the Nizam has also three courses open to him. First, he can grant responsible government and establish a Constituent Assembly and become virtually independent. Second, is to accede to India before 21st June, the date of my departure. This will bring enormous material and economic advantages to Hyderabad. I will obtain a letter signed by the Prime Minister or Deputy Prime Minister, declaring they will not interfere in the internal politics of Hyderabad and will protect the Nizam's personal position whenever responsible government is introduced. His alternative is, of course, to do nothing. He will then, certainly, go down in history as a very foolish ruler.

[The British ambassador Sir Percival Griffiths is announced. The Agent-General leaves]

Griffiths: The Americans are discussing their commercial agreement in Delhi nowadays. I think the Sterling balances delegation should bring up one for the UK as well. I am worried about the Indian proposal that 51 per cent of capital ought to be in Indian hands. It just won't work. Indians expect an immediate return on their capital whereas British firms expect no profits for the first ten years and plough in funds to build up business.

Mountbatten: We must appreciate that in Nehru we have a socialist in a liberal government. Patel is a conservative but his nationalist views naturally make him favour Indian private enterprise.

Griffiths: It is essential that control of any new business should be in British hands for the first ten years. India is not at all attractive at present from the point of view of foreign capital—a sense of security is lacking.

Mountbatten: Chetty, the finance member says that the Congress party statement had shaken even the Indian businessmen's confidence, but I made the government redress that in its official statement on industrial policy. Both Nehru and Patel are making good progress on my advice. [Laughs] The poachers are turning into gamekeepers! Look at our achievements: no action has been taken to leave the Commonwealth; the princes are not being antagonized—in fact, Patel has made many overtures to them; and the government has declared that private enterprise cannot be dispensed with.

Griffiths: I agree entirely, India has come a long way since you took over but I'm afraid British business in the UK doesn't look on India in the same favourable light.

Mountbatten: Well, Nehru is spending the weekend with me at Mashobra. I'll warn him. He is under the impression that foreign capital is waiting to enter the country and when the doors are opened wide there would be a flood.

Griffiths: I hear Hyderabad is hotting up. Our high commissioner is anxious about the safety of the British living there.

Mountbatten: I have a hunch the Hyderabad problem will be settled before I leave India.

Griffiths: From my sources: the real danger is Munshi's activities. The bazaar rumour at present is that Munshi is going to suggest to Patel that India should move into Hyderabad on the plea that Communism is rife in the state and that order needs to be restored.

Mountbatten: This is a quite illogical line of thought!

Griffiths: I think there will be no difficulty in putting over such a line in India.

SCENE 55

In the private sitting room Mountbatten sits alone. Edwina enters with Sheikh Abdullah.

Edwina: Dickie, Sheikh Abdullah was with me to discuss the problems of refugee welfare in Kashmir and wished to see you, so here he is. [Shakes hands with him] Goodbye, Sheikh Abdullah, I will come to Srinagar as soon as conditions permit. [Leaves]

Abdullah: I hope you don't mind, Lord Mountbatten. I have taken the opportunity to meet you now so that we can have a talk off the record.

Mountbatten: I hope you are here to congratulate me on my efforts to improve the atmosphere between India and Pakistan?

Abdullah: Yes, you have played a wonderful role. And you can help me also. I have been thinking, Lord Mountbatten, about the suggestion you made to me when I had dinner with you in October: that Kashmir should stand independent but have close relations with both India and Pakistan. Do you still think independence is feasible?

Mountbatten: I am afraid true independence is not feasible. But I am trying to expand the Joint Defence Council and through it Kashmir can be dealt with as a state acceding to both dominions rather than to only one.

Abdullah: That will be a very good solution. Would both countries accept this solution and give up the idea of a plebiscite? You see, even if the plebiscite is wholly in favour of India, I am certain Pakistan will not give up, the bitterness will continue.

Mountbatten: You should negotiate this with Mr Nehru since you are such great personal friends. The Prime Minister of Pakistan has denounced you as an Indian quisling and asserts that though you may have influence in the valley you have none in Jammu and are detested in Poonch and Gilgit. He forecasts that neither you nor India will get a single vote in these areas.

Abdullah: He is living in the past. Pakistan might have won the plebiscite if they had not encouraged the tribes to come in and massacre, burn and loot so many towns and villages including Muslims. Now they don't have a chance. They might win in Poonch, Mirpur and Gilgit but in Kashmir proper they are doomed to complete failure.

Mountbatten: I will give you a word of advice, Mr Abdullah. The Prime Minister of Pakistan wants proportional representation of Muslims in your administration. Mr Nehru assured him of large-scale autonomy in Kashmir. You should implement that policy.

Abdullah: That is already my intention. But if Liaquat Ali Khan wants that I should invite rebels who have been fighting and massacring to become officials then how can I run the government? I am prepared to put carefully selected Muslims in posts where they will be completely impartial.

Mountbatten: Well, I urge you to release from prison all political offenders who were locked up by the Maharaja or yourself. It would be a good beginning.

Abdullah: In fact I have already met the leader of the Muslim League in prison and promised to release him. I know the massacre of Muslims has created bitterness. The people of Poonch had started a movement for the redress of their grievances—it was not communal. The Maharaja sent in his troops and invited the RSS who are responsible for the killings.

Mountbatten: There is another view on that in India. Sir Dalip Singh, who is the brother of Rajkumari Amrit Kaur, was sent by Nehru to stop the massacres. He admitted that the massacre of Muslims was as high as 10,000, but he maintained that three times more Hindus and Sikhs had been butchered by the Muslims. You see how difficult it is for me to ascertain such things?

SCENE 56

Staff meeting: V.P. Menon, Brockman, Campbell-Johnson, Erskine-Crum, Abell, and Mountbatten present.

Mountbatten: Mr Menon, please read out your note on Hyderabad.

V.P. Menon: I have made the following points which are not noted by anyone. 1. The recent alliance between Communists and Razakars is extremely important. Communists are withdrawing from the Malabar area to the Hyderabad border. They are extremely well organized and well armed and have got hold of a number of lethal weapons from American surplus stock. 2. The Nizam of Hyderabad is completely helpless and is accompanied day in and day out by Razakars. 3. The Agent-General of Hyderabad is no longer trusted by the Nizam and he counts for very little.

Mountbatten: I am sending Alan to the Nizam with a letter and a personal verbal message to be delivered to him alone. In that I will include your point about the communists and emphasize what a great threat they are to the monarchy in Hyderabad.

V.P. Menon: I am very worried about the increase in communist strength—they should be dealt with quickly. Of course, we don't want to embarrass you by military action before you leave India. But by then the monsoon will arrive and no operations will be possible for three months. I think action will have to be taken before the monsoon—as soon as possible.

Abell: The Communist–Razakar alliance is an entirely new concept. So far the whole build-up in the press has been that the Ittehad and the Razakars are the dominant forces in Hyderabad. I foresee that India will be branded before the world as an aggressor.

Campbell-Johnson: I agree. If the Indian government is going to take military action then you, Mr Menon must show—off the record if you wish—all the evidence in your possession to me so that I can condition opinion through the world press. It's no use approaching the *Times* correspondent, but I have useful contacts in the BBC and the *Telegraph*.

Abell: I suppose Mr Menon would have no difficulty in getting hold of certain selected correspondents such as B.L. Sharma and Sri Krishna and convincing them of the Communist danger to public security in Hyderabad. But I cannot over-emphasize the importance of India being branded in world opinion as an aggressor.

Mountbatten: Alan, perhaps you and Abell can go in and prepare a note on this discussion.

[Abell and Campbell-Johnson leave. Laik Ali, Prime Minister of Hyderabad is announced]

Mountbatten: Ah! Mr Laik Ali—I asked to see you because we have a report verified by Major Byrne on the train incident in Hyderabad

State. The attack appeared pre-meditated as all Muslims were asked to leave the train before the others were murdered and looted.

Laik Ali: If the report is verified by Major Byrne, I am prepared to accept the facts.

Mountbatten: Now please don't interpret what I'm saying as a threat. Prime Minister Nehru has no desire to act against Hyderabad and is prepared to go to any lengths to find a solution. Apparently, he alone in the central government is so keen to support Hyderabad because he wishes it to become a centre for Muslim culture. He is also deeply concerned about the future of four crores of Muslims in India. But he cannot stand in the way of mass feeling in the country if Hindu blood begins to run. His position will be much more difficult after my departure. You may save the situation if you are a man of action.

Laik: Lord Mountbatten, I don't understand Mr Nehru's recent reference to Hyderabad misinterpreting India's policy as one of weakness.

Mountbatten: The point is, it is the people of India who are complaining against the weakness of their government vis-à-vis Hyderabad.

Laik: The people of Hyderabad see the Government of India as intent on annihilating 17 million of them.

Mountbatten: You mean two million—which is the number of Muslims.

Laik: They have cut off supplies of salt to our state—that acts equally against all inhabitants regardless of religion. Let India take military action. I am ready to take the whole case to the UN.

Mountbatten: Such a step will only show up the autocratic and undemocratic system in your state. The like of it does not exist in any other country in the world today.

Laik: Hindus in the state are also opposed to the Indian Union. Time will prove this.

Mountbatten: I very much doubt that.

Laik: [Angrily] Now that India has gained freedom why should she object to Hyderabad being free also?

Mountbatten: What do you mean by freedom, the present autocratic rule? If you go on talking nonsense of this sort we will get nowhere.

Laik: His highness the Nizam would prefer to be shot than to accede to India.

Mountbatten: If Hyderabad, my friend, is occupied by an Indian armoured division, there will be very little shooting. It will probably be a bloodless victory. The Nizam will spend the rest of his life in a small house and straitened circumstances: unless he prefers to throw himself under a tank. This is his last chance, so listen carefully. The accession I have in mind is a letter signed by Prime Minister Nehru specifically stating that paramountcy is not being re-established. There will be guarantees for the Nizam and the Muslims in the state. The accession will be strictly confined to the three central subjects of external affairs, defence, and communications. But if you don't use the word 'accession' there will be no peace.

Laik: Why is India so keen on the word 'accession'?

Mountbatten: Because the Ittehad party destroyed the standstill agreement I personally formulated.

Laik: I am not opposed to democratic institutions, I know such advance is inevitable, but I am opposed to responsible government because it will without doubt lead to accession.

Mountbatten: You cannot muzzle the will of the people for this reason! You apparently prefer the immediate extinction of Muslim rule in Hyderabad.

Laik: The people of Hyderabad consider it useless to survive under conditions of Indian paramountcy. They would prefer to go down rather than face that.

Mountbatten: I can understand going down gloriously. But in the face of an army action the end will not be a glorious one.

[Laik Ali bows stiffly and leaves]

V.P. Menon: I had a very difficult time with Sardar Patel yesterday. He thinks there is only one solution... military occupation of Hyderabad. He forbade me to continue negotiations with Laik Ali, whom he considers powerless. I am also convinced that every Hindu in India and in Hyderabad, is in favour of aggressive action against it. If Sardar Patel is forced to resign on Hyderabad I am positive that Pandit Nehru will never be able to hold the cabinet.

Mountbatten: Be patient. I will suggest a plebiscite on the issue of accession of Hyderabad to Laik Ali. I think he will accept it. Perhaps it can be under UN auspices?

V.P. Menon: It is an internal problem: the UN should not be brought in.

Mountbatten: I will get an agreement from Laik Ali—just hold your horses. And see that Munshi doesn't sabotage any agreement with Hyderabad.

V.P. Menon: It is difficult to restrain him until a settlement is reached.

Mountbatten: Come and see me tonight, we'll discuss the tactics of handling Messers Nehru, Patel and Laik Ali… it's tough dealing with them. Have you seen what Nehru has got done in Bihar? A Bill abolishing zamindari! It is a most dishonest act.

V.P. Menon: In my opinion it violates certain provisions of the 1935 Act. It should be sent up before the Federal Court, which is bound to turn it down.

Mountbatten: Exactly my view. We think alike, V.P. Menon.

V.P. Menon: When Rajagopalachari takes over from you I'm not going to have an easy time. I have never hit it off with him. Actually, I consider him intellectually dishonest. He doesn't practice what he preaches.

Mountbatten: I'll advise him to see you regularly so that you can give him the correct advice.

V.P. Menon: Lord Mountbatten, I'm certain the whole government of India would collapse if it were not for the five secretaries of the ministries who keep things going. H.M. Patel, Narhari Rao, H.V.R. Iyengar, B.R. Sen and myself are carrying the whole burden.

Mountbatten: Ronnie, make a note to include the work of the civil service in my handing-over letter. And one of the points for tomorrow's meeting with Nehru should be to recommend ICS men to governorship, in particular Mr Menon.

SCENE 57

Study: Mountbatten and Vernon Erskine-Crum.

Mountbatten: Vernon, who are coming in the Hyderabad delegation?

Vernon: Hyderabad Prime Minister Laik Ali, the Deputy Prime Minister Reddy, Minister Rauf, the Agent Walter Monckton, and the Secretary of External Affairs of Hyderabad Zahir Ahmed. They are outside—shall I fetch them?

[Mountbatten nods and Vernon goes out and returns with all above who bow and are seated]

Mountbatten: Gentlemen, for almost a year now I've devoted more time to Hyderabad than all the other Indian States put together. If you would make a satisfactory settlement, Hyderabad, with the greatest Muslim ruler of all the states and with such high-class Muslim administrators, would be a source of stability to all the Muslims in India. I have twisted and turned in every direction to obtain special treatment for Hyderabad.

Laik Ali: On behalf of the Nizam and the Government of Hyderabad I must say we have great appreciation for everything Your excellency has done.

Mountbatten: Well, I'm very sad that an agreement has not been reached. Do you realize how easy it is for India to take military action? It has an army of 3,000,000 of which only 40,000 are in Kashmir. Their armoured division, which is of a very high-class, is only three days march away from Hyderabad. If I were in the Government of Hyderabad I would pay any price to retain the Nizam on his throne, and with gradual adjustment I would maintain the position of the Muslim landowners and members of the services. Pay full attention to what I'm saying. I am making one last effort and you have one final chance....

[All rise and thanking Mountbatten slowly walk-out]

[V.P. Menon and H.M. Patel rush in]

V.P. Menon: Nehru is in a highly-strung condition—he's having a nervous breakdown after meeting Laik Ali. He was shaking with rage. He asked me to tell you that he will have no more dealings with Laik Ali or with the Nizam or anybody in Hyderabad and you should stop trying to negotiate with such people.

Vernon: [Goes to door on hearing knock] An urgent letter from Mr Patel. [Reads]: '*I am considerably perturbed that even after such bitter experiences of previous negotiations you should still be thinking of finding a formula. The only course we can adopt now is to break off all negotiations. The only solution acceptable to us is unqualified accession to India.*'

Mountbatten: Patel wants war. But I don't take my instructions from him. I thank God I will be a free man in a fortnight. If war comes between Hyderabad and India it will be the result of Patel's opposition to all my efforts. But I can be far more dangerous than people think. Do you think I will break off negotiations? Nehru will now have to choose between me and Sardar Patel!

H.M. Patel: Lord Mountbatten, Sardar Patel feels that if we take a strong line the Hyderabad government will become more reasonable.

Mountbatten: That is ridiculous!

H.M. Patel: What is at the back of his mind is that Hyderabad is following Jinnah's tactics; always waiting for the other side to put up suggestions and then knocking them down.

Nehru: [Entering] What imbeciles! Absolute reactionary bunch! Their draft did not even mention disbanding the Razakars. And whatever number of seats they give to the Congress they will still control all the administration. Though I am a man of peace, I will personally order the army into Hyderabad to pursue the Razakars who come and kill Indian citizens.

Mountbatten: And are you going to order the army against Sheikh Abdullah who is shooting his mouth off on the UN resolution? [Picks up newspaper and reads] *'The object of the mission being sent by the Security Council is to enslave the people of Kashmir. We shall fight tooth and nail.'* What poppycock!

Nehru: Oh dear! What a mess!

SCENE 58

Mashobra, May 1948. Viceroy's Lodge, drawing room. Mountbatten sits in a huge armchair, Edwina and Nehru sitting together on a sofa. A coffee tray is taken around.

Mountbatten: That was a good dinner—well trained chefs. Jawahar, you must try and relax here. I've brought along my project on tracing the interlocking branches of my family tree, it's a perfect tranquilizer.

Nehru: Tell me about your family Dickie. Krishna Menon tells me it sounds like a world federation of all the monarchs.

Mountbatten: Well. In a capsule: Queen Victoria was my mother's grandmother. It is a tremendous thing to be one of Queen Victoria's descendents. They filled the thrones of Europe. Her eldest daughter, Princess Victoria, married Prince Frederick of Prussia, and became empress of Germany. My mother's sister Alex married the Tsar Nicholas II of Russia. Her granddaughter, my cousin Ena, married King Alphonso III of Spain. Another married King Ferdinand I of Rumania; another married King Gustav VI of Sweden, who later married my sister Louise; yet another married King Constantine I of Greece; and yet another one married King Haakon VII of Norway; one of Queen Victoria's great-granddaughters married King Alexander I of

Yugoslavia. On my father's side it goes like this: My father was Prince Louis of Battenberg. I believe I can trace us back through forty-four generations—but certainly to the ninth century, to Charlemagne. My grandfather was Prince Alexander of Hesse and the Rhine, the uncle of the Grand Duke Louis IV, who married Queen Victoria's daughter, Princess Alice, my maternal grandmother. Is your head turning around?

Nehru: I think so. It's quite amazing. A sort of parallel League of Nations.

Mountbatten: World affairs for us have always been very largely family affairs. I became president of the Society of Genealogists—but working out our lineage is a considerable task. [Stands up] I'm going to work on it till late tonight. You two must not talk about all your relief and welfare policies in the refugee camps—there's enough of that in Delhi. Why don't you watch the cinema—Ronnie tells me he's brought along a new film. Meet you at breakfast. [Leaves]

[Silence]

Nehru: I can't tell you how great a support you have been Edwina, everyone tells me you work around the clock at the refugee camps. What is happening to the values we cherished? Where are our brave ideals? I am in danger of losing faith in myself and in the work I do. I needed so much for you to talk to me, talk to me sanely and confidently, as only you can do so well.

Edwina: Since Gandhiji is gone, nothing else soothes me but work. And I know it is much more so for you.

Nehru: On that terrible day, it was only your letter that gave me some comfort.

Edwina: That night when Amrit Kaur and I found you in the dark streets, surrounded by angry men with knives, trying to calm them, I realized that I had to get you away from Delhi for a while. Getting you to Mashobra to talk naturally and informally obsessed me. Oh! Jawaha, I have just discovered what India and you personally have come to mean to me.

Nehru: Life has become such a dreary business that when a bright patch comes it rather takes one's breath away... this morning, as we climbed the orchards my spirits rose for the first time in a year, it was incredible to know that you think of me as much as I think of you. The bright and brilliant sky seemed to enter my heart, you have come and unlocked all its doors and windows.

Edwina: Last evening was perfect—each day more blissful than before—you understand me so perfectly. Talking with you gives me a strange sense of peace and happiness… perhaps I bring you the same?

Nehru: What did you tell me and what did I say to you…? The more one talks, the more there is to say and there is so much that it is difficult to put into words. I have a feeling that I did not say the right thing or did not put it in the right way.

Edwina: It makes me so happy and still slightly incredulous that you should talk to me as you do and I want to do the same… I have never felt in my life that I wanted to, or could, to anyone, till now. The men I have met were always giving women the benefit of their views. The only thought that frightens me is any reservations between us.

Nehru: Your adoring words, they seem so unreal, life will feel lonely and empty when you are gone, leaving behind a fragrance on the air. But we can never forget our responsibilities to other people.

Edwina: That is the only promise we have made. Nothing we do or feel will ever be allowed to come between you and your work or me and mine.

[Edwina moves over to her desk and sits down. Nehru stands beside her]

Nehru: I am convinced that we have to function in our respective orbits or else we will lose our roots and feel terribly unhappy. But… you will soon be gone…a feeling of acute malaise is creeping over me when I look at a picture in my mind of your shaking thousands of hands on the night of the 20th and saying your final goodbye… and I shall wander away….

Edwina: You told me to be practical….

Nehru: And so it will be and has to be. Dickie and you cannot bypass your fate, just as I cannot bypass mine.

Edwina: But I hate the thought of going home now—my heart aches at the thought of leaving. Last night, sitting in the garden with a full moon, I felt… as if ripped apart….

[Nehru moves towards her and upsets the inkstand on her table. They mop it up together]

SCENE 59

Staff meeting: Mountbatten and full staff present except V.P. Menon.

Mountbatten: This I think is our last staff meeting but we do have very important items to take care of. I have already gone over them with Ronnie and as he reads them out you may give your suggestions. Right Ronnie, fire away.

Ronnie: Number one: disposal of wine stocks. Dickie proposes to take the remaining stocks back home. Is that OK?

All: Yes.

Ronnie: Number two: The proposed portraits of Lord and Lady Mountbatten. We have to find out the calibre of the artist.

Mountbatten: I have undertaken to do that myself. After all, the portraits will be the last in the series that began with Warren Hastings and all were executed by well-known artists.

Ronnie: Next: George Abell and Vernon are to list out the final round of dinner parties and banquets that will be hosted by Lord and Lady Mountbatten. Tentatively, it includes the government dinner for the Indian Cabinet; a dinner for the clerical staff; another for domestic and menial staff; and of course, the final reception on the 20th of June. The Governor-General's medals will be given to the servants at their function. Lord Mountbatten will make his farewell appearance to the people of Delhi at the function of the Delhi Corporation.

Campbell-Johnson: Would you make a speech on that occasion, Dickie? I would have to release it to the press in advance.

Mountbatten: Nothing formal Alan. Both Nehru and I can say a few words in Urdu. You can get those translated for me.

Ronnie: Next: The Viceroy's Gold Plate will be presented to the future Governor-General of India at the cabinet dinner. The reception of 20th June will be much larger, with about 3,000 people invited at government house which is now to be known as Rashtrapati Bhawan. On this occasion, everybody will be lined up to shake hands and say goodbye.

Scott: That is going to be a massive exercise. You must wear strong gloves. [Laughter]

Ronnie: A special note to the cabinet on the upkeep of the gardens at Government House. Prime Minister Nehru has informally assured Lady Edwina that the gardens will be kept up and the number of *malis* will remain in permanent employment. He has also accepted Lady Edwina's suggestion that the vegetable growing area could be increased to finance the upkeep of the gardens. The foreign embassies would be a good market for European vegetables and flowers.

Mountbatten: Edwina has made excellent practical suggestions which Nehru has accepted fully but a formal note should be handed over to the cabinet minister concerned.

Ronnie: The next item is regarding the Muslim servants of Government House. It has three sections: 1. It is better for the Muslim servants to stay in Delhi. Those who want to go to Pakistan must be convinced that there is no employment for them there. None of them, in any case, must be allowed to leave before the departure of Lord Mountbatten as the Government of India would take it as an insult—as if only the British were capable of looking after them properly. 2. The object should be to keep the greatest number in their houses on the Viceroy's estate and to continue their employment in Government House or find other jobs for them in Delhi. 3. One member of Lord Mountbatten's staff is to stay on for a month after his departure to ensure that the servants are fairly treated.

Mountbatten: Well, that was quick and businesslike. All agreed on the various items?

All: Agreed.

SCENE 60

Departure of Mountbatten and his entourage.

Spectacle at Viceregal house: Rows upon rows of men in service uniforms, lounge suits, dhotis, sherwanis, turbans and other Princely head-dresses, and a fine showing of brocade and silk by the women guests.

Shaking hands, bowing and curtseying, people mill around as Edwina and Mountbatten are frozen in fixed smile mode.

Flash bulbs pop.

Background music is accompanied by a hum of voices.

Music begins with a soft symphony and ends with a rousing march played by the services band.

THE END

Select Bibliography

Manuscript Source

The Collected Papers of Lord Louis Mountbatten, Broadlands' Archive, Hartley Library, University of Hampton.

Published Source

Mansergh, Nicholas (ed.), with the assistance of Penderel Moon, *The Transfer of Power 1942-7*. Vols. VII–XI (London, 1977).

Printed Secondary Works Consulted

Afzal, M. Rafique (ed.), *Selected Speeches and Statements of the Quaid-i-Azam Mohammad Ali Jinnah (1911-34 and 1947-48)* (Lahore, 1973).

Afzal, M. Rafique (ed.), *Speeches and Statements of Quaid-i-Millat Liaquat Ali Khan, 1941–51* (Lahore, 1967).

Ali, Chaudhri Muhammad, *The Emergence of Pakistan* (New York: Columbia University Press, 1967).

Campbell-Johnson, Alan, *Mission with Mountbatten* (London, 1982).

Gandhi, M.K., *The Collected Works of Mahatma Gandhi.*

Gilmartin, David, *Empire and Islam: Punjab and the Making of Pakistan* (London, 1988).

Ismay, Hastings Lionel, *The Memoirs of General the Lord Ismay* (London, 1960).

Jalal, Ayesha, *The Sole Spokesman: Jinnah, the Muslim League and the Demand for Pakistan* (Cambridge, 1985).

Menon, V.P., *The Story of the Integration of the Indian States* (New York, 1956).

Menon, V.P., *The Transfer of Power in India* (Bombay, 1968).

Moon, Penderel (ed.), *Wavell: The Viceroy's Journal* (London, 1973).

Moon, Penderel, *Strangers in India* (New York, 1943).

Moore, R.J., *Churchill, Cripps and India 1939–45* (Oxford, 1979).

Moore, R.J., *Escape from Empire: The Atlee Government and the Indian Problem* (Oxford, 1982).

Moore, R.J., *The Crisis of Indian Unity, 1917–1940* (Oxford: Clarendon Press, 1974).

Morgan, Janet, *Edwina Mountbatten: A Life of Her Own* (New York: Scribner Book Company, 1991).

Mosley, Leonard, *The Last Days of the British Raj* (New York: Harcourt, Brace & World, 1962).

Nehru, Jawaharlal, *Selected Works of Jawaharlal Nehru* (Delhi: Oxford University Press).

Page, David, *Prelude to Partition: The Indian Muslims and the Imperial System of Control, 1920-1932* (Delhi: Oxford University Press, 1982).

Philips, C.H. and Wainwright, Mary Doreen (eds.), *The Partition of India: Policies and Perspectives 1935–47* (London: George Allen and Unwin Ltd., 1970).

Royle, Trevor, *The Last Days of the Raj* (London: John Murray, 1997).

Wingate, Sir Ronald, *Lord Ismay: A Biography* (London: Hutchinson, 1970).

Wolpert, Stanley, *Jinnah of Pakistan* (New York: Oxford University Press, 1984).

Woolgar, C.M. (ed.), *Mountbatten on the Record* (Hartley Institute, University of Southampton, 1997).

Ziegler, Philip, *Mountbatten: The Official Biography* (London: Collins, 1985).